DOUGLAS JARDINE : SPARTAN CRICKETER

DOUGLAS JARDINE: SPARTAN CRICKETER

CHRISTOPHER DOUGLAS

London
GEORGE ALLEN & UNWIN
Boston   Sydney

George Allen & Unwin (Publishers) Ltd,
40 Museum Street, London WC1A 1LU, UK

George Allen & Unwin (Publishers) Ltd,
Park Lane, Hemel Hempstead, Herts HP2 4TE, UK

George Allen & Unwin Australia Pty Ltd,
8 Napier Street, North Sydney, NSW 2060, Australia

First published in 1984

British Library Cataloguing in Publication Data

Douglas, Christopher
    Douglas Jardine.
1. Jardine, Douglas   2. Cricket players—England—Biography
I. Title
796.35′8′0924   GV915.J/
ISBN 0-04-796083-3

Set in 11 on 13 point Garamond by
V & M Graphics Ltd, Aylesbury, Bucks
and printed in Great Britain
by Mackays of Chatham

Contents

Illustrations

Photograph credits

BBC Hulton Picture Library 11, 17, 18, 19, 20, 22; David Frith
Collection 2; Keystone Press Agency 13, 14, 16; Mrs Fianach
Lawry 1, 6, 21; MCC 7, 8, 9, 15; Sport and General 10, 23.

Acknowledgements

As a complete beginner in this field I was constantly surprised by the kindness and trust extended to me by eminent and busy people who had nothing whatever to gain from a two-hour interview with me. For their hospitality and patience with my awed incoherence I am very grateful. I am grateful, too, to those who allowed me access to private collections of books and letters, and also to those who took the trouble to write to me from all over the world, particularly the late Jack Fingleton, whose interest and encouragement were an inspiration.

I should like to thank especially: G. O. Allen CBE; Rex Alston; R. L. Arrowsmith; Lady Ashton; the late Gilbert Ashton MC; Philip Bailey; Alex Bannister; A. H. Brodhurst; Dennis Castle; J. D. Coldham; Matthew Engel; P. G. H. Fender; the late J. H. Fingleton; David Frith; Alan Gibson; Stephen Green; J. H. Human; Harold Larwood; Fianach Lawry (née Jardine); Laurence Le Quesne; W. H. V. ('Hopper') Levett; Lt Col J. S. McLaren OBE; Major P. M. Nelson; Andrew Nickolds; A. G. Pawson CMG; S. S. Perera; T. B. Raikes; J. Stow; the late Ben Travers; Richard Streeton; Surrey CCC; G. L. Turner; the late Bryan Valentine MC; Rev. C. B. Verity; Cyril Walters; Peter Webb; R. E. S. Wyatt.

And special thanks to those who, to a greater or lesser extent, subsidised the writing of this book: Corbiere, Dishcloth, Teenoso, Shareef Dancer, Habibti, Teleprompter, Gabitat and Timecharter. And of course The Pig.

Preface

During a one-day match at Sydney in 1980, Mike Brearley was booed by the crowd for using a defensive leg-side field. One television commentator confessed himself unable to explain the vehemence of the crowd's behaviour, and it may well be that the booers themselves didn't know exactly why they were so annoyed. They didn't like Brearley's tactics, but did they know *why* they didn't like them? Why have Australians, though once the greatest exponents of defensive leg-theory, for many years regarded it as sneaky and English? The reason is that in 1932, Douglas Jardine transformed leg-theory into the most lethal and effective form of attack in the game's history. It is a measure of his effect on Australian cricket that the appearance of a leg-side field, even as a defensive measure, can provoke feelings of resentment in the hearts of cricket fans born perhaps 30 years after the unhappy tour. Mike Brearley was, for a time, the ghost of Douglas Jardine.

Whatever else he did in his life, Jardine is remembered as the man who gave the world bodyline. The extent to which he was personally responsible for it and the precise nature of his offence I shall attempt to show in due course. Closer examination of his character and the testimony of those who knew him reveal that posterity has attributed to him sinister qualities which he never in fact possessed. His early retirement from the first-class game and his premature death in 1958 made him an ideal scapegoat – a bad egg without whom bodyline could not have come into existence.

It is regrettable, though not really very surprising, that all his other achievements should have been overshadowed by the disastrous events of 1932–33. As a batsman, Jardine deserves to be counted among the best. His success as a defensive player was remarkable, particularly since it derived more from necessity than from natural dourness. He was something of a curiosity in school cricket; the promise and range of strokes he showed were quite extraordinary, and at 17 he would not have been out of place in a county side. Indeed, he was one of the best schoolboy batsmen ever. When he reached first-class cricket, though, he began to cut down on what he considered the more risky of his strokes, so Surrey and, later on, England came increasingly to rely on him as the man to get his head down in a crisis. At the time of his retirement in 1934, he was considered by many to be the best batsman of his kind in the world.

His standing as a captain is less easy to assess. As a tactician he was shrewd and meticulous, although a certain lack of flair prevented him from rising to greatness. But as a leader of men he must rank very highly. His methods were considered strict even by contemporary standards and, while one or two of his players may not have been over-fond of him, they respected him and would have followed him anywhere.

Just as his career ended in controversy, so did it begin. In 1923 he was the unwitting cause of one of those great lbw rows which occur periodically. Words like 'unsportsmanlike' were bandied about even then, although Jardine was doing nothing worse than following the accepted practice of batsmen at the time. Having raged for a few months, the argument died down. It is difficult to tell just how much the affair affected Jardine, but it may well be that it hardened his resistance to any future attacks which the traditionalists might launch in his direction.

Although he retired from regular participation in first-class cricket at the early age of 33, he remained closely involved with the game for the rest of his life. He earned much of his living as an author, journalist and broadcaster and he gave generously of his time in helping out at the less glamorous end of the game.

His love for cricket was intense, passionate even, and therein lay the difficulty, it seems. It emerges quite clearly from the personal memories sought in the preparation of this book that Jardine was a man who provoked strong feelings one way or the other. But in these accounts, references to his 'religious devotion' to cricket occur with striking frequency. If he preferred to abide by the letter rather than the spirit of the law, it demonstrated an unquestioning obedience as opposed to a sharp eye for the legal loophole. His integrity was universally respected, even when his dedication was too zealous for contemporary tastes, and he was held in great affection by those who managed to get to know him.

DOUGLAS JARDINE: SPARTAN CRICKETER

1
Winchester

Born on 23 October 1900, Douglas Robert Jardine was, strictly
speaking, a Victorian by only three months, but in almost every
respect – intellect, morality, even appearance – he was a
nineteenth-century man. His childhood was Victorian, his
schooling fiercely so, and it could be argued that the controversial
'modernity' he brought to cricket was in keeping with the
Victorian passion for innovation.

He was born in one of the great centres of Imperial might,
Bombay. The Jardines lived on Malabar Hill, an area inhabited
mainly by wealthy Parsees. It was as exclusive then as it is now,
but the exquisite wooden bungalows set in large, beautifully kept
compounds have been replaced by high-rise apartment blocks.

His father, Malcolm Jardine, had gone out to India in 1894
after being called to the Bar the previous year. He was following
in the footsteps of his own father, W. J. Jardine, who had risen
rapidly to a place on the bench of the Allahabad High Court via
the Bar and a law professorship. W.J. was a brilliant man who
seemed set for high office when he was struck down by cholera at
the age of only 32. In 1898, M.R. married a fellow-Scot, Alison
Moir.

At the time of Douglas Jardine's birth, M.R. was Perry
Professor of Jurisprudence and Roman Law at the Government
Law School. He became principal of the school in 1902 and from
then on held posts of increasing importance, finally being
appointed Advocate-General of Bombay in 1915. He practised,
fairly lucratively it seems, as a barrister. He and a number of other
English barristers had enough success on what their Indian
colleagues considered to be their pitch to cause a certain amount
of resentment.

The Jardines were well-known figures in Bombay social and

sporting circles. M.R.'s batting on the Esplanade Maidan was greatly admired. One of his finest moments was when he and one 'Jungly' Greig shared a big partnership in the Presidency Match of '98. He was educated at Fettes College and was in the XI for four years, being made captain in 1888, when he also topped the batting and the bowling averages. Three of his brothers played in the Rugby cricket XI.

Malcolm Jardine was lucky in that his first-class career coincided with the very beginning of the Golden Age, so he played in some very illustrious company. Lionel Palairet and Fry were in the Oxford XI with him; he captained Oxford in 1891 and scored his only first-class century (140) in the University match of 1892. He faced Sam Woods at his fastest, hit 54 against Mold and Briggs of Lancashire, took the wickets of Bobby Abel and W. W. Read, was bowled first ball by Bobby Peel and played six times for Middlesex under Stoddart. He played 70 first-class innings between 1889 and 1897 and a career average of 18.35 doesn't really do him justice. Ranji, Fry and Warner all thought highly of him (Fry thought he might have played for England), and he had just started to fulfil his early promise when the need to earn a living took him off to India at the age of only 24.

Short as his career was, M. R. Jardine deserves more than a footnote in the history of the game, and it is for the following reason: when he made his hundred against Cambridge in 1892, much notice was taken of the way he nudged F. S. Jackson's deliveries to leg. Jackson was bowling to a seven-two offside field and clearly thought that Jardine's method was doomed to failure since he did not strengthen the leg-side field. *Wisden* wrote of Jardine's batting, 'His play was marked by very watchful defence and a remarkable power over the stroke which can best be described as the leg-glance.' The slightly deprecatory tone suggests something new-fangled. It was Ranji who brought respectability and even romance to the stroke, but he did not start his first-class career until the following year. It is likely that, with the general improvement in the standard of wickets from 1890 onwards, a number of batsmen were experimenting with variations on the nudge or the glance to leg at balls pitched on the stumps. Jardine can at least claim to have been in the vanguard of that movement.

Both M.R. and D.R. were, it seems, natural innovators, which was a little strange in such conservatively minded men. Their respective contributions to the game are evident today. The modern batsman owes much to M.R. for his staple nudge round the corner, and he has D.R. to thank for the fact that there can be no more than two fielders there to stop it.

Douglas Jardine was deeply attached to M.R. and, in later life, always spoke of him with great pride. The achievements of the son far outshone those of the father but Malcolm Jardine's influence showed clearly in his son's play. All the strengths were passed on but none of the weaknesses. In due course, a number of formidable cricket brains were brought to bear on the young man's progress but it was his father who first spotted and encouraged the exceptional natural ability.

At the age of nine Jardine was sent by his parents to St Andrew's in Scotland to stay with his Aunt Kitty, his mother's sister. She lived in a massively respectable Scottish mansion which was to be his base throughout the major part of his schooldays. Cold and forbidding as it must have been to a little boy thousands of miles from home, he claimed to have been happy there and had a great affection for his Aunt Kitty.

He entered Horris Hill Preparatory School, near Newbury, in May 1910 and to begin with seemed a fairly bright academic prospect. The school's headmaster was A. H. Evans, an old Oxford Blue and a country-house cricketer. He had founded the school for the benefit of those who wanted their sons to have a proper cricketing education. The academic standard was very high and the school was one of the main suppliers to Winchester, as it is still.

Jardine edged his way into the school first XI in 1912, when he was 11, but his first full season came the following year when he took 24 wickets at 6.67 and averaged 45 with the bat. The scorebooks for those early matches still exist and make delightful reading, with good old prep. school names abounding, such as Nosworthy, Hussey-Freke and Tyrwhitt-Drake.

The school's away matches, of which there were perhaps three or four per term, were little adventures. Early in the morning the team would assemble with faces scrubbed, uniforms tidy and pads and boots blancoed snowy-white. They would travel by horse and cart to the station, then after a laborious, stopping, changing train journey there would be another trip by horse and cart to the school where the match was to be played. Sometimes they didn't get back from these games until after midnight, but what fun they must have been, especially since Horris Hill nearly always won.

The ex-headmaster of the school, Jimmy Stow, is amazed by the high scores that were made in Jardine's time: 270 for 3 against Cordwallis in 1914, for example. The matches could not have lasted appreciably longer than they do now because of all the time needed for travelling, and yet these days a total of 150 is usually a winning one.

Jardine was captain in his last year, and so it followed that not a match was lost. In fact, they were all won except for one against a school called Summer Fields. Little Gubby Allen was playing for the opposition, as was Christopher Hollis, who later described the match in his book, *Oxford in the Twenties*. Horris Hill knocked up an impossible score apparently, and so the Summer Fields cricket master told his lads to play for a draw. The little fellows responded eagerly to what must have seemed a very grown up idea and they just managed to save the game. At a cocktail party 40 years later, Hollis reminded Jardine of the incident. One can't tell exactly how and in what spirit Hollis raised the subject, but Jardine did not find it at all funny.

In Jardine's instructional book, *Cricket* (1936), he refers to an important stage in his development:

> The writer still recollects the horrid abstinences necessitated by the laborious hoarding of five shillings in ten consecutive weeks, out of a total income of sixpence a week, in order to acquire Mr. C. B. Fry's great book on *Batsmanship*. Mr. Fry will perhaps forgive it being mentioned in all honesty that the frantic desire to acquire this work was due to an equally strong desire to get a place in a preparatory school eleven, yet, although the place was eventually acquired, it was gained for bowling.

Batsmanship was published in 1912 and it became Jardine's bible. It was quite a radical book in its way, and to traditionally minded cricket masters and coaches, it must have seemed downright subversive. School batsmen had hitherto been instructed to keep the right foot firmly anchored a couple of inches inside the crease and outside the line of leg stump. Fry said that all accomplished batsmen of the day moved the right foot in playing the glance, the cut, the hook and indeed all back-foot strokes. Keen cricket-watching boys were of course fully aware of the existence of footwork but, rather like sex, it was whispered about in the dormitory and experimented with behind the potting sheds – certainly not paraded in the presence of masters. And yet here was Fry, the captain of England, quite openly saying that 'the rule about weight on the right foot seems rather an anachronism', then going on to encourage the Empire's youth to stand with its weight evenly distributed on both feet to aid mobility. Jardine immediately saw the advantages of Fry's method and had the ability to put them into practice. In doing so, as Robertson-Glasgow wrote, he once incurred the disapproval of his cricket master, but the boy stood up for himself, quoting Fry in his defence.

In the first-class game, too, traditionalists were clearly applying a double standard: footwork was fine when it facilitated dazzling strokeplay but an eyesore when used defensively (as in the case of pad-play). This doctrine died hard. As late as 1924, the word 'footwork' was used in a pejorative sense in an article in *The Times*.

In his last term at Horris Hill, Jardine averaged 39.5 with the bat and took 32 wickets at 4.5, including a spell in which he bowled out four of the opposition with consecutive balls. Towards the end of that last summer term, the headmaster's son, A. J. Evans, brought a side down to play against the boys and staff. A. J. Evans played for Oxford, the Gentlemen, Kent, Hampshire and once, though rather luckily, for England. He was an elegant attacking batsman and a medium-pace bowler. He later wrote a book about his experiences in the first world war called *The Escaping Club*. After bowling to the dead bat of young Jardine for some time, he decided that the time had come to put the impeccable technique under a little more pressure. Jardine, tall for his age but with no more than a 13-year-old's strength, played the quicker stuff with a good deal of assurance. As invariably happens in these situations, it wasn't long before the bowler lost his temper and started hurling bouncers, yorkers, break-backs and other nasties, all of which he no doubt imagined to be unplayable but which, owing to his extreme angriness, were probably less than lethal. Jardine was therefore able to treat the bowling with the contempt it deserved. A deeply cross man, with whom one has the greatest sympathy, was eventually obliged to take himself off.

Jardine left Horris Hill and passed, without undue difficulty or distinction, into Winchester College. To enter Winchester in

1914 was to go back 30 years in time. While other schools had dispensed with some of the more austere nineteenth-century customs, Winchester remained unchanged, an upholder of the noble virtues in an age of moral and cultural decline. Life at the school was harsh, monastic and governed by a strict routine. The entire system was based upon the principle of *'mens sana in corpore sano'*. The school's aim was to produce young gentlemen with the minds of philosophers and the bodies of Olympians – a sort of master race. They were not stereotypes, and independent thought was strongly encouraged. There was a common bond, though, and each took an interest in the subsequent successes and failures of the others.

Taking a closer look at Winchester life which Jardine experienced between the ages of 13 and 18 may help to explain some of his later actions. It was a terrifying place for any new boy, although he was treated with marginally less contempt than was usual because of his reputation as a cricketer which had travelled ahead of him. Games were enormously important then, and those who excelled at them enjoyed a privileged status.

Jardine entered 'C' House or, more commonly, Cook's. His housemaster was Charles Little. Like many of his colleagues, Little was unmarried and devoted his life, with religious zeal, to serving the College. He was an academic pure and simple and he left the welfare and day to day running of the house to the prefects, or co-praes. The co-praes frequently abused their powers and to a large extent the authorities turned a blind eye. It was all part of the process by which young men learnt to take life's knocks with a cheery smile. Bullying, though, had been virtually eradicated and, while the co-praes could be brutal, they were not always so. Jardine's first dormitory prefect used to read aloud to his charges. After 'lights out', he would treat them to extracts from *Eric, Or Little By Little*, Dean Farrar's heavily moral school story which elicited howls of merriment.

The first task of a new 'man' (there are no boys at Winchester) was to learn his 'Notions', a secret vocabulary, grammar and code of behaviour consisting at that time of over 1000 items. There were, and still are, similar systems at most public schools but there has never been anything to beat Notions for complexity. It was a means of helping the Wykehamist to regard himself as a superior being right from the word go. The most common form of Notion was a straightforward translation of English into Latin but there were also obscure biblical allusions and some had an old English flavour, while some were artless corruptions of ordinary words: crockets = cricket, Wokhamist = Wykehamist. The behavioural Notions are illuminating: for example, it was a bad Notion to be seen walking alone, for a Wykehamist was a sociable fellow, and the word 'think' was definitely 'non-licet' (not allowed) – a Wykehamist did not think, he *knew*. All this had to be learnt in a fortnight, at the end of which period, immunity from the cane ceased and one became known officially as a 'man-in-sweat'.

The daily routine, into which Jardine slipped more easily than most, was incredibly gruelling: boys were woken at 6.30, or rather, men ceased thoking at corbel. They washed in cold water, even though there was usually a plentiful supply of hot. (In one house, not Jardine's, boys had to run naked along an open passageway to the wash-house and only on the way back were they allowed to drape a towel round their shoulders. I spoke to a gentleman who remembers doing this in the snow.) Work began at 7.00 with Morning Lines; 45 minutes of Latin or Greek, the two subjects which constituted the bulk of the curriculum. Chapel and a practically non-existent snack known as Grubbing Hall were followed by a further four hours of morning school. Lunch was the main meal of the day. It was an unappetising affair at the best of times, but when the wartime food shortages were at their worst, it constituted a serious health hazard. In a privately published memoir, *Winchester 1916–1921*, E. T. R. Herdman (who was in the same house as Jardine) described conditions in 1917:

> Once we were given boiled rhubarb leaves as a vegetable. ... We occasionally had cheese and biscuits instead of a pudding but the biscuits were full of weevils. We used to run races with them. ... We were not supposed to have rationed food sent from home. I brought back a bag of potatoes and boiled them once a week ... they tasted of dirty saucepans, but I got them down with pepper, cold and clammy though they were. They kept me going.

The afternoons were given over to games (ekker). This was generally enjoyable for those, like Jardine, who were in a number of teams, but for those who weren't it meant an endless succession of runs. These runs are remembered as far and away the most unpleasant part of Winchester life.

Washing after strenuous exercise was a practice that had only recently been generally adopted. It had become quite the thing at Winchester and hot water was even allowed. There was perhaps a special significance in this. Hot water, it will be remembered, was not usually permitted in the mornings, but an afternoon spent on the sports field in the service of the God, Fair Play, seemed to warrant something special. A hot bath not only got the mud off, it anointed the body after the sacred act.

One of the things that distinguished Winchester from other schools was its almost total lack of privacy. There were no studies except for partitioned-off boxes in Hall for the co-praes. Everyone else made their home in something called a 'toy', which was a combination of a desk and a locker. There was a dual purpose in this communal, open living: to foster a feeling of team spirit and to eliminate 'beastliness'. In the first case it was successful, in the second less so.

There would have been little enough time to enjoy the luxury of privacy in any case. Spare time was normally spent making frenzied efforts to catch up on undone tasks. During the war there was extra corps drill (a minimum of ten hours a week) and in 1918 boys were required to do a certain amount of labouring on nearby farms.

Discipline was dreadfully harsh and was often merely licensed sadism. 'The ground-ash was the thing', a contemporary of Jardine's told me with a chuckle. Herdman gives an example of prefects fabricating a minor offence simply in order to punish it: the library, said the co-praes, was in a disgusting state,

> so we were all told in turn to bend over and sport an arse, and got six with the ground-ash. Up till then I had tried to avoid getting beaten, but now decided this was impossible, so didn't put myself out any more. I got five beatings in my first half [term]. A more serious affair was a beating by the Headmaster. This was a fairly rare occurrence, and not many men ever had to undergo it. You had to take down your trousers and be beaten on your bare bottom. This always drew blood. One man in our house (Cook's) got his own back. The headmaster had some new chintz covers in his study. After the beating this man sat down groaning on the sofa and bled all over the new chintz.

There are numerous instances of this sort of thing, all related with equal relish. The headmaster, incidentally, was Montague Rendall, who thought up the BBC motto, 'Nation shall speak peace unto nation'.

All this is remembered by people still alive, not so much with affection as with an amused incredulity. There is no bravado but genuine surprise at their own powers of endurance. A sheepish laugh accompanies each recollection. And as these men cast their minds back 70 years, they sometimes slip into the present tense, giving the impression that they have never really left school at all: those arduous five years had a lasting effect on those who lived through them. Wykehamists were taught to be honest, impervious to physical pain, uncomplaining and civilised. It is hardly surprising that in later life, Jardine could be dismissive of minor grievances and impatient with sensitive egos.

The war dominated life at Winchester during nearly the whole of Jardine's time there. There was intense patriotic fervour and a righteous hatred of the Germans such as was not felt during the second world war. *The Wykehamist* magazine contained poems about the glory and fellowship of dying for one's country: 'To a beautiful Boy' and 'Ode to a Tank' were two of the more improbable contributions.

This unanimous support for the war effort waned hardly at all throughout the four years. What amounted to an almost suicidal *esprit de corps* had a lot to do with games-worship which had reached its zenith by 1914. At any rate, the pacifist voice was not heard at Winchester. Corps activity was trebled and, while the extra parades were not relished, talk was nevertheless of doing one's bit and telling the Hun where to get off. Unfit or superannuated schoolmasters were ever anxious to demonstrate their sympathy with those who were fighting: 'What good will you be in the trenches if you can't find your pen?'

By the time Jardine arrived at Winchester in September 1914, most of the older 'men' had left, or were about to leave, to take commissions in the services. For those left behind there began a gradual worsening of conditions and an uncertain wait until military age. And before long came the heavy casualty lists. A contemporary of Jardine's who was in the same house described to me a typical scene with the morning's *Times* spread out on the hall table and, round it, a group of boys studying the lists of dead and wounded. There was an element of ghoulishness in their interest, as if vicarious glory might be won through having known one of the fallen. Much has been written about the innocence and idealism of that generation, but the equanimity with which Wykehamists appear to have faced the future seems incredible.

The Wykehamist published a letter from the headmaster which cannot have inspired much confidence. Rendall asked all boys about to go to the front to 'please send me a postcard stating their unit and rank? This will help us to get our War Roll accurate ...!' No less than 500 Wykehamists were killed in the first world war.

With the premature departure of so many from the upper part of the school, Jardine found himself in the house cricket and football teams at the age of only 14. Being tall, with a long reach and lightning reflexes, he made a good goalkeeper. *The Wykehamist* singled him out for special attention, saying that he kept 'admirably, making quite first-rate saves'. But it was with cricket that his real ambitions lay. In Jardine's memorial address, Sir Hubert Ashton said that from the start he had an unusual air about him, mature and determined. And so, with a sound 33 in his first house match, he began his progress towards an inevitable place in the XI.

He and a boy called Leggatt became, in effect, the house XI. A contemporary bitterly recalls only ever being allowed to bowl once, and that was when Leggatt and Jardine wanted to change ends. It ought to be said that house matches were extremely important during the war. After W. G. Grace's famous letter to the *Sportsman* magazine, county cricket had been stopped and, as a gesture, Winchester and a number of other schools had drastically reduced their first XI fixtures. All interest at Winchester was therefore focussed on the inter-house competitions.

Jardine wrote in his instructional book, *Cricket* (1936), 'There has probably never been a stronger galaxy or combination of coaching talent functioning at one and the same time than Mr E. R. Wilson, Mr H. S. Altham, and Scofield Haigh, who were all at Winchester at the same time.' Scofield Haigh and Rockley Wilson played for England and Altham was a county cricketer, but despite the combined reputations of these three, Winchester cricket was at rather a low ebb in that Eton had been winning by considerable margins in the annual encounters. To make matters worse, Wilson and Altham went off to fight in 1915. Charles Little, Jardine's housemaster, took over a certain amount of the coaching responsibilities. He felt, as people are wont to do from time to time, that the current generation had lost the art of strokeplay – they had become cramped and inhibited. He believed, as did Wilson, that boys should be encouraged to play more on-side shots. Jardine paid many tributes in later life to Wilson's guidance, but he came under his influence for only one season (1919) and so some credit at least must be due to Little, although Jardine must have had a fairly clear idea at that stage of how his batting ought to progress.

His bowling, which presumably fell more within the province of the amiable pro, Haigh, was occasionally deadly. He bowled leg-breaks, but not googlies, with a swinging round-arm action and got his wickets more with variations of pace than with spin. Robertson-Glasgow described his approach to the wicket as halting and pensive. His match-winning performances became rarer towards the end of his schooldays, and then in his early twenties a combination of injury and modesty caused him to neglect his art. But in house matches between 1914 and 1918 he was a terror. When Scofield Haigh died suddenly in 1921, Jardine organised a collection for his widow.

In 1916 he was on something called Flannel Roll, which meant that he was in the first-team squad, but was not picked for any of the six matches. *The Wykehamist* betrays a slight sense of guilt in the reporting of these games. The casualty lists were regularly filling one, two and sometimes three columns of magazine space, and perhaps the editor thought that more patriotic ways could be found of occupying a June afternoon.

At the start of the 1917 season, however, it seemed that nobody was going to be playing in the XI who ought to be fighting in France, and accordingly more fixtures were arranged. Jardine earned his 'Boots' by playing for the 1st XI in some of the early-season matches, and he did well enough to secure himself a place in the side for the big match of the season against Eton. This fixture dated back to 1826 and was played alternately at Eton and Winchester. Eton, being a much larger school, always had the advantage; it was not an overwhelming one but Winchester victories were rare and there had been only three since the turn of the century. During the war the matches were reduced from two days to one day and did not count in the overall total of wins and losses. *The Times* covered this one as always and the match report was situated beside the columns of casualty details.

Jardine opened the Winchester innings and played with impressive fluency. Elegant strokes on both sides of the wicket brought him 30 runs before he was stumped. In the second innings he made a good start but was caught at the wicket on 13. The most interesting feature of the match, which Winchester lost by only one wicket, was the medium-paced bowling of J. d'E. E. Firth, a very short-sighted boy whose pebble-stone glasses used to steam up in the heat of a long spell. He took all ten of Eton's first innings wickets.

Jardine was now a person of some importance in the school. Scholars were respected more at Winchester than at other schools but the real 'swells' were undoubtedly the Lord's men, i.e. those who played for the 1st XI; they were treated with quivering, misty-eyed reverence. They had to work, though, since even the most Corinthian of fellows would be sent down unless he moved up through the school at the required rate. Jardine was quite able to keep his head above water in this respect but he was no scholar.

In the Lent term of 1918 Jardine was awarded his '2nd XI stockings' for football, and within a few weeks he was included in the 1st XI for the important match against Charterhouse. The result was a one-all draw and Jardine acquitted himself well enough to keep his place for the rest of that and the next season. Winchester soccer was very strong at that time, mainly due to the brilliance at centre-forward of C. T. Ashton. Jardine was not often tested but when he did have to make a contribution, he usually earned the approval of *The Wykehamist*. His safe handling and well-judged kicking were often noted. Once, though, in the 1919 Charterhouse match, it had to be reported that 'Jardine gathered the ball, but in throwing it out lost control, and the ball fell at the feet of one of their forwards who had no difficulty in scoring.'

The 1918 Eton match was played on a fast bumpy pitch and the Winchester batting collapsed against the traditionally strong Eton fast bowling. Jardine played 'soundly but tamely', making 6 in the first innings and 4 in the second. He could not seem to pitch his leg-breaks that day either and took a bit of a pasting. Winchester were very lucky to get away with a draw.

In that same year he was made captain of rackets. (This is a thrilling and dangerous game not unlike squash. It is played in a large, hard-surfaced court with a hard ball which travels extremely fast and hurts when it hits you. Timing is the secret, in both hitting and avoiding.) Jardine was thought 'not aggressive enough' in his first season as captain but the following year he won the Public Schools Handicap at Queen's Club and, with R. H. Hill, took Winchester to the semi-finals of the Public Schools Championship. They were just beaten by Marlborough in a desperately close match. Jardine was singled out as the best player by both *The Times* and *The Wykehamist*.

Jardine was not a natural athlete and even appeared to be rather stiff-legged when he ran (Australians were later to take particular note of this). *The Wykehamist* punctiliously records the results of all athletics competitions and nowhere can D. R. Jardine be found except in 1919 when he came second in 'throwing the cricket ball' and was also on the organising committee. Not, then, a runner or a jumper, he possessed a marvellous eye for the moving ball and excelled at any game which required that skill; fives, real tennis and rackets as well as cricket and football. (It was during a brief flirtation with lacrosse that he acquired his slightly crooked nose.)

There was another game at which Jardine achieved a degree of proficiency: a most bizarre activity called Winchester Football. It was a bit like rugger (which Winchester did not play) and could be played with teams of fifteen or six. The scrum was known as the 'hot' and the goal line was known as 'worms'. The hot packed down not in 3–4–1 formation but in three rows of three. The second and third rows, with their heads tucked in, pushed against the bottoms of the men in front rather than being 'meshed' as in a rugby scrum. The middle man in the front row was called O.P. (Over the Pill) and the man immediately behind him was known as Up-Arse. Herdman catches the atmosphere of a game in *Winchester 1916–1921*:

> The start of a match, especially fifteens, was very dramatic. Instead of starting to a whistle, they did so to the chime of Chapel Clock. There is no face on Chapel Clock so you never knew exactly when it was going to strike. The two opposing hots would be formed up, the front row upright, waiting to crash their heads down the moment the clock started to chime the half-hour. Sometimes they would be like this for over a minute, quivering with tenseness.... Then the front row would crash their heads down and try to get them into the stomachs of their opponents before they could do it to them. ... The poor men in the front row frequently got sore heads cracking them against the heads of the men opposite. I generally played O.P. and suffered a lot of this. ... Once Thomas was playing O.P. and the man behind him

started hotting too soon. He slapped back at him calling out: 'Hi, you Up-Arse, stop hotting.' I used to envy the oily little hot watchers. ...

Jardine played in the hot. It was clearly no place for the faint-hearted: the hotters' duties, apart from head-banging, included having to stand in front of an opponent while he booted the ball from point-blank range. Those who flinched – and Jardine was not among them – carried their shame to their graves. Jardine won his colours for the fifteen-a-side version of the game. For 'sixes' he was awarded his 'dress', an odd term for such a manly game; it meant that he never actually played in a match, having to sit instead on the subs' bench.

Jardine's last cricket season was triumphal. He scored 997 runs from 16 innings at an average of 66.46. His average stay at the crease was $2\frac{1}{4}$ hours. As a captain he was tactically sound but there were, to begin with, doubts about his ability to unify the team. Great men were later known to quail before the gaze of those piercing blue eyes but ten supremely confident Wyke-hamists probably needed more delicate handling. He got them together in the end, his own example helping him to assert his authority.

One of the perks of captaincy was the right to use Lord's Box, which was a small, portable escritoire. It was not a great deal of use, as one can imagine, but Jardine was duly presented with it at the appropriate time. Not wishing to seem churlish, he opened it and examined the inside. But what he saw was not meant for his eyes: it was a note written by his predecessor and presumably intended for the master in charge of cricket. On no account, advised the letter, must D. R. Jardine be appointed captain of Lord's. Jardine had incurred the wrath of his three previous captains and they had all felt obliged to discipline him at one time or another. He was precocious, wilful and better than anyone else, a combination that never goes unpunished.

As captain of Lord's and a co-prae, his position inside the school was unchallenged. He had a good many friends but they were mostly in other houses. He was less popular in his own house, where he was thought too authoritarian, especially on the cricket field.

He was determined to win the inter-house cricket cup. Anything less than maximum effort from his side resulted in lengthy sessions of fielding practice. 65 years on, this particular punishment is bitterly remembered. Herdman also makes reference to Jardine's leadership methods:

> ... but he really expected so much of the team, and was so scathing if they made any mistakes, that he had them all on a twitter of nerves. One poor man missed a catch early on in the final, and the man he missed went on to score a century [C. T. Ashton – 107]. For the rest of his career he never heard the end of it, how he lost us the cup.

The match referred to was not the final but the last match that Cook's House played in the 1919 Turner Cup. There have been furious arguments about Jardine's captaincy of Cook's, sparked off by a story in the preface to *The Cricketers' Who's Who* of 1983 which was then reproduced in *The Observer*. At the end of the match, ran the story,

> The Cookite scorer said it was a tie. The College scorer said College had won by one run. Jardine, acting in his capacity as skipper of Lord's, sent for both scorebooks, examined them, found a mistake, beat both the scorers, and announced that Cook's had won by one run, and therefore won Hopper Pot (Turner Cup) 1920. There was of course no appeal from him as skipper of Lord's.

Jardine is then said to have pinned up a notice which normally listed the names of the representative side but which read instead: 'C House Turner Cup 1920: D. R. Jardine, W. M. Leggatt. The following might have been included had they not been unable to bat or bowl, or even to field.' There followed the names of those in disgrace.

Such a match could not have taken place and the story was constructed from remembered fragments of a number of matches played in 1919. Jardine left in 1919 and Leggatt in 1918 and so neither could have played in 1920. The two players did, however, monopolise proceedings when they played together (J. C. Clay, later of Glamorgan and England, had done the same thing when Jardine first arrived at Winchester), but after Leggatt left, Jardine had only moderate support. Although Cook's came close to the final in 1919, they never actually reached one in Jardine's time.

The bit about beating the scorers has an interesting derivation. There was an old Winchester notion that if a match resulted in either a tie or a victory by one run then both the scorers should be beaten. Fortunately for the scorers, the custom survived only in a fairly light-hearted ritual form; the captain of Lord's raised and lowered the ground-ash without actually hurting anybody. There was a tied match in the second round of the 1919 Turner Cup and Jardine did play in it. It may well be that, as Captain of Lord's he administered the ritual beating, but there was no dispute over the score. It is true that he put up a notice with roughly the wording mentioned in the above story. It was a highly unpopular act and he later apologised.

He addressed himself grimly to the task of winning the 1919 match against Eton. Even at the age of 18, his captaincy left nothing to chance – he made all his team go and pray in Eton College chapel the evening before the match.

It was a low-scoring game and Jardine held his side together in both innings by scoring 35 and 89, 'a thoroughly commendable piece of batting,' said *The Times*. So many schoolboy batsmen are basically hitters, and for that reason they rarely succeed in top-class cricket where a good eye alone is not enough. Jardine did not start to acquire the muscle to hit the ball really hard until after he left Winchester, and in that he was probably fortunate since it meant that he had to rely for his runs on timing and a full range of strokes.

Winchester won one of their most famous victories in the Eton match of 1919. It is still known as 'Jardine's match', not just for his batting but for his captaincy as well. When set to bowl out Eton on an easy pitch in the fourth innings, he took a risk in bowling only two of his five bowlers almost unchanged throughout the afternoon and evening, but the gamble paid off.

When the team's train arrived at Winchester station they found a large crowd waiting to cheer them. The College was out in force, of course, but a great many townspeople also turned out to join the celebrations. Jardine was carried shoulder-high from the station through the streets of Winchester to the College gates.

The following week Harrow travelled to Winchester to play a one-day game. The home side knocked up a large score, with Jardine's own contribution being 135 not out. He was widely criticised for not accelerating the scoring rate after he had reached his hundred. *The Times*, *Wisden* and *The Wykehamist* all thought he was unduly cautious. 'Hit out or get out' was not then the anathema it is now. The rain came and ruined the match, and with the benefit of hindsight, everyone said Jardine ought to have declared sooner.

What annoyed the critics in this match, as in many other matches later on at a much higher level, was that his unruffled correctness gave the impression that he could really murder an attack if he only put his mind to it. His calmness frequently led the spectator to believe that the bowling and the wicket were of the very friendliest, when of course they often were not. Quite simply, he played for his side and in this instance, as the leading batsman, he considered it his duty to stay in. If he played cautiously while compiling his hundred it was not through personal ambition but because conditions required caution. And when he made the declaration, he was only three runs short of his 1000 for the season, so he could hardly be accused of selfishness.

The luncheon interval of the Harrow match was stretched to 80 minutes so that all the photographers present had a fair chance of getting their pictures while the light was good. Coming so soon after Jardine's triumph through the streets of Winchester, this episode exemplified the celebrity enjoyed by those public school heroes. And how very enjoyable it must have been, too, with none of the intrusion of privacy and constant recognition that modern teenage cult figures have to suffer. Instead, they commanded the respect of their elders, the veneration of their juniors and, presumably, the murderous envy of their contemporaries.

Their deeds were reported in the national press, also *The Boy's Own Paper* and *The Captain*, two very healthy magazines (the latter, incidentally, was edited by someone who called himself 'The Old Fag'). These magazines frequently published photographs and short biographies of school captains. They were pin-ups really: honest, clean chaps who looked you straight in the eye, firm but fair. They were very different from the pre-1900 hedonists with distant, ethereal expressions, posed in what photographers imagined to be Arcadian scenes – false grass and bits of pillar. After the first world war heroes tended to look more clean-cut and alert, the kind whose pluck had won us the war. Group poses, too, had become more ordered, more military. The two most junior members of the team now sat cross-legged and straight-backed – no more lolling sideways and pouting. Jardine's photograph, taken when he was eighteen, is an unusual mixture of both styles.

Before leaving school cricket for good, Jardine was asked to play in two matches at Lord's during the summer holidays. The first was Lord's Schools against The Rest. Lord's Schools were the eight who played an annual match at Lord's and The Rest were the riff-raff who didn't. Winchester used to play both Eton and Harrow there, but in 1854 there was some unpleasantness and, as a result, the fixture was discontinued. Henceforth, Winchester had to muck in with The Rest.

There was a fair showing of talent in the first match: L. P. Hedges, C. H. Gibson and G. T. S. Stevens, who had all had astonishingly successful school seasons (the latter had even played for the Gentlemen), also A. P. F. Chapman and R. C. Robertson-Glasgow, the Charterhouse express with a run-up as long as his name.

Jardine made a top score of 44 in The Rest's first innings and, after an eventful afternoon, found himself batting again at the end of the first day. He and a chap called Considine (Blundells) survived what *The Times* called 'the mauvais quatre d'heure' before the close, and went on the next day to share a stand of 205; Considine got 118, Jardine 91. The Rest won by 225. *Wisden* said, 'Jardine was deficient in off-side hitting, but apart from that he played a wonderfully good innings.'

Playing for the Public Schools XI against P. F. Warner's XI later in the week, he made 57 (lbw to Rockley Wilson) and 55. The match was drawn slightly in favour of Warner's team. Reggie Spooner made 109, which must have been an education for the lads. *The Times*: 'Mr. Jardine has had a most successful week, and there is no question that he is a very good batsman, particularly on the on-side. ... He watched the ball most carefully, played with the straightest of bats and made the most of his chances of scoring on the leg side.'

Summing up Jardine's season, *Wisden* said,

It must not be imagined that Jardine is a player without strokes. He can and does hit the ball very hard on the on-side and indeed he lets off few chances of scoring. He has, too, the off-side strokes, though he does not use them quite as often as he might. He is a cricketer with an old head on young shoulders, and I [E. B. Noel] shall be very surprised if he doesn't follow his father's footsteps and get into the Oxford side as a freshman.

2
Oxford

Oxford was somewhat overcrowded in 1919. There was a large influx of young men who had had their education interrupted by the war and some of the colleges had to erect Nissen huts to accommodate the extra population. Newly demobbed and with horrors still fresh in their memories, they came up to the University, old before their time perhaps but grateful to be alive and determined to make the most of it. Hearty frivolity prevailed (all the Brideshead campery came later) and the aristocrats were most definitely the Blues.

It was a little more difficult to get in than it had been before the war, and there was now a proper entrance examination. And while there were undoubtedly undergraduates who still managed to sneak in on their batting averages, Jardine was not one of them; he was a most diligent student who would have got in even without his sporting talents.

He was one of 88 freshmen who entered New College in September 1919. This was the most fashionable of Colleges, much favoured by Eton and particularly by Winchester. Shy and not naturally hearty, Jardine found it difficult to mix socially and kept himself rather apart. His high intelligence and greater maturity gave him an air of aloofness and he was even thought snobbish, which he was not at all.

He kept up with his old Winchester friends, the closest of whom was now an exhibitioner of Balliol. His name was Jack Frazer, an extremely popular figure who was to die in a skiing accident when he was only 25. He played cricket and soccer for Oxford and, together with Jardine, for a very strong Old Wykehamist team which won the Dunn Amateur Association Football Cup in 1920. Jardine was given a trial in goal in the Freshmen's Match but did not make it into the Oxford team. He took up real tennis in his first term and made such astonishing progress with this complex and subtle game that only by a whisker did he miss his Blue the following summer. He played rackets less than at Winchester, preferring to concentrate on his new-found passion and in his second term he was included in the six-man Oxford team to play against Prince's Club. He lost his match and Oxford were beaten 5–1, but on very few subsequent occasions was he on the losing side.

The Oxford University Cricket Club had recently appointed the great Surrey and England professional batsman, Tom Hayward, as head groundsman and coach. Since he had been one of the most prolific run-scorers in the history of the game, it was, perhaps not too surprising that one of his first jobs at Oxford was to deaden the wicket at the Parks by treating it with marl. This was the dawning of the age of the super-bats: of the 25 all-time top run-scorers, 16 were playing between 1919 and 1939; it was a bad time to be embarking on a career as a bowler. Hayward's attempt to reproduce Oval conditions at Oxford was not entirely successful to begin with, but by the middle of the 1920 season, the pitch was playing well enough.

Hayward's influence on Jardine's batting was mainly in the area of defence and footwork. There was probably no greater exponent around at the time, but the advice and experience he passed on were to lead Jardine into trouble before very long. At Winchester Rockley Wilson had stressed the importance of getting into line to play the ball: 'When I play back and miss, I like to see the ball hit Wilson.' Hayward took this a stage further and advocated pad-play. He even admitted – and this outraged traditionalists – that his legs had saved his wicket on countless occasions. 'Oh, where were your legs, sir?' he is said to have asked Donald Knight reproachfully after he had been bowled by an off-break. Cardus wrote that in Lancashire before the first world war, they said that a batsman who allowed himself to be bowled by an off-break was either a fool or a hero.

The point was that until 1935, it was impossible to be lbw to a ball that pitched outside the off stump, so if you stuck your leg in the way you were in the clear. More and more batsmen were using their pads to defend their wickets by the start of the 'twenties, and it caused a certain amount of grumbling. But it was Hayward's two pupils, Knight and Jardine, who were the cause of a great lbw row to which we shall come in due course. For the moment, it is enough to know that Tom Hayward's particular kind of professionalism impressed itself on Jardine right from the start.

The University teams were really unknown quantities at the start of the 1920 season. So many people had come up late after the war who had no current form on which their relative strengths could be judged, there was also fierce competition for places. Jardine made a good start to the season with 60 not out in the Freshman's match. He was missed at slip when he had scored 1 but afterwards made hardly a mistake. Tom Hayward's new pitch was far from easy to bat on and Jardine emerged with great credit. In contrast, Greville Stevens, who was later to become a useful England all-rounder, was thought by *The Isis* to be 'most unpromising'.

The following week saw Jardine's first appearance in first-class cricket. It was against Warwickshire at the Parks. Oxford, batting second, had to begin their innings late on the first day when the light was terrible. Jardine opened and was bowled by the fast bowler, Calthorpe, for 0. Calthorpe bowled him again in the second innings, but this time Jardine had made equal top score of 29. Oxford were handicapped by two highly unlikely lbw decisions going against them and they lost by 36 runs.

In mid-May, P. F. Warner brought his Championship-winning Middlesex side to Oxford. He won the toss and, not liking the look of Hayward's pitch, put Oxford in to bat. This was a mistake: Oxford grafted all day and finished with a reasonable score, Jardine making 60 faultless runs. Middlesex were left with about three hours' batting on the final afternoon and failed by only ten minutes to play out time. The defeat was something of an irritation to Warner as he began his season of triumph and the favourable impression that he had formed of Jardine's batting the previous season at Lord's was re-affirmed.

Oxford faced Essex the following week in confident spirits. The captain, Gilligan, won the toss and, not wishing to be caught like Warner, chose to bat. But 'the pitch', said *The Isis*, 'was queer' and Oxford wickets fell quickly (Jardine going for 11). With four down, Gilligan came out to join H. P. Ward and together they retrieved the situation. The Oxford innings closed on the first evening at 331. McGahey and Russell began the Essex reply purposefully, Russell playing particularly well, and by lunch on the second day they were 201 for 1. Gilligan had used all his regular bowlers to little effect. He had even given Jardine five overs before lunch, but this had only resulted in 22 more runs being scored by Essex. Quite what was said in the interval is not known, but when play resumed Jardine continued to bowl at one end while the fast bowler, V. R. Price, operated at the other. The ball apparently came off the Parks wicket a little more quickly after lunch, but that alone could not possibly have accounted for what followed. In a little over threequarters of an hour, Essex went from 201 for 1 to 219 all out. Jardine bowled 7.3 overs of his leg-breaks, conceded six runs and took six wickets, including those of Russell and Perrin.

It was not turn so much as flight, apparently, that did the damage. Jardine suddenly, and sadly only temporarily, acquired the knack of making the ball dip at the last minute. What appeared to be slow, looping full tosses came to earth earlier than anticipated and then did just enough to beat both the swishing and the prodding bat. The match reports were united in the uncharitable belief that this was a once-in-a-lifetime performance. They were right.

The Essex batsmen, thinking a new Sydney Barnes had arrived, made a terrible hash of their second innings. They played Jardine with monumental caution and tried to thrash the other bowlers, with the predictable result that the other bowlers got them out. The regular leg-spinner, Bettington, had a particularly good day, taking 5 for 48 including a hat-trick. Essex went down by 235 runs. (The first batsman out, McGahey, complained that he had been bowled by 'some bugger called Robinson Crusoe'. Thus did Robertson-Glasgow earn his lifelong nickname.)

Jardine was awarded his Blue after making 35 and 70 against the Free Foresters a week later. Then, after a double failure in the match against Somerset, work kept him away from the cricket field for the next three weeks.

One of the big matches of the season was the University match. It generated tremendous interest, and not just among cricket followers. As with the Boat Race, very few people knew the names and strengths of those taking part but everyone supported one side or the other. In 1920 cricket had never been so popular. It represented a return to normality after the ghastliness of the war. The press devoted particular attention to the prospects for the University match, reflecting a national feeling that the proper place for young men was on the sports field, not the battlefield.

The previous season, the counties, fearing a lack of interest in the revival of the County Championship, had experimented with two-day instead of three-day matches. The experiment was unsuccessful. The public clearly wanted cricket, if nothing else, to remain exactly as it had been before the war. 1920, then, was the first proper post-war season and the University match was to be its first high point.

Unfortunately, it was more or less washed out. The first and second days passed without a ball being bowled. On the first afternoon – and this is a measure of the match's importance – it was agreed that play could continue into a fourth day if necessary. Robertson-Glasgow recalled that there was no shortage of cricket in the Oxford dressing room; so intense was the struggle that complaints were made by MCC members who were trying to get some shuteye in the reading room below. Conditions were in fact adequate for play from 4.15 on the second afternoon, but by then the chaps had left in search of alternative amusement and could not be found.

A start was made at three o'clock on the third afternoon. In the limited time available, Cambridge managed to bowl out Oxford for 193 and were themselves 161 for 9 when the rain arrived to put the game out of its misery.

The Cambridge bowler, Marriott, took seven wickets. 'Father' Marriott bowled slow, flighted leg-breaks and googlies, he could turn the ball very sharply and was unplayable on a drying pitch. His many admirers claim that he was the worst batsman in Test, if not all, cricket. This is no idle boast; in his entire career (1920–37) he scored 555 runs. It should be said in fairness, though, that he also took 724 wickets. Jardine thought highly of him and in this, their first encounter, Marriott took his wicket for 13.

Jardine was considered by *Wisden* to have fallen short of the hopes raised by his doings in 1919. This might seem to be a little harsh but it indicates the generally higher standard of school and University cricket then in relation to county cricket. The really exciting prospects in the Oxford side at this stage were Bettington and Stevens, both of whom went on to play for Middlesex in the summer vacation. Bettington was a much better leg-spinner than Jardine, and Stevens, though possessed of nothing approaching Jardine's style, was a more attacking batsman. Jardine's technique was beyond question but, at a time when grafting was more of a tactical move and less of a career in itself, some observers thought he exercised more caution than was seemly in a gentleman at the crease. Part of his problem was nerves; a fear of failure caused him on occasion to tense up, and then he found himself unable to play a stroke for overs on end. These periods of inactivity were sometimes due simply to good bowling or a difficult pitch, but his technique was such that he rarely appeared to be struggling and so it always seemed that he ought to be scoring more quickly. He limited his strokeplay at this stage for the very good reason that he did not feel he had gained sufficient mastery of certain shots, particularly off-side shots, to employ them with safety in a match. He was not going to rush things.

At the end of the University season he was asked to take part in an Incogniti tour to America. The party was surprisingly strong considering the sort of opposition that they were likely to meet. Not that they were household names, but there was a fair proportion of first-class cricketers including such luminaries as T. C. Lowry, who was to be New Zealand's first Test captain, R. St L. Fowler, D.R.J. himself and Major E. G. Wynyard, who took part in the 'industrial action' Test of 1896. They sailed there and back on the *Mauretania* and were away for six weeks in all, playing matches in New York, Toronto and against a number of clubs in Philadelphia. Of their nine games, they won seven and drew two.

For Jardine the tour was one of ups and downs. Against the Philadelphia Cricket Club he had, as the *New York Herald* reported, 'hardly gotten set when he was caught at the wicket for a duck egg'. But his luck changed when he played against S. F. Bretz's New York XI. The *New York Times* was ecstatic – 'The sensation of the first day's play was the wonderful stand of 157 made by P. R. Jardini (*sic*). In compiling this total the Briton made 7 boundaries and a 6, the latter hit being a smash over the fence on the locker end of the field. Jardini was tendered an ovation when he reached the century mark. He was at bat for 3 hrs. 24 mins before he was stumped.' A few days later, he made a hundred before lunch against All New York on Staten Island.

By the time they returned, the domestic season was over. The Championship had been thrillingly won by Middlesex in the final match at Lord's and cricket had most emphatically re-established itself. Even the silent film industry saw that there was money to be made out of the new cricket fever. Two films appeared: *The Hope Of His Side* and *Out First Ball*.

During the close season Jardine represented the University at real tennis and kept goal for his college in the inter-collegiate cup matches. New College had won the previous year's competition and again found themselves in the final in 1921, this time against Oriel. At the end of 90 minutes neither side had scored and so the game went into extra time. New College showed themselves to be the fitter side and had the best of things until, in the one hundred and twelfth minute, Jardine fumbled a high but innocuous shot and a very exhausted Oriel forward managed to score off the rebound. The match report is pleasantly sympathetic to Jardine but takes a slightly unnatural delight in the agonies of fatigue suffered by the other New College players as they tried in vain to save the match.

Encouraged by the success of the 1920 cricket season, the authorities greedily crammed their fixture cards for the following summer. The ones who were to suffer most from this were the Australian tourists. On 29 December the Australian Board of Control agreed that their side should play no less than 38 matches between 30 April and 10 September. It would have been a punishing schedule even under normal circumstances, but the travelling which such a heavy programme entailed was made particularly laborious and uncomfortable by the disruption of train services caused by a miners' strike. The Australians spent much of their time waiting on platforms in the middle of the night. A polite request for a reduction in playing time was rejected and the English authorities held the visitors to the original agreement. Everyone, they said, was experiencing the same inconvenience.

It was true that county sides had sometimes had to take the field after only a couple of hours' sleep the previous night, but those cricketers would have a run of home matches from time to time during which they were able to recover from the long nights of travelling. For the Australians there was no respite. They pressed their case again, this time with a certain lack of courtesy, and bad feeling ensued. All they wanted was a day off before each Test. This was not an unreasonable request but, if granted, it would mean that the matches against Oxford, Gloucestershire and, most importantly, Yorkshire would have to be completed inside two days. Eventually, a compromise was reached: Oxford relinquished their third day, Gloucester reduced the playing hours and Yorkshire – good old Yorkshire – asked for no more than their due, called a spade a spade and made no concession whatsoever to the visitors. The press were genuinely surprised at the Australians' presumption and clearly thought they were a bunch of nancy-boys to want all this rest between matches – Spofforth hadn't needed rest, Trumper had never slept a wink in his life. The English organisers might have been more sympathetic were it not for the fact that the Australians were flattening every side they encountered. Overworked as they were, Warwick Armstrong's men managed to win 22 of their 38 matches.

Oxford came up against them early in the season, just before the first Test. By then, the University had played three matches: they had lost to Hampshire, beaten an under-strength Somerset team and, but for an over-cautious declaration by their new captain, Price, might have beaten Middlesex again. Jardine was in good form, having made 53 and 54 against Middlesex on a difficult pitch and an impressive 60 against Hampshire. This last innings was significant. He had acquired more confidence, it seems, he scored faster than in the previous season and allowed himself a full range of strokes on both sides of the wicket.

The strength of Armstrong's team was already known, even though the English public had not yet seen them in their full horror. Only a few months before, they had massacred J. W. H. T. Douglas' MCC team in Australia, winning all five Tests by huge margins. So Oxford had a fair idea of the sort of people they were up against.

As a small consolation for the loss of the third day, the Australians offered to start play early, a gesture which was appreciated possibly more by the 3000 people gathered around the Christ Church ground than by the Oxford team. Armstrong, massive and unsmiling, led his men onto the field. Since McDonald was not playing, the captain himself shared the new ball with Gregory. Jardine and Bickmore opened the Oxford innings and appeared to play with confidence. Jardine lost Bickmore at 41 and was joined by Holdsworth. They were somewhat hesitant about their running, and declined a number of runs for fear of lightning returns. The score moved along at a brisk enough pace, but at 58 Jardine ran his partner out, an unfortunate but not wholly unexpected occurrence. *The Isis*, which never missed an opportunity to snipe at Jardine, considered him to be not only a very bad judge of a run but slow with it. When Mailey came into the attack, Jardine used his feet well, coming right forward to kill the spin or getting back onto his stumps to anything short. He had made 32 in just over an hour when he played back to a ball from Mailey which did not seem to do anything and was caught and bowled.

Apart from his running, he had as usual looked confident and in control. He never quite dominated the bowling but neither was he intimidated by it. Oxford were all out for 180. *The Times* was not impressed: '... the inexperience and nervousness of some of their batsmen may have flattered the Australian bowlers in some degree, and made them look more difficult than they really were.' 'A pretty poor gallop' was the *Morning Post*'s opinion. Clearly, the might of these Australians was by no means universally recognised as yet. Indeed, even when Gregory and McDonald were scything through the English batting in the Tests, a loud minority expressed opinions to the effect that George Parr, or whoever, would have thought it was his birthday if he'd come up against that kind of bowling. The Australians still had to prove themselves under English conditions, and there is no reason to suppose that they took it easy against Oxford.

The Australians batted through the latter part of the day and for about an hour the following morning, during which time they scored 294 runs, with Macartney making 77 of his best. There was at this stage a good chance of an Australian win, and such a boost to their confidence only two days before the first Test would have been very welcome. Jardine and Bickmore, opening Oxford's second innings, faced the towering hostility of Gregory and the unforgiving length and accuracy of Armstrong. They survived for 35 testing and occasionally painful minutes, and then the rain came. Altogether $2\frac{1}{2}$ hours were lost, and it was not until four o'clock, with conditions far from easy for the fielding side, that Armstrong led his men out again. *The Isis* reporter wrote – and it is as well to bear this in mind in view of what followed – that 'their sporting action was greatly appreciated'.

The Australian captain bowled Bickmore in the first over after the resumption. This left nine wickets to take in a fraction under two hours. Jardine and the new batsman, Holdsworth, got their heads down, Jardine taking most of the bowling. To start with he was finding the fielders with almost every shot, but after about half an hour he began to place the ball to greater effect. The danger of defeat receded and the batsmen started to play their shots, but they were still a little in awe of the Australians' legendary throwing arms and missed a good few runs. There was a fluency in Jardine's batting which made a lasting impression on all those present; it was classical and quite devoid of risk. None of the eight bowlers whom Armstrong tried could unsettle him, not even Gregory, whose short-pitched leg-stump attack was unquestionably nastier than anything he had faced to date. *The Times* said: 'Mr. Jardine was especially good in driving on the on, and in following round short balls on the leg side. Most of his runs were made on that side, but, when he did drive to the off, he hit clean and hard.'

Now we come to an important episode. The scoreboard on the Christ Church ground did not show the batsmen's running totals and, although it was clear by half an hour before the close that a result was not possible, the spectators and the players had no means of knowing about any personal batting milestones that might be approaching. As six o'clock approached, the Australians, being experienced players, would have known that the tall lad had put together a good 80 or 90. One or two full tosses were discreetly delivered, but Jardine declined to hit them. A likely explanation for this is that the young man, for whom this was a very big day indeed, was concentrating so hard on simply playing the bowling that he had not the faintest idea what his score was. As cricketers familiar with scoreboard-less grounds will know, there is often a reluctance on the part of those in the pavilion to let a batsman know when he is approaching a landmark in case it puts him off. It would not at all have been the thing for Jardine to have shouted to the scorers, 'How many have I got?' and it would hardly have been in his nature to do so. And he would, one feels certain, have been suspicious of big, tough Australians bowling full tosses and telling him to hit out for his hundred.

Perhaps there was a signal from the pavilion and perhaps he was too preoccupied to notice. At any rate, he was 96 not out when the bails were removed. *The Illustrated Sporting and Dramatic News* told its readers:

> The Oxford match with Australia was robbed of most of its importance by the two-day absurdity, and is only mentioned to record the fact that D. R. Jardine was not out 96 when stumps were drawn, and that most teams would have given him at least a chance to get his hundred.

From this, and similar accounts, originates the theory that Jardine developed a hatred of all Australians because Armstrong did not bowl him one last over of easy ones. But, as we have seen, the Australians could not have been more accommodating, and there does not appear to have been resentment from Oxford because of the loss of the third day. In any case, Jardine's personality was such that he would not have derived much satisfaction from a hundred which included 'presentation' runs and necessitated an extension of playing time.

In the long run, it was probably best that he had not made those four runs. If he had, the chances are that he would have been thrown into a Test match a few weeks later. As it was, his selection was urged by Warner in *The Cricketer*. While his innings at Oxford was a very good one indeed, it was no preparation for the fury of Gregory and McDonald at Test level. Such an ordeal might have been a serious setback.

Immediately after the Oxford match, the Australians travelled to Trent Bridge where they beat England by ten wickets in two days. Gregory and McDonald took 16 wickets between them. They bowled a lot of bouncers – Gregory actually bowled Tyldesley off his face – and only Holmes and Woolley managed to show any positive resistance.

The selectors, with whom one can only sympathise, cast desperately around for a solution. At that stage, the two highest scores against the tourists had been made by Jardine and Hubert Ashton. Ashton's hundred for Cambridge was not quite as impressive as Jardine's 96; he had not had to face Gregory but had played McDonald pretty well. Young as they were, these two must have been considered for places. But then some of the selectors saw A.J. (*Escaping Club*) Evans make a breezy 69 for MCC against Australia at Lord's and so he became an improbable choice for the Test. One feels that if Jardine had got past the significant three-figure mark, he might well have been picked ahead of Evans (who, in the event, made 4 and 14 and was not asked back). There were five other changes in the England side. A 49-year-old C. B. Fry was even sent for, but he withdrew at the last minute. Australia won the second Test by eight wickets.

Jardine and Ashton remained in Test contention for another month or so. Jardine made a hundred against the Army and a hundred and a fifty against Sussex. Ashton made a hundred in the University match. But the selectors went for experience, and rightly so. The crop of young players was miserably thin as a result of the ravages of war, and such bright prospects as existed were better nurtured than thrown to the hungry jaws of Gregory and McDonald. England managed to avoid a ninth successive defeat by drawing the fourth Test, and a fortnight later they drew the final one, too. Altogether, 30 players had appeared in England colours that summer.

In the second innings of Oxford's match against the Army, Jardine scored his maiden first-class century. He was dropped before reaching double figures and thereafter he proceeded with caution. Most of his runs came from on-side shots as usual, but he also allowed himself some elegant square cuts. He reached his hundred in $2\frac{1}{2}$ hours, then, when quick runs were needed, he took only half an hour to make another 45 before being run out.

In his next innings, which was against Sussex ten days later, he made his second first-class hundred. This was a more dour performance, as indeed was needed by an Oxford team depleted by exams. For over three hours the bowlers hurled themselves at the impenetrable defence. Jardine on the back foot was a particularly depressing sight for a bowler; it was as if the ball, after pitching, slowed down, gave up all ambition and then thudded tamely into the middle of the bat. It was only through a supreme effort of concentration and fakir-like self-control that he was able to play these long defensive innings. It was not really his natural game. It indicated how deeply he cared about any match he played in. He set very high standards, particularly for himself, and always, always he put the interests of his side first. Swashbucklers were two a penny in those days, and amateur batsmen who were prepared to eschew all strokes in any but the direst circumstances were rarities. There were plenty of amateurs who relished a tight situation, but that is not quite the same thing. There was no do-or-die desperation in his batting although he was happy enough to take risks, as indeed he had done in his previous innings, but only when the situation warranted. He was not a man to leave the crease, outwardly ashamed though inwardly pleased, with a snazzy 29.

The description in *The Times* of his 105 against Sussex might have applied to any number of Jardine's innings over the next 13 years: '... impervious to every temptation offered by the bowlers, and yet scoring off anything like a loose ball, and always along the ground. Mr. Jardine in fact must be one of the very soundest leg-side batsmen playing.' His 51 in the second innings was less certain, and he was involved in another run-out.

Jardine's second University match was disappointing both for him and for his side. Cambridge made a record score in their first innings, and this effectively put the game out of Oxford's reach. Oxford, having started the match as favourites on account of their superior batting strength, had to follow on and were defeated on the third morning of the match by an innings and 24 runs. Jardine failed, having got a start in both innings. D. L. A. Jephson wrote in *The Cricketer*: 'One colour, and one colour only, permeated the entire picture, and that colour flourishes on the banks of the river Cam.'

The Ashton brothers played in this match: Gilbert, Hubert and Claude. Ronald Mason wrote that they sounded like a roll-call by Duke William of Normandy prior to his Channel crossing. They are not mentioned much these days, but in the early 'twenties they were a very glamorous trio indeed. They all captained Winchester and Cambridge, and between them they acquired nine Blues and two MCs, the latter being, if not a prerequisite, certainly a great aid to celebrity in those days. The Jardine and Ashton families had been close in India, and the friendship was maintained by the younger generation. They were all batsmen, with different styles, and Claude bowled as well. There is a composite photograph which shows their respective attitudes at the crease. It is rather like a diagram of the evolution of man: Gilbert, the eldest, crouches two-shouldered over his bat, Hubert is side-on but still stoops a little, and Claude, the youngest, stands confidently erect, like 'Civilised Batsman', his shoulder pointing straight at the bowler. They were stupendous fielders, and it was due largely to this that Archie MacLaren picked them to play in his weird team which so astonishingly beat Armstrong's Australians at the end of that wearying season. An inspired piece of selection it turned out to be: between them, they took six catches, two of them breath-taking. Hubert was a *Wisden* Cricketer of the Year of 1921, along with Macartney, Gregory and McDonald. He would almost certainly have played for England at some stage had he not gone out to take up the white man's burden in Rangoon. Gilbert went on to play for Worcestershire and was headmaster of Abberley Hall school for 40 years. Claude was killed on active service in the second world war. There was a fourth, elder brother, Percy, who never seems to get a mention. He played for Winchester and Essex but the loss of an eye in the first war prevented him from matching the achievements of the others, and so no one ever talks about 'the four Ashtons'. The three Ashtons played important parts in the Cambridge victory of 1921; Gilbert was captain, Hubert made 118 and Claude 48.

The Jardine family home was now at Walton-on-Thames and so he had a residential qualification for Surrey. He was invited to join the county after the University season. They were no doubt grateful enough to have his services – he was then eighth in the national averages – but what they really wanted was a bowler. Their success during 1920 and 1921 was amazing in view of their weakness in that department. That they managed to win so many matches was due mainly to the brilliant captaincy of Percy Fender, a peerless tactician who was prepared to take the most outrageous risks in order to secure a win.

Surrey were further handicapped in 1921 by the absence of Hobbs, who aggravated a thigh injury sustained originally in Australia during the winter, and was then stricken down by appendicitis. He was able to play only one Championship match. The makeshift opener, Jeacocke, proved to be a great success, and it is surprising that Jardine took over as Sandham's partner as soon as he started playing. But Jeacocke was a busy man off the cricket field and it may well be that he was glad of a little temporary relief. Jardine was brought in for three matches; in his first, against Lancashire at the Oval, he made 27 and actually opened the Surrey bowling, although it was late on the last day when he did so and the match was very dead by then.

At Blackheath, he took part in Surrey's traditionally unsuccessful away encounter with Kent. The Kent batsman, Hardinge, after being dropped off the first ball of the match, made a double-century and enabled his side to declare at 464. Surrey made an equally substantial reply, to which Jardine's contribution was 19. By the third day, the game was in need of a sporting declaration, but Fender was away on Test duty and so events were allowed to take their course with a stalemate being the inevitable result. It is a little strange that the match was left to fizzle out, for both sides were in the Championship race with two-thirds of the season gone. Kent seemed happy enough to take first-innings points but one can't help thinking that, had Fender been there, he might have persuaded the Kent skipper to live a little more dangerously.

After a failure against Somerset, Jardine was dropped for the next three matches and Jeacocke was recalled. He returned to the side in mid-August, however, and with his fellow-Harlequin, Donald Knight, put on 64 for the first wicket against Northamptonshire. He had reached 30 when he ran himself out. Surrey did not need to bat again and the victory put them at the top of the Championship table, with Middlesex second and Yorkshire third. The match against Yorkshire which followed was therefore crucial to their chances, but they came up against Rhodes having one of his best games of the season. He took six wickets in a mesmeric spell of bowling and Surrey were all out for 129. Jardine made 25 and *The Times* said that he batted 'well but not convincingly. ... There is a staleness in his cricket which one cannot quite understand. He has the strokes and the wrists but he does not use them. Perhaps it was his carefulness which made Surrey bat so badly.' This seemed rather to undervalue Rhodes' bowling. It was to his old master Rockley Wilson, though, that Jardine succumbed. Wilson caught and bowled him with his slower one for which Jardine always had a weakness.

Surrey had a miserable time in the field, bowling badly and dropping most things that came to hand, and Yorkshire were able to build up a lead of 251. Jardine and Knight took a positive approach to saving the match and at the close, after just over an hour's batting, they had put on 81. *The Times* commended their bravery, though only grudgingly in Jardine's case: 'He was not afraid to use the cross-bat to Rhodes – a daring which shows the height of excellence or the depth of stupidity.' Jardine lost Knight the next morning but he continued to play his strokes. When he had made 60, he got a long hop from Macaulay outside the off stump. He tried to clear the off-side field, hit too early and was caught at backward point. Surrey collapsed after that, or perhaps it was more of a steady crumble: eight wickets went down for 129 in 93 overs. Sportsmen that they were, Surrey batted on after lunch in abysmal light to give Yorkshire the chance to secure a deserved win. With ignominy perhaps only an over away, one of the most violent storms in living memory broke over the Oval, and Surrey were saved. Fender's gentlemanly action could, for all he knew at the time, have cost Surrey the Championship. Fond as

Fender was of finding legal loopholes, he respected the unwritten laws of cricketing justice.

The summer of 1921 was exceptionally dry and hot, the word 'tropical' frequently finding its way into *Wisden*'s match reports. The pitches produced plenty of runs and those batsmen lucky enough not to be picked for England took advantage of the helpful conditions. The number of draws in the Championship, though, was surprisingly low. It seems that captains were generally more adventurous then, less afraid of losing. Contemporary critics often deprecated their cavalier tactics, while at the same time bemoaning a decline in pure cricketing skills. But the crowds seemed happy enough with the state of things and came in tens of thousands to the county matches and also to see the slaughter of England's pride in the Tests. The climax of the season came at the end of August when two gripping matches, one at the Saffrons and the other at Lord's, took place simultaneously. Archie MacLaren's victory over the Australians brought to an end Armstrong's run of 39 undefeated matches against English teams. The other match, between Surrey and Middlesex at Lord's, was for the County Championship.

It was to be the sternest test of Jardine's temperament yet. He had succeeded against the Australians and Yorkshire but had failed in the other two big matches against Cambridge. Against Leicestershire, immediately before the Lord's match, he had yet again been run out. Even if he did now pose additional problems for whoever happened to be batting with him, his class was indisputable and he was included in the side with which Fender hoped to take the title. The outcome of the Surrey v. Middlesex match was to decide the Championship for the second year running. In 1920 Surrey could only have helped Lancashire by winning, but in 1921 victory over Middlesex would have left them outright winners. Middlesex on the other hand had only to draw.

A large crowd was already at the ground when Mann and Fender walked out to toss; interest in the match was such that the total turn-out over the three days would now be considered fair for a five-day Test. Fender won the toss and Knight and Sandham opened the Surrey innings. The Middlesex fast bowler, Durston, made a couple of quick breakthroughs and, by the time Jardine came out to join Shepherd, the score was 56 for 3. There would come a time when Jardine's cool approach to the wicket in the middle of a collapse was, for the rampaging bowler, a bit like having a custard pie in the face, but walking out in 1921 as a relative newcomer, he may have given cause for some optimism in Middlesex hearts. He survived, though, confirming Fender's belief that he had the big-match temperament. He and Shepherd played with great care and were content to wait for the bad ball. They put on 144 in 140 minutes, which, interestingly enough, was thought to be rather slow going. If that seems a harsh judgement by modern standards, one should bear in mind that the over-rate hardly ever dropped below 20 per hour.

Jardine was very much the junior partner in his stand with Shepherd, but his role was no less valuable for that. When he was on 55, and having done more than could have been expected of him, he was bowled by Durston. After Shepherd and Jardine had hauled Surrey round to a position of some strength, seven wickets went down for 69.

It was only the second time that Jardine had batted at no. 5 since his first-class career began, and it is significant that he took to it so quickly, since it was as a middle-order batsman that he was to achieve pre-eminence. But for once, it was not an example of Fender's perceptive thinking: Surrey's batting strength was such that when all the best players were fit and available, it was difficult to fit Jardine in any higher than no. 5. Hobbs, Sandham, Knight, Ducat and Shepherd usually batted in the top half of the order, which was fair enough since between them they made over 400 centuries. So competition, particularly for nos 1 and 2, was on the stiff side.

Middlesex made a strange reply: six batsmen got into double figures and yet none made more than 29. The follow-on was only just avoided. Surrey in their second innnings had more or less the same trouble. Jardine had the bad luck to turn a ball from H. W. Lee to forward short leg where was crouching one of the best close fielders in the world at the time, A. R. Tanner. Surrey were in very much the better position at the end of the second day as Middlesex needed a total of 322 in the fourth innings. But Surrey just did not have the bowlers, and Twining and Hearne won the match for Middlesex with a partnership of 277. That was the nearest Surrey got to winning the Championship for the next 27 years.

Off the cricket field, Jardine continued to make rapid progress with his real tennis. He won his half-Blue, which is all the sport is reckoned to merit at Oxford, and played in the University match of 1921. His partner was Victor Cazalet, later to become an MP, and to meet his end with General Sikorski in a mysterious plane crash. They lost the first two sets, but as *The Times* said: 'Two greater fighters on the same side have seldom been seen in a University tennis match than Mr. Cazalet and Mr. Jardine. They won the third set 6–5 then steadily improved.'

In that winter he was one of the Oxford four to play against MCC (there is a court behind the pavilion at Lord's). Oxford won the match 3–1, but not without some difficulty. From *The Times*:

> Unfortunately the conditions were all against the players. A slight fog or haze hung about the court from the beginning, which made the flight of the ball difficult to judge accurately and quickly: but what was worse, the comparatively warm and muggy day following the cold night made the walls and floor sweat, and the floor on the hazard side was so slippery as to be almost dangerous.... Mr. Jardine is a player who, if he could give more time to the game, might conceivably become the best of the younger players. He started very brilliantly against Mr. Leaf yesterday, winning the first six games very quickly: a great point in his game is the certainty with which he finds the dedans when apparently tucked up and in difficulties. In the second set Mr. Leaf played much better. In this set Mr. Jardine was much worried by the sweating floor. He changed one pair of shoes for another after one particularly bad slip, but found those if anything worse. At one time he was playing without shoes at all, but even that somewhat desperate remedy was not wholly effective....

Nevertheless, the apparently sure-footed Leaf was defeated. Without attaching too much importance to this incident, it is worth noting that people who get cross with their shoes, with or without proper cause, almost invariably lose, but Jardine appears to have been able to suppress any feelings of personal frustration in the cause of winning.

Already he was one of the best amateur players in the country of a game in which intellect, judgement and tactical skill are more important than sheer athleticism. Had he been able to put in more practice, particularly on his service, he might have become a champion. He had the ability, as *The Times* said, to 'set a pace'. This seems a dull remark to ordinary folk, but it means the whole world to the man in the court. It is quite impossible to describe unless you have ever been bowled off your legs before you got the bat up.'

3
Injury and a Sense of Responsibility

At the start of the 1922 season fears were expressed, by Sydney Pardon among others, about a weakness in amateur batting. It was felt that the generation of 21-year-olds too young to have fought in the war should now be asserting itself, and wasn't. Budding Ranjis and Frys were demanded as if by right. The fact that professional batting was in a fairly healthy state was in a sense irrelevant, since a Test batting line-up of professionals only would have been quite unacceptable to those who mattered. University batting was criticised for its dullness and lack of enterprise against what was also considered to be a pretty poor standard of bowling. In *Days in the Sun*, Cardus beautifully expressed the general feeling about young amateur batting:

> Cricket at the universities nowadays is certainly not the cricket of swaggering 'bloods'; whatever else it lacks it does not lack brains. Indeed the trouble with university cricket just now is that introspection disturbs the game overmuch: it has the tentativeness which is the mark of the subtle mind. It is the cricket of men fond rather of analysis than action, of men who like to look scrupulously all about them before taking a decisive step – cricket, in a word, not at all out of keeping with the attitude of mind which it is rumoured our young men are cultivating to-day.... Care, that killed the cat, might easily kill university cricket altogether.

This attitude might be termed as post-Armistice depression. Immediately after the war, all was not unnaturally optimism: the national press carried euphoric descriptions of the extraordinary promise shown by this or that 18-year-old. There even appeared a small number of prep. school statistics, and one could almost smell the freshly mown grass in the columns of the sports pages. It is easy to understand this impatience to carry on from where the Golden Age had left off, and it is not altogether surprising that before long, despondency set in. First came the disappointments of the two Australian series, and then the realisation that a new generation of Olympians had failed to emerge. Nevertheless, English Test teams have never been crammed with 21-year-olds. That such a thing should suddenly be expected was perhaps all part of the youth cult fostered by a people in mourning.

MCC had foreseen that English cricket would take some time to recover from the war and had been unwilling to undertake the Australian tour of 1920–21, but a team was sent and was duly trounced. They made no complaints but it ought to have been obvious that more cricketing talent had been cut off in the war than was ever recorded in *Wisden*'s obituary pages. English cricket did not really recover until the mid-1920s.

Great things were expected of Jardine in 1922. He was thought not to have done himself justice in the previous season. Observers felt that his innings against the Australians, good though it was, was not in itself sufficient fulfilment of his earlier promise. What was really wanted was a big innings against Cambridge at Lord's. Jardine would naturally have liked nothing better, but with final exams approaching, it was not going to be easy to spare the time for proper match practice. His intention was to play in just a minimum of games for Oxford before the Varsity match and then trust that he would quickly run into form (his father had this happy knack). Once the Oxford term was over, he planned to spend the second half of the season with Surrey. Unfortunately, none of these things happened.

Early in May, Hampshire travelled to Oxford to play the University. On the second morning of the match the Oxford bowlers were failing to make any impression on the batsmen and so the new captain, Stevens, put Jardine on to bowl his leg-breaks. The ploy proved to be successful and a wicket fell immediately. He had just delivered the last ball of his third over when he collapsed onto the ground clutching his leg.

Semi-qualified medical aid arrived in the form of R. H. Bettington and Jardine was carried to the pavilion where he was found to have displaced his right kneecap. It seemed that he would be out of cricket for at least two months, but within a fortnight he was playing for I Zingari. It was not a very demanding match but he was able to test the strength of his knee. He played one more club game and then, six weeks after the initial injury, returned to first-class cricket, playing against Leicestershire at the Parks. On the third day he was into his seventh over when disaster struck again and he had to be helped off the field. The damage was not quite so serious this time and he was able to play in the next match against MCC. The leg was heavily bandaged and he moved slowly and stiffly, taking great care not to strain it, since at this point any further damage might have been permanent. He fielded close to the wicket and did not bowl. As the match progressed he found a little more freedom of movement, and of his batting on a malicious, rain-affected pitch *The Times* said that he

> played the most collected cricket. Although his bandaged knee handicaps him in the field and also his running, it does not interfere with his footwork. Not out 30 was the score of Mr Jardine. On the day's play he was very easily the best batsman on the Oxford side.... Where most people would have avoided Hearne's bowling, Mr Jardine absolutely courted it!

It is a measure of his standing as a batsman even this early in his career that there was considerable speculation in the press as to whether or not Jardine would be fit for the University match. If the star batsman played, then Oxford would be favourites; without him, their batting looked too fragile.

He decided to give the knee one more outing before deciding, and so he went with the Oxford team to Eastbourne to play against H. D. G. Leveson Gower's XI. He opened the Oxford batting on the first morning and made 26 before being bowled. *The Times*: 'By far the best batsman in the side. He has all the strokes all round the wicket and he placed the ball with delicious accuracy between the fielders on the leg-side. Short runs, of course, have to be avoided. ...' (The man who bowled him, incidentally, was C. U. Peat, his future uncle-in-law.) Fielding on the second day, Jardine was in some pain and eventually had to leave the field. He travelled straight up to London to see a specialist. As he might have expected, he was advised to take a long rest from cricket, yet the next morning he was back at the Saffrons, opening Oxford's second innings.

Right up until the day before the University match it was hoped that he would be able to play. Oxford had two other worries; Stevens had jaundice and Bettington a muscle strain. Without these three, Oxford really did appear to be in for it. The day before the match, it was announced that Stevens and Bettington would play but Jardine would not, it was not considered safe to play him. The match turned out to be almost a carbon copy of the previous year's one, with Cambridge winning by an innings and 100 runs and Hubert Ashton making 90 not out.

Jardine's injury prevented him from taking up his place in the Surrey side, and in fact he did not play again that season until the end of August when he appeared for the Harlequins against The Mote at Maidstone. He made 90 and took three catches, which indicated that he must have been fairly mobile by then. Limiting though his injury must have been to some extent, it does not appear to have necessitated any alteration in technique.

In 1922 *The Isis* nominated Jardine as one of its 'Men of the Year'. There were 32 of them in all and, in keeping with prevailing social order, nearly all of them were Blues. The superiority of the Blues became less secure, however, over the next 12 months. Gradually the more mature men who had come up late after the war all departed, and a younger group of much written about but not all that numerous 'aesthetes' began to assert itself. They challenged and ridiculed all that *The Isis* and its 'Men of the Year' stood for. Hitherto it had been possible to have a foot in both camps, the sporting and the intellectual, but that seemed to change. In *Oxford in the Twenties* Christopher Hollis recalled being the object of his smart friends' derision because he was known to read the cricket scores. Evelyn Waugh wrote of how the Hypocrites, a hearty drinking club whose members were mainly Etonians and 'pipe-smoking Wykehamists' (Jardine smoked a pipe), was taken over by the aesthetes. The club then acquired a reputation for homosexuality, deeply disapproved of then, of course. If Jardine ever had belonged, we may assume that he allowed his membership to lapse at this point.

The brief character sketch which accompanies Jardine's 'Isis Idol' photograph indicates clearly enough that he was not entirely temperate in his social pursuits. He belonged to a dining club called the Boojums, a more conservative though no less enthusiastic group than the Hypocrites. He was also part of an exclusive coterie of notables whom Philip London, the Bursar of Trinity, gathered together in his rooms, salon-fashion. But his circle of friends was comparatively small, as is the case with most shy people. He was not able to form immediate and intimate friendships in the way that young people of similar background and intelligence usually can.

It has been said that it was because of a certain brusqueness and reserve that he was not asked to captain the University XI. This is true, but it is only part of the truth. As a freshman he would obviously not have been considered for the captaincy, and the following year the job went quite properly to V. R. Price, a Blue of three years' standing and a very popular man who was also Jardine's senior by six years. There really was not much chance either of his being elected for 1922, since the real star of the XI was Greville Stevens. Stevens had been even more of a schoolboy phenomenon than Jardine, he had appeared for the Gentlemen, he had played a major part in Middlesex's Championship successes, and again, he was a popular figure. Jardine's class and potential were never in doubt, but he had not yet made quite the same impact as Stevens, who was and remained one of the best amateur all-rounders of his generation. To say that Jardine was not as popular as Stevens is not to say that he was *un*popular; to have got the nod ahead of him, he would have needed to be unusually adorable.

He was passed over for 1923 but it would be wrong to attribute this solely to a quirk of temperament; again, it needs some qualification. As a fourth-year man – he had obtained a fourth in modern history and was now reading law – he was definitely a candidate for the captaincy. R. H. Bettington, though, was in the same position. He was another one who had not quite lived up to earlier expectations, but he could still be a devastating bowler on his day. He, too, had already played for the Gentlemen and for Middlesex. Jardine's injury must have counted against him: he had played only four first-class matches in 1922 and missed the whole of the second half of the season. He was still not fully recovered by the time the election was due to take place, and the club may have been unwilling to take the risk of electing someone about whose fitness there were doubts. Bettington was duly chosen. Jardine's personality very likely lost him support, but it is important to remember that there were other factors involved.

In early march 1923, Jardine put his knee out again playing tennis at Hampton Court and, as a result, he was unable to play cricket until towards the end of May. But mercifully, the knee troubled him only occasionally during the rest of the season. It is almost impossible to say how the injury affected his development as a batsman. Reliable observers such as Robertson-Glasgow and Hubert Ashton, who knew him before and after, have said that it limited his strokeplay and their opinions must be considered, but I wonder if those subsequent restrictions were not self-imposed, irrespective of injury.

When he joined the University side he played cautiously and, as might have been expected, not very successfully. It was not until the latter half of June that the headline 'Mr. D. R. Jardine bats well' appeared in *The Times* (this in reference to an innings of 63 against the Free Foresters during which he hit Percy Chapman for four fours in one over). For the rest of the University season he continued to show good form with scores of 50 and over against Surrey and Sussex. He also played what was described as a 'masterly' innings of 39 in the University match which Oxford won by the record margin of an innings and 227 runs. The weather gave Cambridge no chance at all, but Oxford deserved a bit of luck for once and it was their only win during the whole of the 'twenties. Jardine spent a highly successful second half of the season with Surrey, scoring 127 (his first hundred for the county) against Hampshire and 104 against the touring West Indians. He finished up second in the Surrey averages with 464 runs at 51.55. But what aroused the most interest was the way he batted right back in early June.

It all began when a *Times* reporter, covering the match between Oxford and the Army, described the end of Jardine's innings thus: 'Mr. Jardine stopped one terrible breakback from Captain Hyndson with his pads – *a wonderfully good stroke of its kind* [my italics] – but he was just late with his right leg for a similar ball in the next over.' The writer clearly approved the use of the pads to protect the wicket. Remember, it was impossible at that time to be out to a ball which pitched outside the off stump. A succession of angry letters appeared in *The Times* as a result of 'Our Special Correspondent's' remarks. Sydney Pardon, the cricket correspondent of *The Times*, most definitely did not share his colleague's views and wrote as much in the following Monday's edition. And so Jardine, who had been doing only what a great many batsmen of the time were doing, had to suffer a good deal of unpleasant publicity. 'Pernicious practice' was what R. H. Lyttleton (an old campaigner against pad-play) thought of it, 'a horrible method of play ... detestable'. Critics (mostly older observers) were not, of course, attacking Jardine personally, but the movement of which he was a part. Nevertheless his name was often there amongst the accusations of bad sportsmanship and the scathing allusions to the decline in more or less anything you care to mention since the war. It could not have been pleasant. His well-known distrust of journalists and 'pavilion critics', as he called them, is easily traced to this episode. He did not find it necessary to defend himself publicly or to hit back at the fulminating indictments, being entirely confident of the pro-priety of pad-play, and indeed, he remained for the rest of his life opposed to change in the lbw law. To the critics, Jardine was an unfortunate swept along by the 'new wave', but the real villain in their eyes was Donald Knight, also of Surrey and Oxford.

In 1920, Knight contributed a chapter on batsmanship to the Badminton Library. In it, he said,

> There is nothing wrong or contrary to the spirit of the game in bringing the legs back together in front of the wicket and behind the bat to act as an extra defence so long as the ball has pitched off the wicket.... When leaving the off ball alone it is strongly advisable to keep the bat well up in the air above the head and cover the unguarded wicket with both legs.

This elicited howls of disapproval, mainly, and perhaps significantly, from people who had played little or no first-class cricket. In the 1921 *Wisden*, R. H. Lyttleton condemned Knight's doctrines and re-stated his own long-held belief that a change in the lbw law was needed to redress the balance of power between bowler and batsman: 'There will be quite enough runs got, and the game would be far better, if no individual score of 100 were ever got again. These scores of one, two or even three 100s are an abomination.' In the 1923 *Wisden*, Sydney Pardon, as editor, continued the campaign: 'Surely nothing could be more flagrantly opposed to the true spirit of cricket.'

Knight's crime lay less in his beliefs than in his public proselytising: corrupting the minds of the young and of simple, working folk who knew no better. In the right hands – or rather the right legs – defensive pad-play had, to a certain extent, been tolerated, provided it was used in moderation. Sometimes it added grace to the innings of a gentleman or a Jam Sahib, but there were very, very few to whom this applied. Fry, in his book *Batsmanship* (1912), danced elegantly around the issue. And in *The Jubilee Book of Cricket* (1897), of which Ranji claimed authorship but which was probably written by Fry, the subject was approached with a blush. After a heavily qualified approval of the use of the legs to defend the wicket in an emergency, e.g. 'a very sticky wicket', the author concludes, 'It is not the use of the method, but the abuse of it, that can with any fairness be adversely criticised.' Knight, on the other hand, appeared to advocate pad-play as a stock in trade.

The correspondence in *The Times* which followed the Jardine incident produced a number of interesting suggestions as to how the law could be amended to assist the bowler: a widening of the imaginary track between wicket and wicket within which the ball must pitch; simply giving the benefit of the doubt to the bowler instead of the batsman; a return to the spirit of the 1774 law which ruled a batsman 'out' if he *intentionally* prevented the ball from hitting the wicket by using his legs; and an idea which has been forwarded on a number of occasions and has had such notable advocates as Bob Wyatt and Don Bradman, namely the 'fourth stump'.

The majority of cricketing authorities, though not the crowds, acknowledged that the batsmen were having things too much their own way, but the difficulty was to know how to help the bowler. The argument about the second line of defence had been smouldering like a volcano for nearly 40 years, with periodic eruptions. And since it was the most obvious flaw in the game, virtually nobody looked further than the lbw law for concessions to the bowler. But MCC were rightly reluctant to tamper with the rules. There were those who felt the cause of the trouble was over-prepared wickets – over-marled shirtfronts were to frustrate bowlers for many years – but it would have been impossible to legislate against them without having a sort of Special Patrol Group invested with powers to search and arrest groundsmen. The 'fourth stumpers' did not have much support, mainly for aesthetic reasons. When assistance was eventually given to the bowlers in 1927, it came in the form of a quarter-inch reduction in the circumference of the ball, followed in 1931 by a one-inch increase in the size of the wicket. Neither of these measures had much effect and it was not until 1935 that an experimental change in the lbw law was brought in, a change which was formally incorporated into the laws after its two-year trial period, and which meant that a batsman could be out to a ball that pitched outside the off stump providing that the point of contact with the pad occurred within the imaginary strip between wicket and wicket.

The main argument against this rule change, and one which Jardine and many other players supported, was that it would discourage the batsman from getting properly into line to any ball pitched outside the off stump, thereby flying in the face of the basic tenets of batsmanship. There are a great many people who still believe that the game has been the poorer since the 1935 amendment.

But to return to Jardine's batting in 1923, it seems that for Oxford he played with more circumspection and less fluency than before. Quite why this came about is debatable. The injury handicapped his running and he was unable to bowl, but a more likely cause of the new caution was the fact that the Oxford batting was considerably less solid than in the previous year. Jardine must have recognised that a good total was usually going to be dependent on a sizeable innings from himself. The less gifted batsmen tried to follow his example with varying degrees of success and, in so doing, attracted criticism. But because of Jardine's known ability and range of strokes, most of the adverse comment was directed at him.

His position with Surrey was quite different. He was required to bat fifth in easily the strongest county order of the day: Hobbs and Sandham opening and the next two places being filled by two out of Knight, Shepherd, Ducat or Jeacocke. Consequently, Jardine might find himself coming in with orders to slog for a declaration, or he might just as easily come in in the middle of a collapse, expected to succeed on a drying wicket where Hobbs and others had failed. Fender's daring captaincy made Jardine's position one of great responsibility, and he fulfilled the all-round role with more flexibility than is generally supposed or figures can show.

His 104 against the West Indians in 1923 was described by *Wisden* as 'a masterpiece of defence', while in the same month he was stumped charging down the wicket when he had made only 12, and within a few days he played-on with a wild slash at a similarly early stage in his innings. Such were the different circumstances under which he had to bat.

An innings against Yorkshire towards the end of the 1923 season showed how he could alter his style. Surrey had been limited to 235 on the first day by the mean-armed Yorkshire quartet of Rhodes, Wilson, Kilner and Macaulay. Cardus saw the game and thought the Surrey batsmen were far too respectful; he said that Shepherd's innings was like 'a fossil from paleolithic Kennington'. But Jardine, coming in towards the end of the first day,

> drove the Yorkshire bowling powerfully ... a batsman whose style has been cultivated by observance of pre-war principles. At any rate there is not much of the 'two-eyed' viciousness about Jardine. His position at the wicket gives him liberty to swing his bat and follow through freely whenever he has the confidence to do so.

(He had been criticised earlier in the season for having no back-lift). The next morning, with runs by now even more urgently needed, he took some time to play himself in, much to the crowd's annoyance. But then, when he was ready, he absolutely hammered the bowling. He played all kinds of shots, some awful, some beautiful, he was dropped three times, once so badly (by Rhodes) that everyone laughed, but the point is that he made his own luck. Those Yorkshire bowlers were extremely difficult to get away and Jardine, being no natural hitter, knew that his only chance was to accustom himself thoroughly to the conditions before taking the outrageous risks he did.

As long as Jardine showed this sort of adaptability and willingness to sacrifice his wicket in his side's cause, Fender was content to see him batting in more or less any situation – quite a compliment to a primarily defensive batsman. Over the years this came to be less and less the case but it is worth remembering that in 1923, Fender, who was not at all averse to juggling with the batting order, only once came in ahead of Jardine when quick runs were needed. In an impressively short time he had made the no. 5 position his own, and in recognition he was awarded his county cap shortly after the Yorkshire game.

Having come down from Oxford for good, he set about qualifying as a solicitor, a task which he approached with typical diligence although not a great deal of enthusiasm. There was never any doubt that he would always have to earn his living; the image of Jardine as a rich aristocrat is totally false. There were in fact surprisingly few young gents on the first-class circuit then who were free of that dreary obligation, and for the majority, like Jardine, playing cricket was only made possible by the co-operation of an employer and the burning of a good deal of midnight oil. Jardine's existence was undeniably a pleasant one, though, and there was sufficient family money to install him in a flat in Kensington.

The graph of Jardine's achievement levelled off over the next $2\frac{1}{2}$ seasons: 'not inelegant' 27s and 'redoubtable' 19s formed a large part of a consolidating period during which he remained a valuable member of the Surrey side and took significant steps towards becoming the anchor man of England's Test team.

Others from that vintage crop of post-war University players were developing more quickly; Percy Chapman, Gubby Allen and Greville Stevens were receiving the same kind of press attention that Jardine had attracted a year or so before. Much notice, too, was taken of an even younger generation of players: Duleepsinhji, Dawson, Enthoven and Errol Holmes. Jardine was fortunate in that he was more or less allowed to get on with his batting without the scrutiny which he, in particular, found so distasteful. He reached fifty 10 times in 1924, which was enough to put him third in the final Surrey averages, and he was also picked to play for the Gentlemen. There were fewer strokes, but still the same air of confidence. He was still troubled by his knee, which hindered his running quite considerably throughout the season, and as late as November, when he won a public schools old boys' real tennis cup, he did so with a limp.

His appointment as vice-captain for the 1924 season ahead of Hobbs might seem suspicious to modern eyes, but it really was not a case of committee snobbery. Fender, too, was all in favour of professional captaincy and had publicly denounced as a gratuitous insult Hawke's infamous off-the cuff remark, 'Pray God, no professional shall ever captain England!' But Hobbs, for all his vast experience, knew his place and was only too relieved that there was a suitable young gentleman available to do the job.

In Fender's absence, Jardine led Surrey to a victory over Glamorgan, a draw against Gloucestershire and a draw against Lancashire, whom they would have beaten but for a lengthy

eighth-wicket stand by Richard Tyldesley and Major Green.
When Oxford travelled to the Oval he behaved in a most
uncharacteristic way; perhaps the presence of the visitors
reminded him of the carefree days of his youth, but at any rate he
made 105 and 63 in quick time, playing shots all round the wicket.
He then made a declaration which was sporting even by Fender's
standards, and Oxford won.

There was a common fearlessness to Jardine's and Fender's
styles of captaincy. When they took a risk they took it
wholeheartedly and did not worry if certain of their tactics were
not normal practice or looked odd. They both had a somewhat
eccentric appearance in the field; Fender used to stand in the slips
poised like a sprinter, with his left leg in front of the right and his
hands either spread out on the grass or buried deep under the
biggest sweater in the first-class game if not the world. Near to
him stood Jardine, stiff-legged and bent at the waist like a
clockwork toy which had run down. In their respective postures
they took an extraordinary number of brilliant catches. Theirs
was not a master-pupil relationship by any means. They were two
strong-willed men. They discussed tactics, sometimes agreeing,
sometimes disagreeing, but Jardine was to write:

> The ablest, the quickest, and the most enterprising cricket brain with
> which it has been my fortune to come into contact is that of my old
> captain, Mr. P. G. H. Fender ... Though we occasionally differed –
> generally, I think, because I was too conservative – we always agreed
> that in nearly every game there comes a crisis when gambling is
> necessary.

When Arthur Gilligan's MCC team returned from Australia in
the spring of 1925 having been beaten 4–1, they were received like
children who had failed their scholarships. There were receptions
and speeches, congratulations on the first victory over Australia
in $12\frac{1}{2}$ years – splendid effort. But the head-patting and brave
smiles did not last long and desperate measures were soon being
demanded. A strong body of opinion favoured the cancellation of
the County Championship in order that every cricketing hour
could be spent in preparation for the visit of the Australians the
following summer. The press wanted a change of attitude from
the younger players. *The Times* stated 'The more aggressive
English batting becomes, the greater are its chances of restoring

the game in this country to its ancient position.' Fortunately, by the end of the season most fears had been allayed and English cricket had recovered its self-respect, if not yet the Ashes.

At the beginning of the 1925 season the *Star* urged Jardine's appointment as captain of the Gentlemen. The photograph which accompanied the short paragraph shows the most famous upper lip in cricket history apparently covered by a small pencil-moustache, giving the wearer a spiv-like air. The *Star*'s suggestion was not heeded and, fortunately for Jardine's nearest and dearest, the little affectation was also short-lived. He had a rather disappointing season in fact, his highest score being 87 against Leicestershire. He captained Surrey once, against Cambridge, when he was once again beaten after making a bold declaration. It was his fielding that earned most praise at this time. He used to stand in the slips or the gully and quite often very close on the leg-side, the latter showing alot of courage in view of the level of Surrey bowling. Some observers thought he stood too close and were greatly pleased if a batsman lobbed a ball just out of reach over his head. His knee seems to have recovered, and of his three run-outs in that season, two happened when he was attempting a fourth run and the other was a deliberate sacrifice in order to end the innings and give the Surrey bowlers the best of a vicious pitch.

His father, at the age of 56, still played a good game of club cricket for Harlequins and a Sussex side called Broadwater. Whenever Jardine was able, he liked to play alongside M.R., and a partnership that they shared for Harlequins against Harrow gave them both lasting pleasure. On occasions, Broadwater, who also had a useful googly specialist called B. J. T. Bosanquet, were able to field a very strong team.

Douglas Jardine had a great liking for village cricket and believed it to be quite as important as the Test variety. But he paid for his levelling beliefs when, in early July 1925, he undertook to play for one C. E. McIver's XI at Ashtead near the family home in Surrey. Jardine was batting when an Ashtead bowler attempted what most self-respecting village players, faced with a first-class batsman, attempt – searing pace. The Ashtead wicket being what it was, Jardine was felled and had to retire in pain. At first it was feared that his collar-bone was broken. When the swelling went down the injury was found to be not quite so serious, but it was bad enough to put him out of cricket for the next three weeks. It was particularly unfortunate since it meant that he was unable to take up his invitation to play for the Gentlemen at Lord's. He benefited from the rest, however, and when he returned to the Surrey side for the last third of the season, he made good scores and finished up with just over 1000 runs.

Jardine spent much of the season watching, either from the pavilion or the crease, the progress of the man whom he is credited with being the first to call 'the Master'. Of one of Jardine's innings it was baldly stated that 'He had a fine view of Hobbs for forty minutes.' 1925 was Hobbs' year. In it, he scored over 3000 runs and passed Grace's record of 126 centuries. As he approached the record he was pursued everywhere he went by hordes of newspaper men and film crews who recorded his every word and deed. He was photographed in countless attitudes: picking his bat up, smiling at it, frowning at it, putting it down. There was one priceless shot of him lying on the grass in what can only be described as an abandoned pose; he is supposed to be dreaming of the elusive hundred that will give him the record, and the magic number is rather messily daubed in whitewash on the grass beside his head. He was offered the lead in a film and also a ballet. He was modelled in butter on a stand at the British Empire Exhibition. When he finally broke the record it was reported in one of the French newspapers that he had surpassed even W. G. Grace's feat of hitting a ball into the face of Big Ben. In the vernacular of the period: 'The whole world's gone Hobbs-crazy!'

Hobbs kept the world waiting for four weeks between his hundred and twenty-fifth and hundred and twenty-sixth hundreds, during which time the pressure built and built. There were 31,000 people at the Oval on bank holiday Monday, but when he was out for 54 the ground practically emptied. (This was the innings that produced the famous 'Hobbs fails again' headline.) The queue outside the Taunton ground was said to have been half a mile long when, with his score 91 not out overnight, Hobbs prepared to resume the Surrey innings with Jardine. The batsmen agreed to the Somerset captain's request for a delay so that the crowd might all be admitted. After play began Jardine had to live for twelve minutes with the fear of running his partner out. No doubt he joined in the national sigh of relief when Hobbs turned Bridges to leg and the vital run was completed. Great cheering and hand-shaking followed, but the only pitch invasion came in the form of Percy Fender carrying what looked like a glass of champagne for 'the master.' It was in fact ginger beer, for Hobbs as temperance organisations were proud to claim, was an 'abstainer'. One run later he was out and returned to the pavilion to even more cheering and the congratulations of his team-mates, among them Sandham, whose own excellent season was going almost entirely unnoticed.

The start of the 1926 season coincided with the general strike. Cricket continued, but with a number of fixtures having to be cut to two days because of the problems of travelling. The Prime Minister, Baldwin, wanted the county programme to continue, since he considered that cricket was 'a means of promoting good feeling between all sport-loving classes', while MCC urged cricketers to 'be guided by a sense of public duty rather than affection for their counties'. Many amateurs were unable to resist the opportunity to drive a train or a bus or a milk lorry, and consequently the county sides were well under strength during the weeks of the strike. The Harlequins were particularly active in the volunteer services, mostly as special constables. The chairman of selectors was spotted by *The Times*' cricket correspondent: 'Mr Warner I saw myself, a dapper figure in close fitting blue uniform, doing a twelve-hour spell of work at Scotland Yard.' Jardine preferred to follow the advice of MCC rather than the Prime Minister and he did not appear for Surrey for two weeks.

There was no spectacular advance in his batting in 1926 but he was all the time acquiring greater strength and consistency. The press continued to concentrate their attention on the more glittering lights of Jardine's generation and whether they could or could not win back the Ashes. Jardine had a bad start to the season and he was unlucky to get only one innings (st. Oldfield, b. Mailey, 7) in a closely scrutinised match between the South of England and the Australians. The Test series progressed reasonably well for England and there were few changes in the batting line-up. Consequently, those players who began the season badly had little chance of winning a Test place.

Jardine's only match as Surrey's captain also came early in the season and he did not improve on his uneven record in this capacity. Surrey lost by eight wickets to Glamorgan, and Jardine made a pair (the only one of his career) for good measure.

On the plus side, his knee had improved enough to enable him to bowl, and on one occasion he proved to be a match-winner.

Like so many things in cricket, though, this needs some qualification. Somerset needed 402 to win and were 185 for 9, but a hearty partnership between Peter Randall Johnson and Robertson-Glasgow raised the score to an improbable 324. Somerset's hopes were further raised when, for want of a better idea, Fender tossed the ball to Jardine. Robertson-Glasgow wrote of what followed.

> Let not ambition mock the useful, if somewhat intermittent, toil of bowler Jardine. Let not envy deride the obscure destiny, or question the obscurer intentions of his deliveries.... I chopped, avid but casual – and there was the ball in Strudwick's hands, and Jardine smiling, and Randall Johnson alone in his glory.

Over the last third of the season Jardine began to show the sort of consistency, on all wickets, that is the hallmark of the best defensive batsmen. His last ten innings realised 538 runs. For the first time since his early Oxford days he allowed himself some of the strokes which his classically upright, side-on stance had always promised. His off-driving was of a power and quality which thrilled, but at the same time left the spectator wondering why on earth it was so sparingly applied. It was noticeable, too, that he was able to play with assurance men like Tate and Larwood who, at their best, were simply too good for many county batsmen, although as Richard Streeton wrote in his book on Fender, Larwood's pace caught Jardine unawares at their first encounter. He disheartened rather than dominated the bowling, and if the bowler threw down the gauntlet it was ignored, or occasionally pushed round the corner for a safe single. His defence was based on a precise knowledge of where his stumps were, and in this he was no doubt helped by his stance outside the leg stump. He could judge with remarkable accuracy which balls did, and which did not, require a stroke, and during a match between Kent and Surrey in 1926, even the umpire appeared to bow to Jardine's superior judgement of such things. He was hit some way above the right pad and was given out, but he remained at the crease and before very long the umpire realised that he must have made a mistake and duly reversed his decision.

1926 was his eighth first-class season and he was by now a familiar player on the county circuit. Apart from occasional lapses of judgement in his running, there were no glaring weaknesses in his play that anyone had been able to exploit with any real consistency. Kennedy of Hampshire was the one bowler who really troubled him. In about two dozen encounters over the years, Kennedy got him out 11 times, 8 times for less than 20. Kennedy was a medium-paced inswing bowler who could also cut the ball; he found Jardine a little slow-footed (just as the Australian slow bowlers were later to discover) and he used to trap him lbw or bowl him. He was nine years older than Jardine and his powers began to diminish at about the same time that Jardine approached his prime, nevertheless Jardine only reached 50 against him five times.

The feather-bed wickets of the time ideally suited Jardine's style and, barring rain or a freak delivery, only a mistake on his part was going to get him out. That is not to say that he would have been less successful in another age, since his performances on drying wickets proved his ability to adapt to conditions. Unlike his 'two-shouldered' colleagues, he was well equipped to deal with a spiteful wicket – and better equipped than some of his 'one-shouldered' colleagues. When Surrey played the Australians at the end of July 1926, Jardine was the only player to survive on a pitch which was practically homicidal. Even Hobbs showed no desire to pit his skills against it and was out after a number of wild shots, but Jardine played an innings of 20 not out which was worth five times that amount.

Leg-theory, as used in its most common defensive form, was less than usually effective against Jardine. Normally, an attack directed at a point anywhere between the batsman's left knee and shoulder, and accompanied by a cordon of fielders on the leg-side, was enough to bring the game to a standstill. But Jardine's great strength was on-side play, and his placing was so certain that he was able to penetrate the close fielders and pick up singles in a way that many others could not.

Mr Calthorpe, Mr Wyatt and Smith, it was reported, were absent at the start of the match between an England XI and the Australians at Folkestone at the end of the 1926 season: 'Motoring over from Woking they had been delayed by thunderstorms, and when they eventually arrived they were amazed to find play in progress.' Collins, the Australian captain, and two other members of his side were fielding for the England XI, and behind the stumps, in place of Tiger Smith, was D. R.

Jardine. Larwood, with the wind gusting behind him, was bowling very fast. He was still only 22 and was to acquire even greater pace over the next few years, but as it was he was quite nasty enough for the Australians, and Jardine's unhardened hands must have been tingling by the time Smith relieved him.

Larwood had shown in the recent Test series that he could tear the heart out of the batting, but here he gave a glimpse of further terrors. Woodfull was the first to fall, caught in the covers by his own captain. Then Ponsford was given an awful roasting with short-pitched deliveries and was eventually bowled round his legs as was to happen again in his meetings with Larwood. Bardsley alone played him with any certainty, making 55, but then Larwood produced the sort of ball which batsmen are much better to pretend does not exist. It was just short of a length and, needless to say, quick. It reared and Bardsley managed to get underneath it but left his bat in the air. The ball knocked it out of his hands and into his stumps, then continued without pitching into the wicket-keeper's gloves. One wonders if any Australians in the dressing room were unkind enough to ask Bardsley how he was out. In all, Larwood took 7 for 95, his other victims being Collins, Ryder, Hendry and Oldfield.

When the England XI began their innings, the field-placings had a flavour of revenge. Not for the first time, poor old Frank Woolley had to face Jack Gregory bowling short. Gregory had failed in the Test series and was not quite the force of old, but he was still only 31 and on this occasion he was distinctly hostile. Wyatt was immediately caught at the wicket and Jardine came out to join Woolley. Together they wore Gregory down and played until the close.

Only 20 minutes' play was possible the following day and so on the third morning the batsmen resumed their partnership at 57. The sky did not look promising and it seemed that the match would quietly die. If any English players were entertaining thoughts of motoring back to Woking early, such was not the case with the Australians, who were out to restore some of their self-respect after losing the Ashes. They approached their task with considered determination. Jardine's predilection for on-side strokes was already known to them and it seems that a plan was formed to dismiss him by feeding his strength. Shortly after play began, Gregory bowled a slightly overpitched ball on about the line of leg stump. Jardine came forward and played a pleasant glide, but Oldfield had anticipated the stroke and was already moving across. He caught the ball, diving full-stretch to his left. That the catch was in the miraculous class does not alter the fact that the plan had worked and that Jardine had been 'thought' out. His 38 proved to be the top score of the innings. The match was drawn, but for Jardine, it had been a most instructive three days.

With the increasingly widespread doping of wickets in the late 'twenties and 'thirties, the plight of the bowler worsened. Again the arguments sprang up as to how to redress the balance, but not everyone was agreed that the cause of the problem was, as seems so clear with hindsight, the wickets. The letters page of *The Times* smouldered with old grievances and attacks on current methods. R. H. Lyttleton took up his campaign for lbw reform with renewed vigour and a great many other solutions were offered. MCC appointed a special sub-committee to investigate the possibilities and as a result of their findings the maximum circumference of the ball was reduced by a quarter of an inch to nine inches. Bowlers found the new size easier and more comfortable to grip, but the change in no way diminished the might of the bat.

Jardine's bat especially flourished and 1927 was the first of his great years; if one judges by figures alone, it was his greatest. His Championship average for Surrey was 114.33 and he also headed the national averages. Less deservedly, his haul of three wickets for 64 put him at the top of the Surrey bowling averages. Work, however, allowed him to play in only 11 first-class matches but he seemed to thrive on irregular appearances. An afternoon in the nets or a gentle club game, and he was back in form.

By now he was a fully fledged solicitor, but strangely enough, he was never to practise. At this time he worked as a bank clerk in the City and later on was employed by Cable and Wireless. While possessing in abundance the mental capabilities for success either in the legal profession or in business, he had no great ambitions beyond cricket. Cricket was his passion, and with it lay both his hopes of success and his fears of failure. To no other activity did he offer such devotion and in no other field did he aspire to excellence with such determination. This did not, as often can happen, make him narrow-minded; he led a very busy social life outside cricket and his breadth of reading put him on sparring terms with C. B. Fry. And like Fry, he was never entirely free of financial worries.

Many amateurs of the time led this strange sort of double life – adding up columns of figures with the fellows in Accounts one day, and modestly raising one's cap to the cheers of thousands the next. Those of Jardine's amateur contemporaries who have been kind enough to talk to me find it difficult, not surprisingly, to express their commitment to cricket in a word. 'Hobby' seems to be pitching it on the short side, particularly in the case of, say, Gubby Allen who, at the time of writing, has served the game for the best part of 65 years. 'Profession' it most definitely was not, in spite of the stories about shamateurism, and it says a lot about the times that for an amateur to turn professional was almost unknown.

To many, Jardine was the epitome of the old-fashioned amateur – the patrician good looks, the stance, the high back-lift and, of course, the Harlequin cap. Yet his application to the business of scoring runs was professional, his back-play in particular was of a certainty unparallelled outside the professional ranks, and he served the interests of his side as if his livelihood depended on it.

He began the 1927 season with a century in each of his first three games. Before, his batting had been assured; now, it was commanding and he began to attract the attention which had been lacking over the last couple of years. Observers' minds were very much occupied with the next MCC tour of Australia. It was still almost two years away but the building of a team to retain the Ashes was a matter of obsessive discussion and speculation. Jardine was very much in contention for a place.

He captained Surrey against Cambridge again, and it was noticeable that this fixture used to bring out the gay desperado in him. This time there was no daring declaration, but instead an innings of rare abandon; he reached 50 in half an hour and at the end of 90 minutes he had made 118 including three sixes and four fours. Unfortunately rain frustrated any further plans he may have had and the match was left drawn.

In fact, the weather remained awful for the rest of the summer. Only a day and a half's play was possible in Gentlemen v. Players match at Lord's, but it was a far from pointless exercise from Jardine's point of view. He made 123 'in the manner of a master,' according to *The Times*, and in front of all the right people. He was picked to play for England against The Rest in the Test trial at Bristol. At the last minute Chapman had to stand down because of business commitments and so Jardine found himself captaining England. The purpose of the match was to help the selectors pick a side for the forthcoming tour of South Africa and, since Jardine's professional commitments prevented him from taking part in this, it seems that his function was to test The Rest's bowling. The Rest batted first on a blatantly marled wicket and the expectations were for a very long, slow innings. Jardine opened with Tate and Larwood, who achieved a measure of success by bowling short. Wickets fell fairly regularly and the run-rate never rose above three an over. By the close, The Rest were all out for 248, and the captain was praised for skilful handling of his resources. It was quite tricky to get the best out of Larwood when the pitch was as unresponsive as this one, and it is significant that Jardine was shrewd enough not to overbowl him.

The main feature of the second day's play was the bowling of E. W. Clark, a fast left-armer in the Frank Foster mould. He employed a leg-trap and his tactics were the nearest thing to bodyline seen in England before 1932. On his good days he could be very awkward, but he had rather too many bad days to be classed among the very best. In spite of Clark's effective bowling, Jardine's side was able to knock up 461 and he declared at the close.

On the third morning, Sandham and Holmes went out to open The Rest's second innings. The prospects for the day's play at this gloomy ground were unexciting to say the least, for the match was obviously going to be drawn and rain was forecast. To even the keenest cricket watcher the scene was one of unrelieved dullness, yet there were two interesting incidents during the two hours or so of play before the rain came. Those two incidents are worth a little consideration since they constituted the first phase in an extraordinary partnership, the first time that Larwood 'found a bit extra for Mr Jardine'.

Holmes was the first to go. His middle stump spun like a weighted dagger towards the wicket-keeper and then stuck upright in the hard ground about 15 feet behind the wicket. The ball that bowled Sandham did not have such spectacular effect but was no less disturbing for that. The wicket, though not splayed, was obviously broken and yet the batsman quite irrationally refused to believe he was out. He stood at the wicket looking angry and then after a few seconds he came to his senses, made his excuses and left. The laughter which one might have expected from the fielders under the circumstances was not forthcoming. Instead there was an uneasy silence. And Larwood was still not yet at his fastest.

Shortly afterwards he ricked his knee and had to leave the field, an injury which put him out of cricket for the rest of the season. It was a momentous half-hour, and in a way it was a microcosm of his whole association with Jardine, which was to finish just as it had begun, with an injury.

Neither of them could have known then that they would become one of the most awesome combinations in the history of the game. In fact, neither of them really acknowledged that theirs was a partnership as such, for it might have been difficult for them to do so. Larwood, perhaps, did not wish to appear presumptuous nor Jardine patronising; there was a vast gulf between them off the field, as may be imagined. Those who toured with them in 1932–33 tend to dismiss the idea that Jardine had a special effect on Larwood, and some even say that he handled him badly and that Larwood played as well as he did in spite of Jardine. But in viewing the relationship, tiffs and all, at such close quarters, the fact may have been overlooked that Larwood under Jardine was so good that they had to change the rules.

Wisden named Jardine as one of its Five Cricketers of the Year for his batting in 1927:

> Standing fully six feet high, and blessed with great power of wrist and forearm, Jardine has always possessed the qualifications essential to the making of a fine batsman, and to these he has added style and footwork the better to give effect to the mental gifts for cricket which he possesses in abundance. He is not the master of all strokes, indeed, he is definitely restricted in his off side play. But as to his strength on the on side and to leg, there can be no two opinions. Nobody plays with a straighter bat; few hit harder in defence whether in a forward or backward stroke, and not often does he lift the ball. As with all really sound batsmen, fast bowling possesses no terrors for him. Above everything else stands out his splendid defence: the manner in which he watches the ball right onto the bat, stamps him as an accomplished player. Provided he can spare the time, nothing appears more likely than that he will be in the next team that visits Australia.

The tourists in 1928 were the West Indians, who had just been elevated to Test status. They possessed, in Constantine, Francis and Griffith, the most hostile attack in the world – they were fast and great triers even on the hopeless wickets that were in vogue at the time. On the rare occasions when they found a sympathetic pitch, they were very awkward to play. On these occasions a fair number of batsmen, with the tour of Australia in mind, allowed themselves to be hit by the short-pitched deliveries, but not many actually played the bowling with much confidence. Jardine was one of the few. He was picked for the first Test at Lord's but, within the context of his overall record for the season, his first appearance for England was unremarkable – he made 22 before trying to turn a straight one from Griffith to square leg and was lbw. Play finished for the day with England 382. The West Indies made a good start to their reply and were 86 for 0 at lunch on the second day, but then somebody must have put something in their ham salads because they lost 16 wickets in the last two sessions and ended up losing by an innings and 58 runs.

England won the second Test by an innings as well, and Jardine did rather better this time. He reached 83 in his most commanding style and it seemed that only an act of God would stop him reaching his maiden Test hundred. This is where Maurice Tate enters the picture. Jardine played Scott down to long leg for an easy two, but Tate thought there was only one in it and would not be persuaded otherwise. Jardine, whose call it was, charged down the wicket shouting, but Tate kept his head and stayed his ground. Even when Jardine was actually standing next to him he would not budge. Eventually the ball was thrown and the bowler's wicket broken, by which time a certain frostiness existed between the two Englishmen. The amateur left with dignity.

Jardine and Tate were never on very good terms with one another, and although it might be a mistake to point to this incident as being the cause, it could not have helped the relationship. Tate was a somewhat moody individual, who, on occasion, gave less than his best. Jardine had no time for that.

The Gentlemen relied heavily on Jardine at the Oval and at Lord's. In the first match he played a huge innings of 193 which at times moved certain sections of the crowd to impatient barracking, such as when after lunch he took half an hour to score 2, yet at other times they were on their feet cheering him – he made his last 50 in half an hour. At Lord's he could not quite save his side from defeat, even though he again scored more runs than anyone else on either side.

He liked to make runs when his side was in trouble, and he enjoyed having his ability stretched to the limit. Often his patience would unobtrusively turn a losing position into a winning one, seeing through an hour or two on a drying pitch or taking the heart out of a bowling attack whose spirits had been raised by early breakthroughs. Yet his was a more positive approach than those batsmen who are at their best only when their side is losing, who can find psychological release only in a lost cause: as we have seen, he was often quite happy to take advantage of favourable conditions.

Perhaps Jardine's best innings of the summer was for The Rest against England at Lord's. He captained The Rest and top-scored in both innings. On the last day he saved his side with 74 not out against Larwood and Tate bowling at their best on a wicket that was flying. His batting was of the very highest quality and confirmed the opinion held by many that all it needed was some hard Test experience against Australia and Jardine would be batting at no. 5 for Earth v. Mars.

4
Australia

The job of the selectors in picking the party for Australia was as difficult as ever, perhaps more so because they had to choose not simply the best 17 players available but those who were likely to succeed under arduous Australian conditions. The Tests might last for seven or eight days and so endurance was one of the most important qualities looked for – batsmen who could bat for six hours, fielders who would keep chasing for $2\frac{1}{2}$ days with temperatures up in the hundreds, and bowlers who could deliver 100 overs in a match. To this end certain sacrifices had to be made but the selectors, greatly to their credit, did not play entirely for safety. Larwood was included as the only fast bowler; his knee was still suspect and it was somewhat doubtful that he would get through a gruelling tour without breaking down, but it was a risk which simply had to be taken. He was supported by Geary, himself not 100 per cent fit, Tate, Staples and Hammond. The two spinners were White, the vice-captain, and another risky choice, Freeman, whose leg-spinners and googlies had been rather clobbered on the previous tour.

The batting, by contrast, was monumentally strong: Hobbs, Sutcliffe, Hammond, Hendren and Jardine were the first five with Mead, Tyldesley and Leyland as reinforcements. The fact that the great Frank Woolley had to be left out in favour of Leyland, a nimbler fielder, supports the view that this was the strongest English batting side ever to tour Australia. Woolley's omission caused a bit of a stir and so, to a lesser extent, did that of Charlie Hallows, who had scored 1000 runs in May and finished up with 11 centuries that season. But apart from these two quibbles the selectors' choices met with an unusual degree of approval.

After a calm voyage on the *Otranto*, the team's arrival in Perth created enormous interest. There were crowds to greet them and the press eagerly noted their every word and deed. It was reported among other things that Hobbs had not been seasick and that Jardine had won the deck-tennis. There began the lengthy succession of civic receptions and parties. Two of their earlier treats ashore were a performance of *La Bohème* at a local theatre and a gala evening at the Prince of Wales cinema, where they were shown slow-motion film of Australian cricketers practising.

With Percy Chapman in charge, the spirits of the team were bound to be high, and their confidence may be judged from the scrupulously tactful and charming speeches made by both the captain and the experienced manager, Frederick Toone, on their arrival. Tributes were paid to the beauty of the landscape, the brilliance of Australian cricketers, the generosity of their hosts and the impartiality of the press. Indeed, it is strange that the ever-sensitive Australians did not feel patronised by such effusiveness, but it was all much appreciated. To Australians, Chapman was a straightforward sort of a bloke who did not give himself ideas and, most important, he liked a few beers. He hardly put a foot wrong during the tour and, even though England gave Australia their biggest hiding to date, he was and probably remains, along with Freddie Brown and Arthur Gilligan, one of the most popular English captains to tour Australia.

Some of the team were familiar to Australian crowds: Hobbs, Sutcliffe, Chapman, Hendren and Tate each had their following but rather less was known about the others and so, from the start, they were closely examined for signs of individuality. Styles of play were on the whole of less interest than mannerisms and characteristics. It seems that Australians were a little ahead of the English in wanting to know more about players' personalities and off-the-field lives. Jardine was the first new 'character' to emerge and he was in fact the most talked-about player during the first month of the tour. This was because his batting form was such that he spent more time at the crease than anyone else, and so the public had ample opportunity to size him up. They noticed all the things that one might have expected: the stance, the aristocratic profile and of course the Harlequin cap with its blue, maroon and buff quarterings. He wore it at the start of the tour when he was batting, not as a deliberately provocative gesture but out of mild superstition; as long as his unprecedented run of high scores continued, he was reluctant to change the headgear. The crowds were also especially tickled by what one journalist called his 'stork-like' run. Old newsreels show Jardine's run as being not unlike that of David Gower, not nearly so fast but with the same slightly unathletic quality.

The ringside comments which Jardine's appearance provoked at this stage were fairly good-natured. They sent him up, certainly, but a player who scores a century in each of his first three innings on his first tour is hardly an object of scorn and derision. To begin with, Jardine took it all in good part. During his innings of 109 in the very first match a spectator shouted to him to take his hat off, and Jardine is reported to have smiled and touched his cap in mock obsequiousness, an action which got a very good laugh indeed from the crowd. But then things started to go sour. The mildly funny remarks became fewer as the wits of the four main cities turned their energies to putting Jardine off. He was no longer the 'jolly old bean' in a funny hat who could bat a bit; rather, he was likely to prove a serious obstacle to the recapture of the Ashes.

Jardine received his first dose of barracking at Melbourne in the third match of the tour. He was often in difficulties against the slow left-arm bowling of Ironmonger but fought his way to 104 in 4 hours 18 minutes. It was an innings of great patience and determination, as those in the outer well knew, but their demands for quicker scoring were no less vociferous for that. 'The wolves are out,' remarked Hendry to Jardine who offended those within earshot by saying that he did not care what the crowd thought.

It ought to be said that by today's standards the barracking was of a pretty mild order. It was to increase over the next few years, but the noise of a one-day final lay decades ahead. Be that as it may, Jardine did not like it – others thrived on it but not him. In the Melbourne match the unruly element, or 'larrikins' as they were known, sank further in Jardine's estimation when, during a break for rain, they commandeered the heavy roller and battered down a fence in order to get into the more expensive grandstand seating area. They constituted only a small proportion of any crowd but they made their presence felt to a degree hitherto unknown to Jardine, since their English counterparts, the 'roughs', tended to seek amusement in places other than cricket grounds.

At this stage there was no real malice intended in their treatment of Jardine and it was a little strange that he did not realise it, especially when the tourists played the fourth match of the tour, at Sydney against New South Wales. He opened the batting with Sutcliffe, and Jack Gregory, for the last time, summoned up his old fire. Both batsmen received knocks and each was beaten twice by rising balls, much to the crowd's delight. But Jardine soon dashed the home supporters' hopes by attacking Gregory and the medium-paced Kelleway with a series of blistering drives; one of them nearly took Gregory's hand off and another crashed into the bowler's wicket before anyone could make so much as a token move towards it. He played shots all round the wicket, including the cut, which showed considerable confidence in only his third innings of the tour. Kippax, the New South Wales captain, had to strengthen his off-side field, a measure which Jardine hardly ever forced upon his opponents. His placing was as sure as ever and it was noticed that he regularly managed to push the ball into areas patrolled by the less agile fielders. During the afternoon, which was rather cold and windy, the barrackers kept up their attack and the band, which was playing selections from *The Gondoliers*, was barely audible above the noise.

Once Jardine had passed his hundred he accelerated, batting with arrogant ease. He had reached 140 in 3 hours 40 minutes when he played a rather tired shot to the medium-pacer, Hooker, and chopped the ball into his stumps. Bradman, who was playing in the match, was later to say that this was one of the finest exhibitions of strokeplay he had ever seen. It was one of Jardine's greatest innings – not *THE* greatest perhaps since the pressures were not as they might have been in a Test or an important county match, nor was the game at a critical stage and nor was he fighting for his place – but without a doubt his most attractive innings, and when he left, the cheers easily drowned the boos and catcalls.

When he got back to the English dressing room he met Patsy Hendren on his way out to bat. Referring to the crowd's earlier behaviour, Hendren said, 'They don't seem to like you very much over here, Mr Jardine.'

'It's fucking mutual,' said our hero, unbuckling a pad, for he had had nearly four hours of it.

I am indebted to the late Ben Travers for this morsel. He was actually present at the exchange, as he related in his book, *94 Declared*. However, he favoured me with the unexpurgated version at his home shortly before he died. Travers, with *Plunder* safely ticking over at the Aldwych, was fulfilling his life's ambition to travel to Australia and watch an Ashes series. Amazed at such enthusiasm, the English players welcomed him into the fold and he became an unofficial member of the party. Naturally he got to know the players fairly well over the weeks, particularly Percy Chapman, with whom he even shared a bath once. Travers got on well enough with Jardine, although they were not on back-scrubbing terms, and he noted with disapproval that Jardine would not sit with the professionals at breakfast.

Jardine was never very good at being one of the lads, finding it difficult to pretend to be something he was not. The attempts he made at mateyness with the 'professors' were usually awkward and mutually embarrassing. He was painfully aware that, as a highly intelligent and articulate man, he might easily appear patronising or overbearing, and it was in the interests of both parties, not for snobbish reasons, that he kept himself apart. In fact he was rather a solitary figure throughout the tour. The only other amateurs, Chapman and White, mixed quite happily with the professionals but Jardine did much of his socialising outside the MCC party. In consequence, and contrary to popular belief, he made many friends in Australia.

After four weeks the team had shown themselves to be the strongest to tour Australia since the war. Sections of the English press were behaving as if the series was already won and the Australian press devoted a lot of space to contradicting those reports. As part of the general cricket fever, the capital cities of the two nations were linked by the magic of Beam Wireless, and at five o'clock on the morning of 11 November, Jardine and several other early risers from the England party sent messages home from the 2FC studios in Sydney. Jardine's was the only message that was received in full. He paid tribute to the form and spirits of the team and spoke of the 'sporty' crowds they had encountered. The others were inaudible through the static, except for Herbert Sutcliffe who broke through for a few seconds, only to be stopped in mid-flow and told that he had exceeded his time and the broadcast was at an end.

Jardine's run of hundreds ended in the match against an Australian XI at Sydney. His old Oxford team-mate, Reg Bettington, was playing for the home side and got him out for 6 and 13. In the first innings Jardine studiously watched a leg-break all the way round his legs and onto his middle stump, while in the second innings he was trapped leg-before. Bettington was loudly cheered for cutting Jardine down to size at last and he was very nearly chosen for the first Test on the strength of this alone. Jardine's failure did not greatly matter, as MCC won comfortably in the end. Neither side was at full Test strength but it was an important blow for the English team and the effect may be judged from the following extract from an article which appeared in the *Sydney Morning Herald* the next day:

> The national ego is in a bad way. It can stand the assaults of those who, after spending a short holiday in Samoa, go back to England and assert that Australia has no artists, no writers, no peerage, no butlers … But to have our cricket team swept off the wicket in one afternoon for 231 runs, that kicks our conceit fairly and squarely, buckles it up, flays it and humiliates the pieces.

The writer then went on to discuss the scientific probability of a meteorite falling on Jardine, Hobbs, Tyldesley and Sutcliffe.

The English team had a couple of problems of its own. Staples had developed rheumatic trouble on the boat over and his condition had worsened to the extent that he had to be sent home. Geary had sustained a broken nose while batting in the first match of the tour and had had no cricket for nearly a month. Fortunately all the front-line bowlers were fit and the wisdom of the selectors in including four all-rounders plus a wicket-keeper batsman (Ames) was being borne out.

The first Test was to be played at Brisbane, which in 1928 was a bit like a wild west town with its dusty streets and wooden buildings. The city had not staged a Test before and thousands had made the journey from the outlying areas of Queensland, crowding the hotels and boarding houses. As Jack Gregory started his run to bowl the first ball of the series there was silence all around the ground, and then as he accelerated into those long, leaping strides, all the insecurity of a young nation exploded in a thunderclap of exhortation. The ball thumped into the turf and Hobbs, the calmest man on the ground, lifted his bat and watched it sail past his off stump. It was evident that the pitch, like all good products of the Empire, was built to last. A week's gate money and 1500 runs was what the authorities were after.

Gregory, whose bowling action was a supreme example of the power of mind over body, was hard-pressed to get the ball to rise above stump height.

Hobbs and Sutcliffe put on 85. The Australians kept at them, though, and a brilliant catch by Ponsford on the boundary ended Sutcliffe's innings. Shortly afterwards Don Bradman, playing in his first Test, ran out Hobbs. It was a significant little episode. 'The Master', on 49, was completing a third run from a Mead cover drive when a tremendous throw caught him yards adrift. The age of Hobbs was not quite over but the age of Bradman had begun. Mead was then lbw to Grimmett for 8 and so, with the score at 108 for 3, a real crisis under those conditions, Jardine walked out to play his first innings in the kind of cricket that matters most.

His job was simply to stay there and wear down the bowling. In timeless Tests this was something batsman frequently had to do, since scoring runs was just not worth the risk of losing wickets. Jardine played his most cautious game, with Hammond at the other end scarcely less obstinate. Valuable as these long defensive innings of Jardine's were, they did on occasion flatter the bowling. He would abandon all strokes except for the push to square leg or point, and even these were sparingly used. A bowler's spirits are apt to rise under these circumstances, especially if his half-volley is met with an unerringly dead bat. Grimmett and Ironmonger gave him a fair amount of trouble, or appeared to at any rate. Ben Travers, who was in and around the English dressing room, claimed in *94 Declared* that Ironmonger's bowling was rather relished and that his action was also thought to be suspect. 'Of course he throws,' Jardine said, 'but don't, for God's sake, tell anybody so.' They succeeded in getting Ironmonger picked for the second Test but he was dropped after that. In fact, he was a much better bowler than the story suggests, taking 74 Test wickets at under 18 apiece. It is surely inconceivable that Jardine, in his first innings against Australia, would have attempted anything so flash as affecting to struggle against a bowler. His remark was probably harmless bravado, but unfortunate nevertheless since Ironmonger was to get him out five times in eleven Test innings between 1928 and 1933.

Hammond and Jardine put on 53 for the fourth wicket, and when Hammond left, Hendren came in to join the struggle. After batting for two hours, Jardine hit a straight ball from Ironmonger hard and straight to Woodfull at silly mid-off and was caught. He had made 35 of the 109 runs scored while he was at the wicket and, within the context of the game, it was a major innings.

Australia definitely had the better of the day's play, even though Hendren and Chapman took advantage of some tired bowling towards the close. The next day Hendren was given wonderful support by the tail. Larwood, who must have been about the best no. 9 around at the time, made 70 and England were finally all out for 521. It was a comfortable total but no more than that in view of the state of the pitch. And Australia had a strong batting line-up: Woodfull, Ponsford, Kippax, Hendry, Ryder and Bradman. The English selection committee, of which Jardine was a member, had deliberated late into the night before the match over whether to play four bowlers or five. They had settled on four, a decision which, by teatime on the second day with the prospect of perhaps two days in the field, may have given them an anxious moment or two.

With an hour left to play on the second day, Woodfull and Ponsford walked out to begin the Australians' reply. Larwood was to open the bowling and the wind was blowing from on to off, helping his away-swinger. Woodfull prepared to receive his first ball as Larwood ran in lightly, on his toes, which was always a danger sign. The first three balls screeched down the wicket, completely beating Woodfull. The fourth took an outside edge and Chapman, leaping to his left from gully, brought off an impossible catch; the impetus took him to where short fine leg would have been. Such bowling combined with such fielding (Hobbs said it was the best catch he ever saw) could not have inspired much confidence in the Australian dressing room.

Larwood then yorked Ponsford, with the batsman being seen to draw away. Chapman sensibly rested Larwood after his fourth over and in the meantime Tate caught and bowled Kippax. Larwood had 15 minutes in which to renew his strength and then Chapman brought him back to attack the new batsman, Kelleway, who had come in as a night-watchman. He made every effort to get out of the way of the first ball, but it took the shoulder of his bat and streaked over the slips for four. He waved his bat at the next two and the fourth uprooted his off stump. Bradman was due in next but fortunately for him, the captain, Ryder, came in instead. He survived the last two balls of the over, but when Larwood was about to begin his sixth over, Ryder appealed against the light. According to Percy Fender, who was covering the match for a London newspaper, the sun was shining in a cloudless sky. The appeal was upheld, however, and the players came off.

Larwood did not manage to bowl quite like this again during the series, but then he did not need to – his spell of five overs, nine runs and three wickets was a major contribution to the retention of the Ashes. Others, Hammond and White for instance, maintained far greater consistency and, without taking anything away from their remarkable records in their respective departments, it would be true to say that the Australians did not recover from this devastating early blow to their morale until it was too late.

Australia were all out for 122 just before lunch on the third day. Larwood took 6 for 32 and England eventually won by a record 675 runs. In the second innings Jardine made 65 not out under not much pressure, but it was an ideal innings for the situation in that he scored a single off nearly every ball he received, so giving the strike to his more quick-scoring partners.

England included a fifth bowler, Geary, in the side for the second Test. Australia made three changes, none of them successful as it transpired. One of them was to drop Bradman – fair enough at the time but a bit comical in retrospect – and another was to bring in a chap called O. E. Nothling. Larwood broke Ponsford's hand, thus putting Australia's leading run-scorer out of action for the rest of the series. (He had also been instrumental in ending their main bowler's involvement, for in trying to take a return catch off Larwood at Brisbane, Gregory had injured his knee so badly that he never played Test cricket again.) Jardine and Hammond came together under circumstances similar to those at Brisbane and turned the game round with equal success. They put on 83 before Jardine was late in responding to Hammond's call for a single and was run out. Hammond went on to score 251, O. E. Nothling did nothing and England won by eight wickets.

The Australian press demanded new blood, and with some justification since the average age of the side was 34½. What was really lacking was a fast bowler, and the absence of new talent in this department was felt all the more acutely against a batting side as strong as England's. It is interesting to note that in such times of crisis the English press tend to moan and talk about the old days, whereas their Australian counterparts take a much more positive though no less high-handed attitude.

The third Test was at Melbourne, where there was slightly more hope for the bowler since the pitch had not been quite so over-prepared. Because a state game had taken place immediately before the Test, the groundsman had not had as much time as he would have wished for watering and rolling. The Australian selectors injected some young blood as requested; E. A. A'Beckett was picked for his first Test appearance and Bradman was recalled.

It was fairly level pegging after each side had batted. Hammond made his second consecutive double-century and Jardine scored 62 in $3\frac{1}{4}$ hours. The pitch, however, was proving to be just as lifeless as the previous two and by the close on the fifth day the third innings of the match had still not been completed.

There was just enough rain overnight to ruin the wicket and so, for the first time in the series, the Australians looked certain of winning. Their score was 347 for eight overnight and, if they could get England in quickly, they would surely have them beaten by teatime. Chapman did his patriotic duty by saying that he considered conditions unfit for play, but the umpires disagreed and play began at 12.30. Since this was a timeless Test there would have been no point in the English bowlers keeping the Australian tail-enders batting until the wicket improved – that would merely have put England's fourth-innings target still further out of reach, and so White, with ominous ease, took the last two wickets. Hobbs and Sutcliffe had only two overs to face before lunch. They survived but Hobbs himself doubted that England would manage 100, so vicious was the pitch.

In the first over after lunch Hobbs gave a straightforward catch to Hendry at slip and Hendry dropped it. It was an error in the Fred Tate class. Thereafter the two batsmen played the innings of their lives, Hobbs taking most of the strike and using his brilliant footwork not merely to survive but to score runs as well. Sutcliffe at the other end was less flamboyant and, if anything, more secure. The danger came not so much from the turn of the ball as from the unpredictability of the bounce. In defending against a good-length ball they simply had to get into line and then wait for the sting as the ball hit them, Hobbs was even hit in the neck once. The only forcing stroke either batsman attempted was the pull. Each delivery made a crater as it pitched and, with the wicket drying hard all the time, it was as if a strip of corrugated iron had been laid diagonally in front of the batsman. Anything pitched short often bounced over the heads of both batsman and wicket keeper.

The spectators, so full of good humour during the luncheon interval, turned nasty. They barracked Sutcliffe when he prodded the pitch, they even barracked their own side, and their disappointment was heightened by the fact that Australia had no left-armer to exploit the conditions to the full. Just such a bowler was Ironmonger, who might have bowled England out in an afternoon, but he had been dropped almost by public demand after the second Test because of his age, and was now sitting watching from the pavilion.

Sutcliffe and Hobbs added 78 in the afternoon session and continued bravely into the evening. The thought occurred to Hobbs as the total mounted that England now had a minute chance of winning the game. With this in mind, he signalled to the pavilion, ostensibly for a new bat. Jardine took several out to the middle and waited attentively while Hobbs tried each one in turn and then decided to carry on with the one he had been using. The object of the little pantomime was to pass a message back to Chapman. Hobbs thought that if another wicket fell Jardine should come in ahead of Hammond, Chapman or Hendren since – and this must have been embarrassing for Jardine to relay – he was the least likely to get out under the circumstances. The captain, however, was not in the dressing room since, according to one reliable source, he was enjoying the play from a more convivial vantage point unknown to his team-mates. The senior players present discussed the plan and, without the captain's approval, decided to support Hobbs.

At 105, the most stirring of all the famous pair's partnerships came to an end. Hobbs, having scored 49, was given out lbw to Blackie, a decision which Fender in the press box thought incorrect since the ball in his opinion would have passed over the top of the stumps. Jardine came in next, as suggested, and was immediately badly beaten by Blackie, the ball fizzing inside his bat and onto his pads. 50,000 people appealed and Jardine, benefitting perhaps from any doubt lingering in the umpire's mind about the Hobbs decision, was given not out. He played a few more deliveries uneasily and then went down the wicket for a long talk with Sutcliffe.

His discomfort showed just how bad the pitch was and how great had been the achievement of the openers, especially during the afternoon when conditions were even worse. Jardine had the character to hang on, even though he really struggled against Grimmett. During the weeks of the tour he had tended more and more to remove his bottom hand from the bat handle in playing defensively and also in playing certain of his leg-side strokes. The practice had been fashionable briefly in his time at Oxford and he had used it intermittently since then, but he now found it particularly effective against Grimmett. In this way he managed to stay with Sutcliffe for the 68 minutes until stumps were drawn. By then he had scored 18, and it is unlikely that anyone will ever make a more valuable 18. Had Australia managed to dismiss Jardine quickly, it is quite likely that they would have had the rest of the side out by the close, instead of which, England looked certain of victory. In *The Turn of the Wheel*, Fender said this of Jardine's batting: ' ... it is no reflection on any other member of the side when I say that I doubt if any other could have coped with conditions in the same way.' The Australian press were so cross with their own side's failure to bowl out England on a drying wicket that the three heroes of the day received scant praise for their miraculous fight-back, and neither was the full awfulness of the wicket appreciated – except, of course, by the tiny collection of Englishmen present.

Sutcliffe and Jardine resumed their partnership the next morning amidst a feeling that England had already won the match. They needed only 160 runs with nine wickets still standing. The wicket had improved and was now merely untrustworthy. The batsmen were severely tested although, once again, this was not appreciated. They raised the score to 190 and then Jardine was bowled off his pads by Grimmett for 33, having batted in all for 115 minutes. Less valuable triple-centuries have been made.

Hammond and then Hendren stayed with Sutcliffe to take England to within 14 runs of their target, by which time the Australians had given up. Sutcliffe, having batted in all for 6½ hours, swished across a straight ball from Grimmett and was lbw for 135. His return to the pavilion was greeted with silence by the spectators whose generosity of spirit was so often praised: they might have managed a small ripple in view of the state of the game. The atmosphere in the English dressing room, on the other hand, was lively, perhaps a little too much so. Fender takes up the story:

> Chapman came in and slashed wildly at several balls then shut up like an oyster, and began playing pat-ball and refusing long singles. Perhaps he was trying to give Hendren a chance of his 50 before the end came. If so it was a very foolish thing to worry about ... Hendren was bowled last over before the tea interval with only 6 runs wanted ... Resuming after tea, Tate came out with Chapman, the batting order having been altered and, with 1 added, Chapman attempted to hit Ryder for six, and was caught easily at extra-cover by Woodfull.

Tate and the new batsman, Geary, ran a bye, then Geary decided to finish it off with a big straight drive. He connected and Tate, unaware that Bradman was lurking thirty yards behind the bowler, set off down the wicket. Bradman returned the ball and Tate was easily run out – England needed four to win with three wickets standing, $2\frac{1}{2}$ in effect, since Larwood was pretty well out of action with an ankle injury. One may imagine the feelings of Hobbs, Sutcliffe and Jardine towards their team-mates at this point. And to Jardine, the advantages of firm leadership and a disciplined approach must have been more apparent than ever. Meanwhile Geary was quite unruffled by the sudden upsets, he wound up for the next delivery and thumped it through mid-on for 4, bellowing, 'Dammit, we've done 'em!' It was an appropriate way for a side under Chapman to win the Ashes.

Afterwards the captain made the proper speeches to the effect that beating the Australians had been no easy matter and that they had certainly had him worried on not a few occasions. His next goal, he said, was to win the last two Tests and thereby level the overall tally between the two countries. The team certainly wanted to maintain their unbeaten record and any noticeable relaxation would have put that at risk, as well as being rather tactless. But inevitably, their lust for blood waned somewhat over the second half of the tour, and the Australians, who were ever on the look out for slights, occasionally found them.

Not long after the Test, the MCC team travelled to the mining town of Bendigo in Victoria for a two-day match against a local XIII. The game was played in an amicable spirit, even through a dust-storm on the first day, and by the final session on the second day England were nearing the end of their second innings with a draw inevitable. Chapman persuaded the local captain to agree to end proceedings as soon as England were all out. It is easy to see how Chapman's request might have sounded high-handed, and it seems that one of the umpires, a Mr Pearce, took offence. The MCC last-wicket partnership continued with commendable seriousness well into the final session, until 20 minutes before the close, Jardine dollied up an easy catch to square leg. The Bendigonian fielder trotted in to take it but Umpire Pearce, not yet appeased, mischievously pushed him out of the way and took the catch himself, the purpose being to cause the ball to be 'dead' and the MCC innings to continue. Jardine is said to have looked 'puzzled' and the umpire must have felt a little foolish, for Jardine could look witheringly puzzled sometimes. The game continued to the appointed time and two weeks later Umpire Pearce was busted – stripped of his white coat and pebbles. It is sad when such men are lost to cricket.

The team played two matches against Tasmania, whose side at the time was rather below State standard. The first match was at Launceston. After a rough overnight crossing from the mainland, the tourists found themselves having to field for most of the first day. Tasmania were able to take advantage of the condition of their opponents to the extent of scoring 229 runs. The following day, Jardine went on to make the highest score of his career, 214 in 4 hours 8 minutes. He shared a glorious two-hour stand with Mead which produced an astonishing 224 runs. Nor was the bowling all that easy; in the next match Tasmania were to bowl out MCC for under 250 and a fast bowler named Ward so impressed observers who had come over from the mainland to watch the match that he was tipped to open the bowling for Australia in the next Test (but he did not). Jardine's innings was of the same quality as those he had played at the start of the tour before a series of awkward situations in the Tests had demanded more caution, and he displayed once more the full range of strokes which had moved M. A. Noble to describe him as the finest stylist ever to tour Australia.

He did not play in the second match at Hobart, but instead was taken by his host into the interior of the island on a fishing trip. Fishing was a lifelong passion of Jardine's, first inspired when he was a small boy in St Andrew's by Andrew Lang, the classicist and man of letters. Lang was in his late sixties when Jardine entered his life and he developed a great affection for the boy. As Jardine wrote in *In Quest of the Ashes* (1933):

We were in complete agreement that the two 'C's' – Cricket and Classics – were the two most important things in the world.

One day Mr Lang staggered me with the announcement that he felt we should add Fishing to the two 'C's', and I shall never forget the shock I suffered on listening to this unabashed declaration of heresy.

Even a present of the wherewithal to buy a rod hardly weakened my contempt for the 'new religion'.

I am bound to confess that to-day I rank that one-time heresy above the two 'C's'!

(This was written immediately after the bodyline tour, when cricket batted pretty low down in his order of things.)

The conditions that Tasmania offers for fishing are among the best in the world, and large areas of the countryside remained uncharted even into the 'thirties, so there was a pleasant sense of venturing into the unknown. The party camped on the banks of the Penstock, a stretch of water which at the time contained so many fish that anything under 4 lb was thrown back. When Jardine returned to fish there during the bodyline tour, he found that his friends had grown tired of repeatedly wading back to the bank after every catch to add to a mounting pile of brown trout. They had discovered the more efficient method of reeling the fish in, then clubbing them over the head with a blackjack and hooking them onto a belt.

The team left Tasmania after a week and with their departure ended the toughest assignment yet for the two cricket correspondents of *The Illustrated Tasmanian Mail* – 'Veronica' and 'Gumleaf'. Back on the mainland, Jardine made 114 against South Australia. Most of his runs came off the bowling of Jack Scott, a fiery fast bowler now a little over the hill, who bowled what, in the absence of a better word, is referred to in this book as 'bodyline'. Scott had first bowled it in 1925 when he was playing for New South Wales, but his State captain, Collins, loathed the tactics and so Scott was only able to employ them when Collins was away on Test duty.

Eventually Scott moved to South Australia where the captain, Vic Richardson, allowed the bowler complete freedom to practise his art. If anyone bowled at the man it was Scott. He was fast and inaccurate, a combination which was very effective against timid or inexperienced players but not against accomplished batsmen. Ponsford, for instance, who was Larwood's rabbit in Australia, appeared quite comfortable against him, and to Jardine he was practically a joke. Photograph no. 5 shows the extent to which Jardine was intimidated by short-pitched bowling. The innings against South Australia gave him the distinction of having scored a century against each of the three principal States.

With the Ashes lost, the Australian selectors felt they could afford to be a little bolder in their choice of side for the fourth Test. Archie Jackson was picked for his first Test at the age of only 19. The England team remained unchanged. There followed seven days of heavy scoring, with Hammond rumbling up and down the wicket for days on end like a heavy roller – unstoppable, taking the life out of the bowling.

In the first innings Jardine was given out lbw to a ball he was clearly heard to play, and England were bowled out for 334, the lowest total of the match. The Australian selectors' faith in Jackson was more than justified, as he scored 164 in a way that caused people to wonder in all seriousness whether there had ever been a better batsman. When England batted again it was the familiar story; Jardine came out to join Hammond at 21 for 2.

> Throughout the series (wrote Fender), Jardine seemed always to be faced with the necessity of supplying the stability which the batting of the side had not only appeared to lack on paper, but also in actual practice. The opportunity had never so far occurred to him to play an innings free from the greatest necessity for restraint, and once again he found himself placed in a most difficult situation.

Fearing a third successive double-hundred from Hammond, the Australians went onto the defensive and bowled leg-theory. The scoring rate slowed appreciably and the barracking started. A state of mutual contempt between Jardine and the cheap seats was by now well established, and even though he was outscoring Hammond, nearly all the hooting and shouting was directed at him. By the close they had raised the score to 206 and England were back on level terms.

Resuming the partnership the next morning, Jardine survived an anxious moment when, in the first over, he played a ball from Grimmett onto his pads as he had done in the first innings. The bowler appealed, the umpire's arm went up – and then down in realisation of the error. For the home supporters, then, the day began badly, and when the run-rate became even slower than on the previous day, there was no doubt in their minds as to who was to blame. Jardine's daring efforts to counter Grimmett's leg-theory by sweeping him one-handed on the full met with renewed outbursts of what has since been described as friendly raillery.

The two batsmen continued their partnership into the afternoon session and, with the temperature above 100°, Hammond began to tire. Jardine took most of the strike and in so doing managed to move his own score up into the nineties. He had reached 98 when, to the unbounded glee of the crowd, he was deceived by a slower one from Oxenham and drove a hard catch to Woodfull at silly point. His partnership with Hammond had lasted 5 hours 47 minutes and produced 262 runs which, at the time of writing, remains a record for the third wicket by England against Australia.

England rather folded after that, and Australia were left with a target of 349 to win. They only failed to make it by 13 runs, White being the cause – he took eight wickets with his easy 'ones' and his overall match figures have a period feel: 124.5–37–256–13.

If Jardine's relationship with the crowd sank to new depths in this match, Chapman remained as popular as a winning England captain can ever be. It is interesting how the crowd reacted to the two men. Just as Jardine often wore his Harlequin cap, Chapman wore his Quidnuncs cap, the Cambridge equivalent. It was less garish but just as symbolic, one would have thought, to those in the outer. There was an element of mischief on the part of both men in wearing these things, and it was noticeable that they both on occasion fielded in them, which was strictly 'non-U'; the custom in those days was that one might bat in a 'fancy cap' but one fielded in the colours of one's side, and neither player would have departed from the convention unless it was for a particular reason. In the fourth Test, Chapman went even further and appeared at the crease topped off with a riot of colour. It was a cap presented to Cambridge undergraduates who made a 'pair', with on the front two large noughts and on the back the word 'Chaps'. The crowds knew that Chapman was only teasing, but with Jardine it was different: his humour was too subtle, he lacked the common touch in a land where no such expression was necessary and where his sort of diffidence was as familiar as a snowdrift.

The fact that he spent so much time fielding on the boundary aggravated the situation. With close-fielding specialists Chapman and Hammond in the side, it was necessary for Jardine to do a lot of work in the outfield. He was quite unsuited to this, although by hard practice and sheer determination he achieved a measure of competence. One may imagine the crowd's reaction to his early efforts as he strenuously bounded round to cut off a four, his face a study in concentration, and one may imagine their delight if he misfielded or if his throw bounced three or four times before reaching the stumps. Nobody likes his humble struggle to improve being derided. When he was batting he was in command, or confident at any rate, and therefore the barracking was no more than an irritation, but when he was down on the boundary it was barely tolerable. In the second Test at Sydney he was fielding just in front of the Hill and was subjected to a constant stream of abuse. He took not the slightest notice until Chapman rescued him and told him to go to another position, then before he walked away, he turned his head slightly and spat on the ground. It was mutual, all right.

Those best qualified to know have said that, had he but given the barrackers a friendly wave, all would have been well. It certainly worked in the first match of the tour, but once the crowds turned against him, the Harlequin cap became a symbol of the Imperial order, something which was believed to be the cause of many ills at the time. Upright and apparently imperturbable, Jardine was the image of the British establishment. Other players of less patrician bearing might easily win over the crowd with friendly waves and dashing play, but that simply was not Jardine's way.

In 1979–80 Brearley was the barrackers' prime target for similar, though quite mistaken reasons. He tried the friendly wave and had beer cans thrown at him.

Even Chapman incurred the displeasure of the mob towards the end of the tour. They barracked him at Ballarat for allowing the non-bowlers to bowl, and they barracked him at Melbourne for turning Larwood on the no. 11, Ironmonger. During the latter outburst, Chapman sat his side down and waited for the noise to subside. When it did not, he went and spoke to the aggreived section but this had no effect. Only a declaration by Ryder enabled play to continue. Jardine was present on both occasions and himself received further attentions during his match-saving innings in the game against Victoria. A young tyro called H. H. Alexander was bowling a crude form of bodyline and

Jardine pointed out that he was scuffing up the pitch in his follow-through, which indeed he was; in fact it was the bowler's regular practice to do so. The umpire supported Jardine's complaint, much to the annoyance of the crowd. Alexander then went round the wicket and proceeded to try and knock Jardine's head off, which was the height of folly, and the result was another Jardine hundred.

Chapman stood down for the final Test for reasons which still remain unclear. He had a dose of 'flu just before the match but could have played had he really wanted. His form had been erratic, if not so 'deplorably ineffective' as *The Times* stated, and it seems that he felt he was not worth his place and should make way for Maurice Leyland, the young left-hander who had not played in any of the previous Tests. It is also possible that the treatment Chapman received after the fourth Test, at Ballarat and then at Melbourne, where he was jostled and insulted in the members' enclosure, may have influenced his decision to pull out. These were isolated incidents in an otherwise happy relationship with the crowds, but when he returned to England he indicated that the atmosphere had in general been too highly charged for his liking.

White took over the captaincy and Leyland fully justified his inclusion by making a hundred on his Test debut. The match turned out to be a marathon, running into an eighth day which made it then the longest Test match in history. Over 1500 runs were scored but Jardine, promoted to open the batting with Hobbs since Sutcliffe was unfit, failed to take advantage of conditions, being dismissed for 19 in the first innings by Wall, and then in the second innings the same bowler got him first ball. At long last Australia managed to win and so avoided being beaten by what would have been, for them, an unprecedented margin.

Having completed both his innings, Jardine left this match at the end of the fifth day and made his way across Australia to catch a boat for India where he had planned a holiday. It had not been announced before the Test that he would be leaving when he did and it seems that he simply decided that he had had enough. His departure was most abrupt and unexpected. One cannot help but wonder what might have happened if a professional had decided to leave early.

He may on the other hand have privately told his captain that he would be leaving after the fifth day but this possibility does not reflect very well on the Englishmen. It suggests that they were trying to pull a fast one by picking their strongest batting side (which meant dropping Chapman) without weakening the fielding (since Chapman was Jardine's substitute). At any rate the Australian captain was none too pleased when White asked if Chapman could field in Jardine's place and only agreed on condition that Chapman did not field close to the wicket. It was as well for diplomatic relations that Chapman did not take a vital catch and that Australia won the match.

The Australian press tried to get Jardine to talk about his sudden departure but he refused, saying that, while there was a great deal he would like to say, he would not comment until the tour was over. Before the press had time to launch an attack on Jardine for running away from the 'friendly ribbing' of the crowds, Australia had won the Test and all was euphoria.

And so Jardine's relationship with Australia came to the end of its first phase. There was no follow-up to the story in the press and he did not reveal the extent of his grievance until he wrote an attack on Australian crowds in the 1930 edition of the Lonsdale Library's *The Game of Cricket*:

> Cricket, when all is said and done is a game for twenty-two people, and no game that I know of, unless community singing be a game, is improved by thirty or forty thousand people endeavouring to take part in it ... With the exception of the Manchester crowd, which in the author's opinion has no superior, Australian crowds are better judges and keener critics of the game than most English crowds, it will be a thousand pities if a generation is allowed to grow up in Australia which allows a well-earned reputation for sound criticism and fair play to be discounted by partial and unintelligent barracking. There are only two possible attitudes for the individual to take up towards the barrackers, one is to jest with them, the other is to take no notice. The former is more diverting and it is not difficult to 'score', but the latter, though less diverting, is probably safer, since it is less distracting.

From left: Emily Leggatt,
lison Moir (mother), Edward
eggatt, Grandmother Moir,
.R.J., M.R. Jardine (father).

(above) Jardine as captain of the
inchester XI, 1919.

Jardine at Oxford, before his injury.

No. 564.

DOUGLAS ROBERT JARDINE (New College).

O.U. Cricket Club.

Unlike many other famous Scotsmen, D.R.J. was not born North of the Tweed, but in Bombay. On the 23rd of October, 1900, the prospects of the world were brightened by the arrival of a child of magnificent physique and figure. But our Idol did not long remain in India: he found time, however, to open his first season on the verandah by resisting for three minutes the fast inswingers of his kitmugar, and since that day has never looked back. We next hear of him at Horris Hill, where he soon became a prominent figure in both Cricket and Soccer XI's, becoming Captain of the former in his last year. This early promise was fulfilled on entering Winchester College, where in 1917 he gained his place in the XI, and represented the School the following winter as goalkeeper. Besides this, he found time to play for Houses VI and captain the School at racquets, at which game he nearly won for the School the Public Schools Racquet Competition. His last year was crowned with success when, as captain of 'Lords,' not only did he lead

his side to victory in 'Eton Match,' but ended the season with an average of 66. Had his work and other athletic distinctions allowed him time, no doubt he would have won the Senior Steeplechase, but suffice it to say that he did not enter for this event. In October, 1919, he came up to New College, and the following summer gained his Blue as a batsman, which honour he at once celebrated by taking six wickets for 27 against Essex. But it is not only at cricket that our Idol thrives; his agility in goal earned him an invitation to accompany the Varsity Soccer team to Queen's as reserve goalkeeper, while at Real Tennis he can look back with pride on the occasion he beat W. Renshaw. But our Idol is also human, a first-class connoisseur of spirits, as many will testify; he can never yet be said to have disgraced the Mitre or the George, and the Proctors lay their traps in vain. At Bridge he has few creditors and fewer partners, while as an early-riser he is the despair of his scout. He has not yet taken up rowing seriously, but when he does, a brilliant future is assured for him in that direction, for has he not as great a variety of strokes in a boat as he has in the Parks! But we nearly forgot our Idol's greatest triumph when, at the end of his first academical year he defeated the Examiners after a desperate struggle lasting, he tells us, no less than 75 minutes.

In conclusion, we may wish this redoubtable figurehead every success, and express a tender hope that his shadow (at present pretty considerable) may never grow less.

I am dining with Wilmer this nite tonight & shall look forward to seeing Small Peter.

Thy;

Xmas 1928 —

am happy — ~~more often~~ get ½ a chance.

Hearty Greetings for Xmas and the New Year

from

"A Happy Family" in Australia

Douglas Jardine

M.C.C. AUSTRALIAN TEAM 1928-29

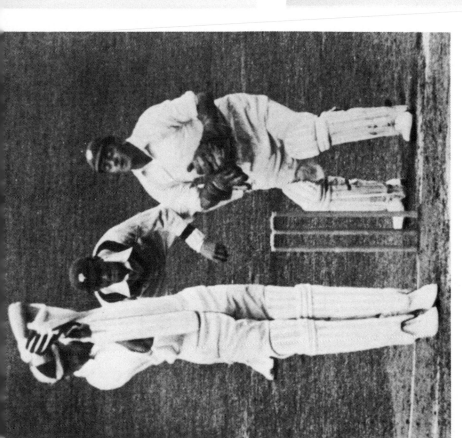

5 Playing a rising ball in one of his early games for Surrey.

6 (right)   A card home from one of Chapman's 'happy family'.
Back row: G. Duckworth, L.E.G. Ames, C.P. Mead, M.W. Tate, E.H. Hendren, G. Geary. Middle row: M. Leyland, S. J. Staples, W.R. Hammond, F.C. Toone (manager), H. Sutcliffe, H. Larwood, A.P. Freeman. Front row: E. Tyldesley, J.C. White, A.P.F. Chapman, D.R. Jardine, J.B. Hobbs.

7 & 8 That sticky dog at Melbourne, 1928–29. Jardine falls forward to Grimmett (above) and tries vainly to sweep the same bowler one-handed (below).

9   Intense concentration as Jardine catches Ryder off Larwood in the Brisbane Test of 1928.

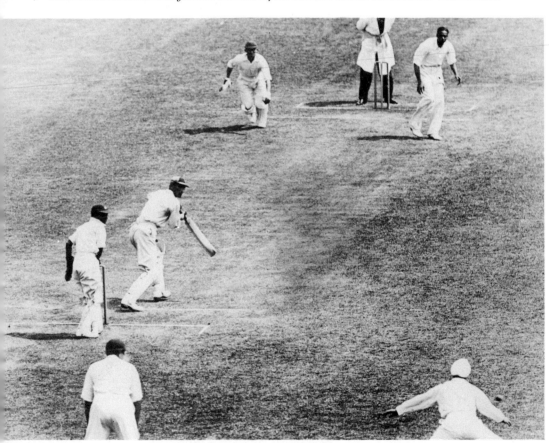

10   A couple of runs off Amar Singh in the Lord's Test against India, 1932.

11 (above)   The 1932–33 MCC team about to sail for Australia on RMS *Orontes*. Left to right: Allen, Jardine, Brown, Capt., O'Sullivan, Bowes, Duckworth (head turned), Larwood, Leyland, Mitchell, Paynter, Sutcliffe, Verity, Voce, Wyatt.

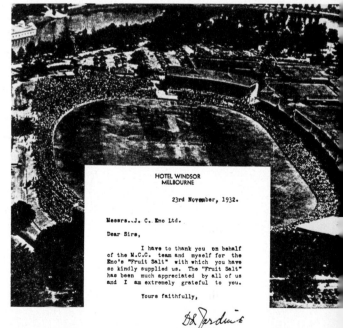

12   How the 1932–33 MCC party ensured that their systems were clean and their blood pure.

13 & 14   Harold Larwood in action.

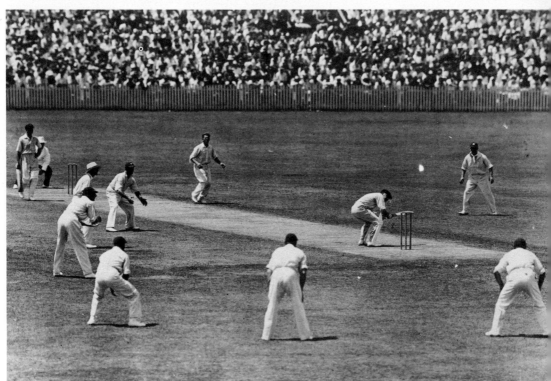

15 & 16   Two views of Woodfull batting against Larwood in the fourth Test of the 1932–33 series, in each case with a bodyline leg-trap.

17　The armour worn by some of the Australian batsmen during the bodyline tour.

18 (below)　Fender seeing Jardine off with the MCC team for the Indian tour of 1933–34.

19 A face in the crowd. Queueing outside the Oval on the first morning of the final Test between England and Australia, 1934.

20 (below) Jardine and his fiancée, Margaret, at a garden party three months before their marriage.

21 Jardine on holiday in Scotland holding his first child, Fianach.

22 (below) Jardine presents the County Cricketers' Billiards Championship trophy of 1936 to Ewart Astill with Alf Gover, the runner-up, between them.

23   One of the last photographs of Douglas Jardine, at National Book League v. Authors, 1958. Back row: Ian Peebles, Ben Barnett (Victoria, Buckinghamshire and Australia), Percy Fender. Front row: Len Hutton, D.R.J., Bob Wyatt.

5
Captain of England

1930 was Bradman's year. His incredible achievements during that summer have been described by the best writers on the game and I shall not attempt to re-tell the story here. When all is said and done, he was the greatest batsman of them all. This was his Test record in 1930: 5 matches, 7 innings, 974 runs, top score 334, and an average of 139.14. He was only 21 at the time and it was his first experience of English conditions, which were then quite different to those in Australia.

And yet, when one quotes his record to those who saw him play, it almost invariably provokes the reply, 'Oh yes, but ...' followed by some quibble about his performances on sticky wickets, his fallibility against fast, short-pitched bowling or even the assertion that there was an inevitability about his batting that made him less exciting to watch than some of the less consistent stroke players. Fortunately, a quantity of newsreel footage showing the young Bradman still exists. Viewed in short clips and from a distance of 50 years, his every movement seems sheer grace; it is as if the bat is making the strokes and Bradman is following with his hands and feet in perfect sympathy. Perhaps, though, even in cricket one can have too much of a good thing. One feels that if he had not been so assured, if he had got himself out trying to play left-handed or if his trousers had fallen down once or twice or even if he had simply scored fewer runs, there might never have been any doubt about his greatness. Instead of which, he has so often had to suffer the title of 'the greatest run-machine ever'.

The 1930 Australians did not go rampaging about the country quite as Armstrong's side had done in 1921 or as Bradman's was to do in 1948, and in the Tests the sides were evenly matched,

Bradman aside. England won the first, Australia the second and the weather the third. The fourth Test, also spoiled by rain, was remarkable in that Chapman had a bad match as captain. The selectors' nerves had been set a-jangle by his rather risky batting in the second Test and, since the final encounter was to be played to a finish, they seized the opportunity to make a change. So after leading England to nine wins in eleven matches, Chapman was dropped, much to the Australians' delight and everyone else's surprise. Wyatt was appointed in his place and did all that was required of him and more, but England were caught on a bad wicket in the fourth innings and Australia won the Ashes.

There can be no doubt that, had Jardine been in match practice, he would have been given the captaincy ahead of Wyatt. He had captained a side on only 12 occasions in first-class cricket but his tactical skill and powers of leadership were obvious to anyone who played with him. Moreover, his record against the Australians was excellent. But as it was, he played only eight innings at the start of the season and then pulled out of the running for a Test place. Knowing in advance that his business commitments would allow him very few Championship appearances, he had turned down the Surrey vice-captaincy at the beginning of the season and Maurice Allom had been appointed in his place. Even with their wealth of batting talent, England missed Jardine, particularly in the second Test where his steadying influence in the middle of the order might have made the game safe. On the whole, though, it was in bowling that England were deficient or, more specifically, they lacked a bowler who could get Bradman out.

Jardine came up against the tourists twice within 10 days at the start of the season. Rain spoiled both games; in the Surrey fixture only one innings was possible (Bradman 252 not out) and in the other a strong MCC side performed well and even appeared to have a chance of winning. Jardine was lbw to Wall for 25. This bowler had a good record against Jardine; he bowled to him on nine occasions and got his wicket five times.

The Times correspondent, reporting the MCC match, made what in the light of future events was a significant observation:

> The deepest impression left on my mind by my first sight of the Australian batsmen is that, generally speaking, they have anglicised

their methods. On Saturday a notably large proportion of them walked in front of all three stumps while the bowler was in the act of delivery, and planned to make most of their runs by pushes and glances on the leg side. In particular Woodfull, Jackson, Kippax, Richardson, Fairfax, and the three tail-enders adopted this scheme of play, some more obstinately than others.

It had become increasingly clear to batsmen that, with the universally friendly wickets and the prevalence of off-theory bowling, there were rich pickings available. By moving across the stumps, under cover to some extent of the existing lbw law, they would play the ball safely into the comparatively undefended on-side area. In playing both forward and back this method was effective, but whenever possible back-play was used, since it enabled the batsman to commit himself late to the shot and to watch the ball right onto the face of the bat.

The emphasis was on the elimination of risk. Hammond had shown in Australia that huge scores could be made by curbing artistic inclinations and relying almost entirely on two or three safe, back-foot strokes. Effective as his method had been, it was thought to be unnecessarily self-denying since in Australia the ball stopped swinging after four or five overs and thereafter forward play involved a minimum of risk. But in England, where the ball might continue to swing all day, the advantages of back-play were abundantly clear. Bradman's name is missing from *The Times'* correspondent's list but that did not mean he shunned the new tactics. Far from it, but his genuis allowed him to play several different types of game. Against MCC, it seems, he went for old-fashioned strokeplay.

With this further strengthening of batsman's defences, the day of the bowler's revenge moved a little closer. MCC's efforts to maintain the equilibrium were rather like those of the Dutch boy trying to plug the dyke. Two alterations made in 1930–31 were the enlargement of the stumps and a legal amendment so that a batsman could now be out lbw even if he snicked the ball onto his pad. The former innovation was well received and there were indeed fewer unfinished games. Neither measure was employed in the matches against the Australians. The doping of pitches continued unabated despite the disapproval of MCC and *Wisden*. Funnily enough, the county clubs, in their eagerness to attract big gates, were frequently cutting their own throats. The specially prepared

featherbed wickets that provided all the runs were so dense with
marl and dung and so on that they took ages to dry, so a lot of
time and interest in the matches was lost through waiting for the
effects of rain to wear off.

Jardine did not achieve much on the cricket field in 1930 but he
made his first appearance as an author. He contributed two
chapters on batsmanship and Test match cricket to a volume in
the Lonsdale Library series of sports handbooks. In its review,
The Times said, 'He shows a most remarkable power of analysis,
an equally austere discrimination between the grain of practi-
cality and the husk of sentiment.' The writing bears the stamp of a
classical education both in construction and in the liberal use of
Latin quotations. In fact, the influence of Winchester is evident in
this and in two other instructional books he wrote in 1936. At an
early age he was, as we have seen, influenced by the writings of
that great technical analyst, C. B. Fry, and he never departed from
those opinions formed while he was at his preparatory school.
Consequently, the three works are necessarily similar although
not repetitive in the way that, say, Warner's books are.

In dealing with batting, he not surprisingly favoured
orthodoxy. Those players who were successful but unorthodox
in their methods would, he believed, have greatly enhanced their
natural ability by adhering to the accepted canons of batsmanship. Like most batsmen, he was at pains to point out that there is
no mystery about bowling. He was rather less forthcoming about
how wickets might be taken but he emphasised the importance of
accuracy and, again, orthodoxy. Fielding, too, he regarded as an
art which, given a basic cricket sense, could be mastered with
assiduous practice and strict observance of the correct principles.
He clearly attributed his own success to these elements since,
again and again, he cites 'stupidity' as the cause of failures and
mistakes in all departments. 'It is in tense moments that good
training in and knowledge of the game come to the rescue of the
individual, in the same way that discipline may save a coward.'

Bravery and all-round toughness were perhaps more commonly
praised then, and they were certainly qualities which Jardine
valued highly and which he possessed himself in abundance. After
the bodyline controversy he became more outspoken on the virile
virtues, encouraging fieldsmen to take the manlier course when
faced with a scorching drive and addressing batsmen on the
desirability of 'standing up to any bowler and taking his knocks

with a rub and a smile. Grown men who constrict their freedom with thigh pads and chest protectors are faintly ridiculous.'

A further reminder of his Victorian upbringing came in *Cricket: How to Succeed* (1936). He included some advice on the general care of one's body, words which could have been written by C. B. Fry himself:

> As soon as you get up, or better still, as soon as you wake up, brush your teeth and wash your mouth out thoroughly, and then blow your nose twice.
>
> Now strip, take a rough towel and rub yourself all over for half a minute. You will find the skin begins to tingle pleasantly all over.
>
> Slip on your shirt and pants, and standing with your heels together, circle your arms from back to front ...

etc. If this seems a bit alarming, it should be remembered that it would not have been thought strange at the time. Fry, too, was a great one for 'physical culture' and even occasionally wore lederhosen, according to Cardus.

While one would have to term Jardine an imperialist, he held strong views on the role of politics in cricket:

> For years it has been assumed by successive after-dinner speakers that a sporting tour abroad invariably serves to forge links and bonds of sympathy and community between different countries and races engaged in friendly rivalry. There has been in consequence a tendency to place too heavy a burden on sport and to expect too much from it as a result. At the top of the tree, keenness and rivalry breed too much partisanship to produce the best results; and the somewhat chequered history of the Olympic Games should serve as a warning.

And in 1934 he wrote:

> What Liberal politicians of a century ago would have dubbed 'healthy rivalry' has all too often been allowed to drift into an exhibition of rampant nationalism on the part of the spectators and the press of the countries involved.

But in his 1930 essay he had relished the 'gloves-off' atmosphere of Test matches, the sternest trials of a player's skill:

> May they always be played in a spirit worthy of the place they hold in

the world of cricket. An atmosphere of 'great deeds done in so knightly a fashion, that there is no arrogance in triumph, no chagrin in defeat, but only calm of mind all passion spent' – such at any rate has been the author's happy experience.

In his post-bodyline works, however, it is apparent that Test cricket had lost much of its appeal. He disliked the huge partisan crowds and he disliked even more the necessity of having them. Like the Golden Age amateurs, he played the game for his own amusement, not for the benefit of the crowd. Of course, the game, could not survive without the paying customers and Jardine knew it, but it seemed to him that they were being accommodated to an unacceptable degree – the over-preparation of pitches to provide run-feasts, for example, and the increase in the number of overseas tours. 'It is the humbler manifestation which is infinitely more important for the sport as a whole, and the choice between clicking turnstiles and the village green is in reality no choice at all: the village has it every time,' he wrote.

The changes that took place in the game undoubtedly contributed to his early retirement. It was the amateur game he loved in later life – on the village green, with as little at stake as possible. In fact, apart from the weather, he disliked any influence or attempted influence on the game that came from outside the field of play. A distaste for the press lessened as he joined its ranks, but he maintained an unflagging contempt for 'pavilion critics' – those who had either never played or who had played but were only interested in re-living mythical deeds of their youth.

> At best [Jardine wrote] talking and writing only amount to inactive participation in the game. The speaker who delivers the usual type of well-worn oration, bringing in the overworked clichés about 'playing the game' and 'not cricket', may fancy he is doing some real service. But mildly bombastic references to the flag and to the game have a habit of sounding a little out of tune when the oration concludes with a peroration to the effect that, though many have played the game better than the speaker, none can have loved it more. Such things, if said at all, may strike a false note and in any case are better said about others than by speakers referring to themselves.

Technically, Jardine was at his most interesting when discussing captaincy. In *Cricket*, he takes the reader through the fourth innings of an imaginary match, the action being seen through the eyes of the captain of the fielding side. Each alternative is weighed up as carefully as a captain would have time for in a real situation. The account is both instructive and painfully true to anyone who has ever tried to captain a side. He attaches great importance to operating to a plan, however vague, and also to assessing the strengths and weaknesses of the opposition. Nearly all the fictitious captain's tactical moves fail, although some succeed indirectly and on one occasion, simply doing something different brings a wicket. In his efforts to get the best out of his bowlers, he ends up having to bowl both his quicks alternately from the same end since they are both under the delusion that there is a 'spot' to be exploited. The advantage tilts back and forth and it actually gets very exciting, but then the rain comes and ruins the pitch, and the next day the batting side are skittled out 50 short of the target. The humour of the situation is subtly expressed and the captain's struggle to control man and nature is obviously drawn from personal experience. The reader is left with his knowledge of captaincy greatly extended.

M. J. K. Smith is quoted as saying in reference to the England captaincy that it isn't a crown you wear, it's a coconut. If anyone was set up and then knocked down it was Jardine. Other captains have been mauled by the press – their tactics criticised, their honour called into question and their resignations demanded – but with the passage of time they receive whatever credit is due and, since there is an element of nostalgia in all cricket discussion, they often receive more than their due, and why not. But this is not so with Jardine. To say that he was a great captain remains somehow a provocative statement, and one which is made without qualification by very few people – almost exclusively those who played with or under him. Any disinterested assessment of Jardine's standing as a captain, however well-meaning or unbiased, is necessarily coloured by the fact that bodyline has been illegal since 1935 – there is a feeling that if bodyline was reprehensible, then so must have been Jardine's captaincy. But there was nothing illegal about it at the time. Jack Hobbs scored 61,000 runs under the old lbw rule but no one would be so silly as to suggest that he was any the less great because of it. Lillee and Thomson bowled more bouncers in 1974–75 than would now be permitted, but who would belittle their achievement? The reader is asked to forget for the moment that bodyline was outlawed and to make his own judgement on the basis of the facts as they emerge.

Jardine's appointment to the highest office in English cricket at the start of June 1931 received a mixed press. Only one Test match was scheduled, and that against New Zealand, so the selection of a leader might have been approached in a number of different ways: Carr would probably have been the safest bet if the object was winning the match as an end in itself; under Chapman, the England side seemed to play with more sparkle, and he had many supporters even though his batting average at the time was only 9; Lyon of Gloucestershire was another swashbuckler not worth his place; and then there was Percy Fender who had been an unsuccessful candidate for the job for seven years and who would have been a good man to force a win inside the three days allotted for the Test. But with the tour of Australia in 1932–33 uppermost in their minds, the selectors rightly decided to give a younger man a chance. That narrowed it down to Wyatt and Jardine.

Wyatt was in his second season as captain of Warwickshire, he had already captained England creditably, and he was having the best season with the bat of all the county captains (except Duleepsinhji, who was not really eligible for the England leadership). Jardine, although inexperienced as a captain, was an even better batsman, and this is where posterity has been particularly unkind to Jardine. Certain writers have found it convenient to say that Jardine was hired like a hit-man to travel around 'wasting' disaffected colonials. There is a tiny element of truth in this theory, but it always seems to overlook the important fact that he was the best defensive batsman in the world at the time and therefore an essential member of the English side. His career Test average was higher than Woodfull's, higher too than those of Woolley, Leyland or Hendren, and as a fighter in a crisis he had no equal.

On the morning of 11 June, *The Times* received Jardine's appointment thus:

> As a Test match batsman, his ability is indisputable, but for the moment, with so many others claiming the honour of captaining England, his claim has yet to be proved. Those who have chosen to attract popular opinion are at once dismissed but there are others who have played the game long, and always as it should be played, who have been passed over.

The slight suggestion that he might have been amongst those who did not play the game as it should be played may well have caused the Jardine breakfast cup to clatter back into its saucer. (*The Times* correspondent at the time was Sydney Southerton, who had been in Australia with the 1928-29 tourists as a Reuter's correspondent. Perhaps there had been a little friction between the two men then, although there is a photograph taken towards the end of that tour which shows them standing amicably beside one another, both dressed in filthy old clothes having just been shown round a gold mine.) 'Those who have chosen to attract popular opinion' probably meant Chapman, or it may have referred to Bev Lyon and F. E. Greenwood, the Yorkshire captain. In order to achieve a result in a rain-restricted Championship match, these two had decided to declare their respective first innings closed at 4 runs and then play the game as if it was a one-innings match. Only by doing this would the winning side receive maximum points (the law was later changed to make arranged declarations unnecessary). Their action met with popular acclaim but official disapproval. Later in that very wet summer Fender and the Glamorgan captain, Maurice Turnbull, came to a similar arrangement with the same results.

Writing in the *Star*, Fender approved the selectors' choice of captain, and hoped it meant Jardine would be available to lead England in Australia in 1932-33. Richard Streeton wrote in his biography of Fender that Fender even offered to resign the Surrey captaincy in order to give Jardine some experience of the job, but the Surrey committee turned down the offer.

There are several important questions, some of which can never be answered with complete confidence, relating to Jardine's appointment. Warner said in the *Morning Post* at the end of the 1931 season that the selectors (of whom he was the chairman) had set out with the intention of building a side for 1932–33. Did they, then, ask Jardine if he would be available for selection when the time came? And if so, what was Jardine's reply? My own feeling is that they did ask him and that Jardine, while agreeing on the need to build a new side, was unable to give an assurance as to his own availability so far in advance. The selectors were unlikely to have insisted on a commitment from Jardine, and in any case the rebuilding of the side would not have been much affected if one had not been given. The methods and capabilities of Wyatt, the other candidate, were regularly on view at Edgbaston and a trial period was not so necessary for him as for Jardine.

A number of things would have influenced Jardine's thinking, such as his rather unhappy experience of Australian crowds in 1928–29 and his professional commitments. Set against these considerations was the almost irresistible opportunity to become only the fifth England captain to win back the Ashes in Australia (only six have done it to date). Another attraction from his point of view was the selectors' determination that the tour would need to be run along more disciplined lines than the previous one under Chapman. The side would be younger and, on paper anyway, weaker, and it was going to need a concerted effort to beat the Australians, whose rebuilding process was now complete. Chapman's tour had been quite an easy-going affair. All that had to change.

Another point in Jardine's favour was that the selection committee, Warner in particular, came to value his contributions to their meetings. Not only was he a very good judge of players' strengths and weaknesses but he also had an extensive knowledge of cricket history, a very rare quality in first-class cricketers and one which endeared him to his three colleagues, all of whom were over 55. His Winchester and Oxford background also made for freer discussion across the table. Therefore, even if his availability was uncertain, he was an ideal fellow to have around at the planning stage.

It is difficult to tell what exactly were his intentions regarding the task that lay ahead. At the beginning of 1932 he was to be involved in a slightly puzzling sequence of events. As Richard Streeton pointed out in his book, Fender had fallen from favour with the Surrey committee for a number of reasons, among them the arranged declarations and his habit of selecting match-fit professionals ahead of the many amateurs who might have liked a bit of a knock. Fender said he was told at the end of January that Jardine would be taking over as captain. The change was undoubtedly being made for the wrong reasons, but it was a sensible one nonetheless. Fender supported it and expressed his willingness to play on under the new captain. There was a good deal of speculation in the press about what was actually going on, and then on 26 February there appeared in the papers an announcement by the Surrey Club which began,

Owing to conflicting statements which have appeared in the press with regard to Mr Fender and the captaincy of the Surrey XI, the committee of the Surrey County Cricket Club desire to state that nothing has been decided except that the committee are of the opinion that the time has come when a change of captaincy is desirable, provided a suitable successor to Mr Fender can be found.

And it was another $2\frac{1}{2}$ weeks before it was announced that Jardine would lead the side in the 1932 season.

The most likely explanation for all this, although it cannot be proved, is that the committee had assumed that Jardine would accept the captaincy at the time of the initial meeting with Fender. Whether or not the offer had been made by then is impossible to say, but that there followed a period of uncertainty suggests that Jardine delayed giving an answer. It is understandable that he should have taken his time; if he accepted the Surrey captaincy it would be taken as a declaration of intent to lead England in Australia, something about which he had reservations. But accept he did. We shall come to that summer of planning and intrigue before very long, but first, Jardine's performances as England's captain against New Zealand in 1931 need to be assessed. He began the Lord's Test nervously and a little too anxious to assert his authority. Perhaps he did not want to make the same mistake as Wyatt, who had embarked on his first Test as England's captain intending to lean on Hobbs for tactical advice and had then got a nasty shock when he found that 'the Master' was totally silent on the subject. Ian Peebles has left a good description of Jardine's first day in charge:

We lost the toss and had not been long in the field before the first signs of friction arose. Instead of putting Frank Woolley at slip – his accustomed position – Jardine sent him down to fine leg. Habitués of Lord's will know that each stand or section of it is distinguished by a letter, starting with A on the left of the pavilion and going clockwise around the ground. The letters are large and displayed at convenient intervals along the railings. Douglas, wishing to station Frank accurately, called out 'B, Woolley,' but it was clear that Frank was unaware of the lettering so the message had no meaning for him. Using his own judgement, he stationed himself by chance under the letter C. As the bowler, Wally Hammond, was running up Douglas stopped the game and called out in stentorian voice from mid-off, 'I said B, Woolley – not C.' Frank's confusion was not lessened by Wally Hammond's pointing in both directions at once, all of which led to a

certain hilarity amongst us young. But Frank was very much
affronted and felt that he had been humiliated in front of a large
crowd.

'Relations between the two worsened when, having disposed of the
New Zealanders for 224, Douglas went to the professionals' dressing
room to discuss the batting order. 'Woolley,' he said, 'you will bat at
number five and I shall bat at number six but, if there is a crisis, I shall
bat at number five and you will go in number six.' As we lost three
wickets for 31, and four for 62, there was a crisis, and Douglas
preceded a now thoroughly disgruntled Frank.

Jardine and Woolley retrieved the situation somewhat, but with
the score at 188 for 6, Peebles went in as night-watchman – and
was stumped for 0! This greatly amused two fans of Peebles'
batting, Hammond and Walter Robins. Jardine, however, failed
to see the funny side of it. In the dressing room the next morning
Robins was sternly ticked off by his captain, who said his
behaviour was 'rather fourth form'; Robins' discomfiture was
increased by the fact that all the other amateurs were trying to
make him laugh by pulling faces through the glass door behind
Jardine.

England were saved from embarrassment by the brilliant batting
of Les Ames and Gubby Allen; in $2\frac{3}{4}$ hours the score moved
from 190 for 7 to 436 for 8, and their stand of 246 is still a world
Test record for the eighth wicket. Allen had only been selected to
play in the match at the last minute when Larwood had to pull out
through injury. When the news of Larwood came, P. A. Perrin
and Warner were watching a match at Lord's. Fortunately Jardine
was playing and so a hasty meeting of the selection committee, or
threequarters of it anyway, took place. The fourth selector,
Higson, was at that point on a train somewhere between
Manchester and London. Later that evening he found out what
had taken place and was absolutely furious. Warner wrote that
'Like Bret Harte's chinaman, his language was 'frequent and
painful and free', but, turning the other cheek, I told him the
circumstances....' Poor old Warner, people always seemed to be
shouting at him. It was therefore doubly fortunate that Allen was
successful, since New Zealand proved to be rather stronger than
expected.

Their second innings gave Jardine some good experience of
captaining a fielding side when things are going badly. Two
century partnerships and one of 99 were added before Lowry, the

captain, declared on the third afternoon. In order to win, England would have had to make 240 in 140 minutes, and naturally the challenge was not accepted. It was a sign of the times that Jardine was criticised for not chasing the runs. As it was, England lost five wickets before the close.

On the strength of New Zealand's performance at Lord's and in some of the other matches, two further Tests were arranged. At the Oval the tourists were beaten by some inspired fast bowling by Allen in the first innings and a nasty pitch in the second. Ian Peebles described what happened in the final match at Old Trafford:

> After two and a half days of rain play surprisingly began on the third afternoon. The England team were all present thinking there was to be a farewell lunch but the New Zealand players, thinking there would be no play, had dispersed to celebrate. The New Zealand players finally gathered, some being in no fit state to bat, so it was agreed that England should bat out the remaining time. An element in the crowd started calling for a declaration. Lowry sent a message back to DRJ begging him *not* to declare but the protesters continued until DRJ opened the window and gave them one of his looks – the barrackers fell silent!

At the end of the Test series the selection committee was left with a number of problems still unsolved. An opening partner for Sutcliffe had not emerged although, to be fair, those who were tried in that position were not given much of a chance. And the middle-order batting, strong as it had seemed against New Zealand, lacked 'concrete' as Jardine liked to call it. On the plus side, there was the erratic but occasionally devastating bowling of Gubby Allen and the promise shown by the three young leg-breakers, Freddie Brown, Walter Robins and Ian Peebles, and the latter had already proved that he could get Bradman out. Further reassurance came at the end of the season in the match between The Rest and Yorkshire at the Oval. Jardine played one of the best innings of his career, 104 in 4 hours 25 minutes without a chance. In saving the game, he was helped by Bob Wyatt who stayed with him for nearly three hours, batting with a broken bone in his hand. Bill Bowes was bowling short and both players took a battering, in fact Jardine went so far as to pat down a spot well inside the bowler's half of the wicket. In Wyatt it seemed that England had found the necessary 'concrete'. He himself remembers that Jardine was most impressed by this innings and remained for many years a great Wyatt admirer. *The Times* said, 'If a man can bat one-handed against Yorkshire he is a player made for Test matches.'

Bowes' performance in taking eight wickets in the match did not meet with unanimous approval and nor did it suggest that he was an England prospect. If a bowler could make the ball rear off a length, then all well and good, and Bowes was able to do this given only moderately helpful conditions, but too often for some observers he resorted to bowling persistently short. Not that it was considered unfair, merely unattractive. If the batsman was fool enough to allow himself to be hit then that was his look-out, but while short-pitched bowling might be effective against the incompetent or the faint-hearted, it was unlikely to present any difficulties to top-class batsmen such as Woodfull, Bradman and Kippax, the players who were uppermost in people's minds at that time. No, Warner said in the *Morning Post*, as far as the tour of 1932–33 was concerned, 'the strength of England's bowling today lies in our young amateur spin bowlers.'

6
Bodyline:
The Background

Bodyline was a stage in the game's evolution. So many factors influenced its appearance that it is futile to attempt to attach responsibility to any one individual. It is so inextricably bound up in the continuous process by which the bowler sets a problem which in time is overcome that it is possible to trace the origins of bodyline back to the 'shabby play' of Ring and Taylor, who in the 1780s used their legs to stop the ball hitting their stumps. The bowler has never ceased to develop new tricks: round-arm then overarm, swing, the googly, leg-theory, bodyline, seam and the modern bouncer, but not all have been mastered simply by an adjustment in batting technique. The improvement in the standard of pitches towards the end of the last century helped the batsman, just as protective equipment has come to his aid a hundred years later. And in the case of bodyline, legislation saved batsmen, groundsmen and manufacturers the trouble of working out a defence.

All this is not to say that it was merely one of those little vicissitudes to which the game is subject from time to time. Technically it was hardly more important than the arrival of Bosanquet's googly or Hirst's 'swerve', but the ruthless, cold professionalism it represented and the element of danger it carried caused the most acrimonious upheaval in the game's history. It would not be quite true to say that the game was never the same again – bodyline left its scars, but the repercussions have been greatly exaggerated over the years. If the affair did go to cabinet level, there is no mention of it in the minutes. Similarly, there is no evidence to support the theory that Australia tried to secede from the Empire, or that they refused at one stage to accept an English-born Governor General.

What bodyline did do was to provide a glimpse into the future – baying crowds, chants of 'bastard, bastard', batsmen ducking, swaying and being doubled up with pain. In this respect, and only in this one, Jardine was ahead of his time, for in 1933 they were not ready for that kind of cricket.

Over the last few years so much has been written and said about this subject that one almost expects to find diagrams of field-placings pinned up in post offices. Nevertheless, a brief explanation of the technicalities of the bodyline attack is necessary. Larwood's bodyline field looked like this:

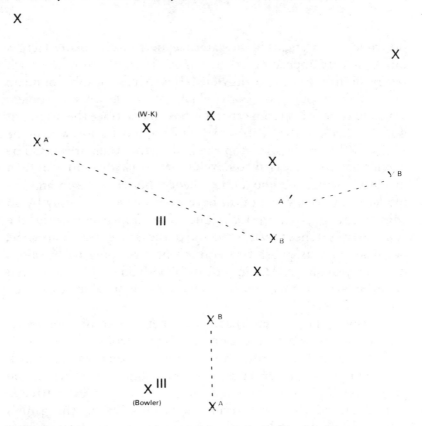

The bowler's line was on or outside the leg stump. The length depended on the ability of the bowler to make the ball get up and, of course, the state of the wicket. Voce and Bowes, for example, tended to pitch on the short side while Larwood could pitch the ball further up and still make it rear. For some reason it is much harder to judge the exact line of a leg ball than one bowled on or outside the off stump; many batsmen are experts at allowing the latter kind to pass within inches of the wicket, but with a leg-stump attack, 'leaving' is a rarity since, apart from the difficulty of picking up the line, there is the added danger of being bowled off one's pads.

The first advantage of bodyline, then, was that the batsman had to play at nearly every ball if only in defence of his body. The fact that the majority of deliveries rose above waist-height meant that the shot offered by the batsman was frequently either involuntary or incautiously aggressive, hence the ring of four, five or sometimes even six close fielders on the leg-side.

This is an over-simplification of a method which has inspired, at a rough calculation, over ten million words. The basic principle is there, though, and has to be understood before all the ramifications can be. It was undoubtedly an intimidatory method, but that in itself need not be taken as a condemnation, the word need not necessarily be a pejorative one. It can be argued that a batsman has a bat with which to protect himself and that to deny the fast bowler the use of the bouncer is unfair. On the other hand, should cricket be allowed to become a sport for which the most valuable qualities are recklessness and indifference to pain?

Anyone who plays cricket at any level knows that it is a very hard game and that intimidation is an essential part of it. A player may fear for his physical safety, his wicket, his dignity, his bad leg, his place in the side. Any number of personal vanities and apprehensions may affect his performance, and his opponent is praised if he manages to exploit them. Physical pain holds no terrors for some who may become immobile with anxiety faced with a 60-year-old leg-spinner. Any village opening bowler will vouch for the sense of despair induced by the sight of an opening batsman with spotless pads, a pink face, glasses and some university cap with roman numerals on it. That is intimidation, as is the placing of close fielders and the batsman's attempt to hit the ball at them as hard as he can. It is said that Charlie Macartney always used to try to hit his first ball straight back in the bowler's face. No-one would claim that bodyline was pleasant, but as long as there was one batsman in the world who could play it (and there were several), was it unfair?

There must come a point where intimidation is unacceptable and nowadays only a handful of people would deny that bodyline went beyond that point, and it would be foolish to ignore the weight of expert opinion. But was it the tactics that offended or was it, in reality, the genius of Larwood? Bodyline as bowled by Voce, Bowes and later on Constantine and Martindale was nasty to face, often dangerous and on the whole rather dull to watch. I imagine it was a bit like bobsleighing – holding a ghoulish fascination for a few minutes, but five days of it...? When used by Larwood, however, it was lethal. That a bowler could make a mockery of the basic principles of batting was unacceptable, particulary to the Australian people who, at the start of the 1932–33 tour, were relishing the prospect of Bradman making a mockery of the English bowling. Their disappointment was the most powerful influence on the whole affair.

At the beginning of the 1932 season, most people subscribed to the Australian view that England were the underdogs for the coming series. C. Stewart Caine, *Wisden*'s editor, said in his 'Notes' 'At the end of the forthcoming season we have to send a team out to Australia and it would be idle to suggest that the undertaking is being approached with great confidence.' It ought to be said that this was not wholly representative of national feeling. There were optimists; Warner, of course, who was optimistic about most things, and also Fender, whose opinions appeared regularly in the *Star*. Caine continued:

> There remains the big question of who shall captain the side. A year ago everything pointed to the probability of the post being offered to Jardine. The old Oxonian not only possesses the experience born of a tour in Australia but can look back upon a series of fine performances out there.... On the other hand he does not seem to have impressed people with his ability as a leader on the field.

Quite whom he had failed to impress is difficult to say. There had been one or two grumbles in the press over his disinclination to chase 240 runs in 2 hours 20 minutes in the first Test against New Zealand, but the selectors appeared to have every confidence in him. Peebles wrote that there had been misgivings in inner cricket circles about Jardine's appointment but then he was writing 40 years after the event and, after all, misgivings are expressed about most appointments. Jardine's style of captaincy could not have been more different from Chapman's and the sudden change may have been difficult for some to accept. Chapman's was just the kind of dare-devil approach that is remembered with affection and, even though it was barely a year since he had lost the leadership, his reign was being regarded through rose-coloured specs.

Jardine began cautiously as Surrey's captain but as the season progressed he became a little more adventurous and the county finished up having their best season for six years. Most notably, he appeared to have overcome a slightly gingerish approach to the use of spin. Freddie Brown, though he always felt Jardine might take him off if he got hit at all, became the spearhead of the attack, bowling 112 overs more than the next man, Fender. Jardine's field-placing, too, became less conservative; during the Gentlemen v. Players match at Lord's he maintained an attacking field while Hammond was making a thundering hundred. Taking over the Surrey captaincy under slightly mysterious circumstances and needing to prove himself capable of leading England in Australia could not have been easy. Fender was still very much part of the side and many of the players continued to call him 'skipper', which could not have helped Jardine much. But from the start it seems that he commanded the respect of his men, even if they didn't always show it.

Surrey lost only two matches in 1932 Championship, both times to Yorkshire. Jardine had the greatest respect for the northern counties – Yorkshire, Lancashire and Nottinghamshire – and relished the hard atmosphere of those games. Even if he did not play in quite as many of these fixtures as is commonly believed, he regarded them as the acid test of a cricketer's ability, something he was keen to impress upon his fellow-selectors. Surrey's second defeat by Yorkshire came at the end of what had otherwise been an extremely successful August in which they had beaten Northants once and Middlesex and Hampshire twice each.

The game against Middlesex at the Oval was a real classic: fractionally under 1200 runs scored and fractionally under 400 overs bowled, a dozen or so wickets falling to leg-spin and the result in the balance until the last possible ball. Surrey gained a huge first-innings lead over Middlesex, mainly due to a flawless century from Jardine and a fearsome innings from Freddie Brown of 212 in 200 minutes, in which he managed to clear the Oval ropes seven times. Middlesex made a better showing in the second innings, with Hendren and Sims making hundreds. After a day's batting they managed to work off the deficit and establish a small lead. They were all out half an hour before the close on the last day, 56 ahead. After the statutory 10 minutes in between innings, Surrey were left with 57 to get in 20 minutes. In those days there was no such slight to a chap's honour as a minimum-over requirement in the last hour and so Surrey had no idea how much bowling they were going to get. Jardine sent in Shepherd and Brown, the first over from Durston produced a wide, seven off the bat, a dropped catch and finally Brown's wicket, caught at slip. Fender then hopped off the pavilion table and trotted out to the wicket and was caught first ball. By then Jardine had his batsmen lined up by the gate in front of the pavilion, ready to sprint out when wanted. Spencer Block, described by *Wisden* as 'hugely strong', was the next in. He and Shepherd hit 36 off 25 balls and were then both run out in the sixth over. The position when Jardine came out to join young Ratcliffe (down for the vac) was that there was time for only one more over and 11 runs were needed. Under the existing rules, if a wicket fell before the end of the over the match would finish and would therefore be left drawn. Ratcliffe faced the first ball from the experienced fast bowler, Durston, and managed a single. Jardine hit the next two straight to fielders – 10 to win off three balls. He lofted the next one to deep mid-off where Enthoven dropped the catch and they ran two. Jardine then late-cut beautifully through the slips for 4. The last ball he drove straight back to the pavilion rails.

Middlesex, under the captaincy of Nigel Haig, had given Surrey seven overs in 20 minutes, and that with two fast bowlers operating and four wickets falling.

In contrast to his dramatic 10 not out, Jardine played a seemingly interminable innings of 44 earlier in the season for MCC against the visiting Indians. He made his side's top score but was harshly criticised for going at such a slow pace. There was, however, a very good reason for his caution. If the New Zealanders had proved stronger than expected, the Indians very nearly caused a major embarrassment. In the early 'thirties they were as good as they have ever been at any time, if not better. Their record in 1932 of played 26, won 9, lost 8, drawn 9, does not adequately reflect their performances. The pitches and the climate were vastly different from the conditions they were used to; in addition, they were not accustomed to playing so much cricket and found the programme very tiring. But they might so easily have beaten England in their very first Test match (the only one allotted that season). They were terribly unlucky with injuries to two key players but even then they might have won if it hadn't been for two stern innings from Jardine.

Having taken the trouble to size up the opposition earlier in the season, he was able to withstand the unexpectedly hostile bowling of Nissar and Amar Singh, who deserve to be counted among the best opening pairs. His two innings of 79 and 85 not out constituted 30 per cent of England's runs. He knew his enemy and remained imperturbable, meeting everything in the middle of the bat. He might have been a District Commissioner putting down a spot of local trouble. England's winning margin was comfortable enough in the end and honour was thought to have been satisfied on both sides. Sydney Southerton remarked in the 1933 *Wisden*, 'Wherever they went the tourists made friends, not only by the fine regard they had for the traditions of the game, but by their modest and correct demeanour at all times.'

A week after the Test it was announced that Jardine had been invited to lead England in Australia. It seems that until the last minute he still had doubts about taking it on. The selection committee is said to have enlisted the help of his father to persuade him to accept, but his acceptance was more likely his own decision than the result of any pressure from outside. It cannot have been an easy decision to take: in addition to the prospect of renewing an unhappy relationship with the Australian crowds, there was the financial consideration. A seven-month tour was an expensive business for an amateur, though exactly how expensive is hard to say. Arthur Carr claimed that the South African tour of 1922–23 cost him £500 and he believed that the captain, Frank Mann, ended up about £1000 out of pocket. The amount varied, naturally, according to the means and tastes of the individual, but Jardine certainly enjoyed the good things in life. Perhaps he had told himself 'never again' after the 1928–29 tour, but if such resolutions were not broken, the world would probably stop.

It has been said that, given his known antipathy towards Australian crowds, the committee were wrong to pick him and that he was equally wrong to accept. Hindsight makes it possible to point to this and several other events in 1932 as signs of trouble which were culpably ignored, but at the time a catastrophe on the scale of the bodyline affair must have seemed as probable as another war with Germany. MCC took their Imperial responsibilities very seriously, cricket tours playing a vital part in the strengthening of links between the 'red bits', but the twin needs for success on an ambassadorial as well as a sporting level had hitherto not come into conflict, at least not to any really troublesome extent, and so there seemed to be no need for extra caution in this case.

There was also a strong feeling in English cricket circles that the Ashes might stay with Australia for a good few years unless the Bradman problem was solved. Just when English cricket had regained its rightful position after the ignominies of the early 'twenties, Bradman had come along and upset everything. Something had to be done, and MCC were as keen to redress the balance as anyone. It was important for Britain to maintain friendly relations with her Dominions, but not at the expense of national prestige; British superiority was, after all, an essential part of the Imperial ethos. Sending a team under the leadership of an amiable diplomat might have made for a convivial series but it would not have been seen as being in British Imperial interests. It would also have provoked a national outcry. A determined leader they wanted, and a determined leader they got.

In his book *Moreover*, Hugh de Selincourt typified English reaction to Jardine's appointment. Far from having misgivings, the cricketing public firmly approved the selectors' choice and delighted in trying to fathom what was going on behind the famous poker face.

> Watching Jardine at Hove with a lynx eye helped. One got the feel of the man. One saw the way he spoke to the men, his courtesy to the man by the little gate (he was called to the phone), his punctilious return of the ball to the wicket-keeper, his general alertness, his suppressed annoyance at bad fielding (there was one long sinner on the side). And I thought, as he stood within ten yards of my seat by the wicket-gate, waiting after his phoning, to go back onto the field: 'My goodness! I'd like to have an hour or so's chat with you!' However, there I sat among hundreds of other humble folk who were sizing him pretty shrewdly up, in their intense keenness on the great games to come in which he had been chosen to represent them. I came away more convinced than ever that he was the man for the job, for feeling ran high whenever cricket was talked, on who ought by rights

to be England's Test Match Captain. I had seen not primarily a good chap, out mainly to be a lad and popular, but what is a very different thing, a man graciously and firmly poised on his own feet, not to be turned an inch from his course by opinion or prejudice however loudly voiced; a leader, in fact. I was awfully glad to have watched him.

De Selincourt was writing shortly after the bodyline series, by which time he had met Jardine and taken to him. The match described in this passage could only have been the friendly between Sussex and Surrey which took place nearly three weeks before Jardine's appointment was announced. That de Selincourt remembered it as he did indicates that, to him at least, Jardine was a cast-iron certainty to lead England in Australia. Their meeting took place in August, probably on the first or second day of the action-packed Middlesex match. On receiving Jardine's invitation to dine, de Selincourt remembered, being in a flurry of nervous excitement, to the surprise and amusement of a German friend he had staying with him. In explanation, de Selincourt drew the analogy of a private soldier receiving an invitation to dine with Hindenburg, but even that did not seem quite right since Hindenburg was only a field marshal. Modern leaders were, in his view, either puppets or so reliant upon the advice of committees that they were not worthy to be called leaders. Only on the cricket field could leadership in the old-fashioned sense of the word be found.

He arrived at the club to which he had been invited and found his host in the bar with the burly Block and the extremely tall Maurice Allom and was naturally a little disappointed not to have Jardine all to himself:

> One watched and listened to escapade talk of lads together which is much the same the world over, but made interesting by the noticed fact that my host embarked on a story and got lost in it through shyness, and, with the dour persistence of a man who, though he can't get going won't get out, continued the quiet narration. That was a delightful something.

To his further delight, Allom and Block went before very long and he and Jardine were left to dine alone. Beyond saying that Jardine was a perfect host and that he had found it almost impossible not to laugh when the host offered him a sardine from the hors d'oeuvre tray, de Selincourt maddeningly confines his description of the evening to what he said to Jardine and the reader is left to guess at the nature of Jardine's replies – if he managed to squeeze any in, that is.

A week or so before this, a more significant dinner took place. This was the famous occasion at the Piccadilly Grill Room when Jardine, Carr, Larwood and Voce met to discuss tactics for the forthcoming tour. Bodyline was not born at that meeting, for as we have seen, the seeds were sown a long time before, but there was an exchange of ideas, albeit a tentative one, which was as important as any of the many happenings in the summer of 1932 when progress towards the discovery of bodyline accelerated. The dinner took place on what one might term neutral territory, in an atmosphere somewhere between that of the pavilion bar and the gentleman's club. By all accounts it was sticky going. But as Kevin Perkins indicated in Larwood's autobiography, *The Larwood Story* (1965), the most revealing and absorbing of all the accounts, things did warm up once they got on to the emotive subject of Bradman. That was something everyone could talk about.

A number of astute observers, including George Duckworth and Percy Fender, fancied they had seen Bradman flinching during a hostile spell from Larwood in the Oval Test of 1930 when, for a brief period after rain, the wicket was lively. Nobody at the time really supposed that the answer to the Bradman problem had been found, since after all he did go on to make 232, but at least it was something. Jardine was aware of the incident and it had been much discussed among cricketers. In addition to this, Fender had received letters during 1932 from fellow-journalists in Australia who wrote that the Australian habit of moving across the stumps and playing the ball into the on-side was on the increase. As Richard Streeton explained in his book, Fender took these letters and showed them to Jardine when he spent a week-end at the Jardine family home at Walton-on-Thames. Jardine later thought about the implications of these two pieces of information but did not arrive at any immediate conclusions. There was the possibility of using a leg-stump attack with a leg-side field to feed the Australians' strength and to contain it at the same time, and then there was the strong likelihood that, possessing no bowlers of any great pace themselves, the Australians would be susceptible to fast bowling and, in at least one player's case, short fast bowling.

These theories were discussed at the dinner. It was suggested that Voce should try the leg-theory tactics he had been using for the last couple of seasons in England. Given the harder and faster pitches of Australia, he might get the ball to rise more and therefore put the batsmen under greater pressure. Primarily, though, the plan was a defensive one, its main object being to cut down Bradman's scoring. Jardine then asked Larwood if he could bowl leg-theory, making the ball come up into the body so that the batsman had to play the ball into the on-side. Jardine reckoned that if Larwood's extra speed could unsettle Bradman, then it would be likely to have the same effect on other Australians. Larwood agreed that it was possible and that it was certainly worth a try.

Larwood was in fact willing to try anything at this stage. He felt that Bradman had got the better of him in 1928–29 and also in 1930, and if reports were correct the lad was actually improving, his last five Test innings having realised over 800 runs. Larwood's difficulty was that in Australia the ball would only swing for, four or five overs and after that he was, in his own words, 'just straight up and down'. That was still testing enough for plenty of batsmen, but not Bradman, and Larwood had a nightmare vision of himself bowling over after over on those rock-hard pitches, temperatures up in the hundreds and Bradman flogging him into the parched outfield until the ball became like a bundle of old rags. He had a good chance of getting Bradman out if an early wicket fell and he could get at him while the ball was still swinging, but otherwise he could see only gloom ahead. Leg theory offered at least a hope of keeping Bradman quiet.

Larwood had had an excellent season with Nottinghamshire in 1932 and topped the first-class averages with 162 wickets at 12.86 and yet, despite those exceptional figures, he was still not certain that he would be picked for the tour. He thought it possible that only one fast bowler would be taken and that it might be himself, Clark, Nichols, Bowes, Allen, Farnes or Voce: a surprisingly modest attitude for the fastest bowler in the world, but then he was, and indeed still is, a man of great modesty.

The Australians had no doubts that fast bowling would form the basis of the English attack and that Larwood would be the main strike bowler. In fact they even seemed to sense this before the English themselves had decided upon any sort of plan. The fact that they were walking across their stumps and cutting down

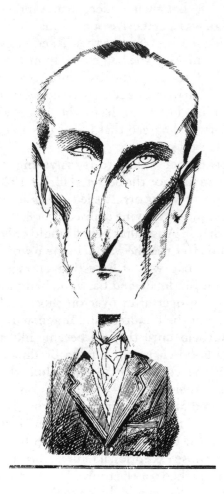

DINNER WITH JARDINE

Contrasting views of Jardine: an
Australian cartoonist (left) sees him
as humourless and ruthless, whereas
the illustrator of Hugh de
Selincourt's *Moreover* (above)
portrays a more genial side.

on the off-side strokes indicated that they were anticipating some
fast bowling, short-pitched fast bowling too. But their methods
were conceived to counter off-theory, not leg-theory. The
principle was that the batsman would be in a good position to
leave anything outside the off stump and at the same time to force
the straighter deliveries into the – supposedly – thinly defended
on-side. Such a method gave the genuine fast bowler a chance of
hitting the leg stump, but it did not seem to occur to the
Australians that the English might use leg-theory. In its most
aggressive form, as bowled by Scott, the South Australian, it was
invariably expensive, especially against top-class batsmen. This
was unrefined bodyline – dangerous, fast but inaccurate and
therefore ineffective at Test level. The defensive kind of leg-
theory seemed equally inadvisable since, in a timeless Test, there
was not much advantage to be gained from slowing down the
scoring, and all the time the bowlers would be getting more
exhausted.

The method which Larwood agreed to try was, he thought, no
different to the kind of leg-theory that had been in use in England
for years. He hoped that he might again be able to trouble
Bradman with the sharply rising ball on the leg stump, but on the
whole he thought that Voce was more likely to succeed in
Australia.

Voce was a big strapping chap of 6 feet 3 inches. He possessed
a powerful body action that enabled him to achieve fearsome pace
and lift off the pitch. As a fast left-arm leg-theorist, he was heir
to an honourable line. George Hirst had been a practitioner of the
art, as had Frank Foster, and both men bruised, or 'pinked' as
they sometimes called it, plenty of the great Golden Age
batsmen. Where Voce differed from his predecessors was that he
bowled so much of his leg-theory from over the wicket. He was
widely criticised for doing this, since he had a good inswinger
which might have been more effective if delivered round the
wicket in the approved manner. He did sometimes bowl it round
the wicket and achieved considerable success in doing so, but he
found it easier to maintain his accuracy by bowling over the
wicket, and as Jardine emphasised at the Piccadilly meeting,
accuracy was essential in Australia. The Tests were to be timeless
and therefore the batsmen were able, except in special
circumstances, to score as slowly as they wanted too. Any
delivery wide of the stumps was a sheer waste of energy: the

batsmen, said Jardine, had to be made to play the ball.

Carr had Larwood and Voce trying out the new method at Leyton, a few days after the meeting with Jardine. The Essex batsmen were thoroughly battered and shaken up, and one poor man, O'Connor, had his box knocked inside out. Larwood, not accustomed to bowling leg-theory, was very erratic. He did not take many wickets but his bowling was probably more physically dangerous then than later on by virtue of its unpredictability. The Essex batsmen managed to survive and saved the game which, on form and with Larwood using his normal methods, they ought to have lost. Carr was really sticking his neck out by allowing the experiment since Nottinghamshire still had a small chance of winning the Championship at that stage. As it turned out, it probably cost them third place and nothing more than that. Nevertheless, it was a brave gesture by Carr and showed how keen he was for his boys to do well in Australia. Indeed, he might have been on the losing side of the bodyline argument, but he showed greater loyalty and integrity than certain of those who brought about its demise.

Three weeks after the unsuccessful experiment at Leyton, Larwood tried the new method again at Cardiff. Glamorgan were putting up a good score on a batsman's pitch and Notts could not make a breakthrough. Larwood switched to a leg-side field and started to bowl to it more accurately than he had done against Essex. But Maurice Turnbull and Dai Davies played him without difficulty and Glamorgan were able to score 502, breaking several club records in the process.

In the next match against Lancashire further progress was made, Larwood taking 7 wickets at 11.5 apiece. But then they came up against some brave and somewhat fortunate batting at Scarborough and some resolute hooking at Folkestone. These matches were between members of the MCC Australian team and sides representing the rest of England. Woolley (aged 45) and young Bryan Valentine took several knocks from Larwood in the first innings of the Folkestone match but they managed to hit nearly four an over of him. Woolley is said to have walked down the pitch and asked, 'Are you trying to hurt me, Harold?' But in the second innings Larwood gave those present a fleeting glimpse of what the Australians would have to face over the next few months. Both Hone and Nichols had at least one stump knocked back as far as Duckworth, who was standing halfway to the boundary. His figures of 10–1–32–3 were respectable enough, but they do not give any indication of the terrifying pace at which he bowled.

It is useful to bear in mind such physical details as flying stumps when attempting to compare the relative speeds of fast bowlers of different generations. Everyone knows that Larwood was among the fastest of all time, but it is logical to suppose that, since we can run faster and jump higher and further than we ever could before, we must be able to bowl faster. Nevertheless, if cricketers have evolved, the physics of the game have surely remained the same; then as now, certain groundsmen watered the base of the stumps to help uproot them, but a stump presumably weighs roughly the same now as it did in 1932, and to send it spinning 60 or more feet across the grass would be quite as impressive now as it was then. Once, in 1929, Larwood managed to send a bail 66 yards, not quite a record, but he wasn't at his quickest when he did it. When Notts were playing at Lord's in 1931 a succession of three wicket-keepers had to be used, such were the bruising effects of his deliveries. Several times over the years he knocked the bat spinning from a player's grip. And as far as it is possible to tell, the West Indian wicket-keepers seem to stand no further back to Michael Holding than Ames or Duckworth did to Larwood.

It is impossible to make a judgement as to his exact ranking in the speed league table, but then if such a thing was possible it would put an end to much pleasant speculation. Some of the surprising results produced by modern speed-measuring techniques show that 'pace' is an imponderable which exists largely in the eye of the beholder. One can only say that, to those who faced him, Larwood was the quickest ever.

Add to this the exceptional accuracy which enabled him to develop the technique that became bodyline. The development process was not all plain sailing, but the remarkable fact remains that he bowled to a bodyline field on less than a dozen occasions between the meeting at the Piccadilly Grill Room and the date when the first cable of complaint was dispatched by the Australian Board of Control.

Short-pitched bowling had been on the increase over the previous two seasons and more batsmen were getting knocked about. Looking through the papers of the time, it is hard to find much condemnation of the practice. It seems that the bowler had every sympathy at this stage and if a batsman could not defend himself with his bat, then not much pity was wasted upon him.

One notable exception was Bill Bowes, whose bowling methods were often criticised. His offence was that on occasion, he bowled short even when conditions favoured keeping the ball up to the bat. It was blatant intimidation. When he opened the bowling in the Test against India he began bowling short immediately, an act which did not impress the *Times* correspondent: ;'Bowes started bowling from the Pavilion end, being given a sufficiently long trial to demonstrate that neither in pace, length, nor anything else is he the bowler for whom England is looking. His is a sheer waste of a new ball.' He had begun the season by laying out Wazir Ali, the Indian opener, and had carried on 'pinking' throughout the summer. His name did not appear in the first batches of names to be released by the tour selectors, but during August he took 77 wickets for Yorkshire and finished his season off with an awesome display of hostility in the Champion County match at the Oval. Without pitching particularly short on this occasion, he took seven wickets in 14 overs, and might have improved on those figures had not the selection committee, thinking no doubt that this Bowes was labouring the point a bit, told him to leave the game and make preparations to sail for Australia in five days. By contrast, Larwood and Voce were unable to extract any life from this Oval pitch and took only 2 for 119 between them.

Warner approved Bowes' selection even though, a fortnight before, he had vehemently criticised his intimidatory tactics in the Surrey v. Yorkshire match at the Oval. Hobbs was on the receiving end of a concentrated short-pitched attack with five men on the leg-side. He was hit several times, once on the head, and was visibly annoyed. 'That is not bowling,' wrote Warner in the *Morning Post.* 'Indeed, it is not cricket.' Hobbs, incidentally, although in his fiftieth year, managed to score 50 in 45 minutes and saw Bowes off. Warner continued, 'I appeal to Bowes and to others, if any, who may have influenced him to his present style, to get him back to orthodoxy.' And yet, according to one account, when it was decided at the last minute to take another fast bowler, it was Warner who suggested Bowes to his fellow-selectors. Ever the optimist, he may have hoped that the Oval incident was merely a temporary lapse of taste on Yorkshire's part. But what must he have thought about Larwood's experiments?

One of the most important things to remember about this whole affair is that nobody wanted to win back the Ashes more than Warner. He had brought them back in 1903–04 and (though not participating) in 1911–12. When the party left in 1932 he had with him the same old MCC flag he had taken on his previous trips. Notwithstanding any misgivings he may have had about bowling methods, his first priority was to ensure that the strongest possible team was on board that boat when it sailed for Australia.

The selection process was a lengthy one in those days. This particular party was announced in seven stages, invitations being dispatched at fortnightly intervals, and two months elapsed between Jardine's appointment and Bowes' late call-up. It is difficult to see what advantage was to be gained from picking a side in this way. It would surely have been easier to balance the side if selections were made in one go, from a pool of players who had already declared themselves available. As it happened two players pulled out: Robins because of business commitments and Duleepsinhji because of ill-health. But by clever thinking and perhaps a little luck, the selectors were able, if not to replace them, at least to maintain a balance. Here, then, is the full team:

	Age	Caps	County	
D. R. Jardine	32	11	Surrey	Right-hand bat and captain
R. E. S. Wyatt	31	15	Warwickshire	Right-hand bat, medium right-arm bowler and vice-captain
G. O. Allen	30	4	Middlesex	Fast right-arm bowler and right-hand bat
F. R. Brown	21	3	Surrey	Right-arm leg-break bowler and right-hand bat
The Nawab of Pataudi	22	0	Worcestershire	Right-hand bat
Sutcliffe	38	39	Yorkshire	Right-hand bat
Hammond	29	31	Gloucestershire	Right-hand bat and right-arm bowler
Tate	37	37	Sussex	Right-arm medium bowler and right-hand bat
Duckworth	31	19	Lancashire	Wicket-keeper

	Age	Caps	County	
Larwood	28	16	Nottinghamshire	Fast right-arm bowler and right-hand bat
Leyland	32	15	Yorkshire	Left-hand bat and slow left-arm bowler
Voce	23	11	Nottinghamshire	Fast left-arm bowler
Ames	27	9	Kent	Wicket-keeper and right-hand bat
Paynter	31	2	Lancashire	Left-hand bat
Verity	27	2	Yorkshire	Slow left-arm bowler and right-hand bat
Bowes	24	1	Yorkshire	Fast right-arm bowler
Mitchell	30	0	Derbyshire	Right-arm leg-breaks

A great side, greater in retrospect of course than it seemed at the time. One or two mighty reputations were yet to be made. With an average age of 29, it was the youngest to tour Australia since Warner's 1903–04 side, but it was generally thought to be the strongest possible representation of the available resources, and modern selectors might look with envy upon the contemporary press reactions.

Without Duleepsinhji the batting looked less commanding than it had done, but it did not lack experience and the men who effectively took Duleepsinhji's place in the Tests achieved great success; Pataudi scored a hundred on his Test debut and Paynter rose from his hospital bed to make a match-saving 83. Paynter, like Bowes, was a late selection and not an obvious one, since he was a fair way down the national averages and was not the most consistent of players. But he was a great man for the big occasion and for the crisis. He shared a vital stand with Jardine in the second innings of the Test against India in 1932 and, significantly, he had a good record against Yorkshire; without a doubt he was Jardine's selection. The Australians already knew plenty about the big guns – Sutcliffe, Hammond, Jardine and Leyland. Tamed they may have been in 1930 but there was still the memory of 1928–29. Wyatt had played only one Test against Australia but was experienced, fearless and very effective.

The bowling had an aggressive look to it with four fast bowlers, and the Australians can have been in no doubt about what to expect. Voce and Bowes were perhaps nearer to fast-medium than fast but Allen was capable of real pace. He was another interesting selection; at the end of the English domestic season he lay fifty-ninth in the bowling averages and two hundred and twentieth in the batting, so the selectors showed foresight in picking him. Against him was the fact that he had played first-class cricket so infrequently (four Championship appearances for Middlesex in 1932), and there was also uncertainty about whether he had the stamina for a seven-month tour. As it turned out, he thrived on the intensive programme of matches and was able to build up his form and consistency to a standard that he hardly ever matched in England.

There remained a belief in the theory, born in 1930, that Bradman was vulnerable to leg-spin, and this was reflected in the composition of the side. But Robins and Peebles, the two men who had supposedly exploited his fallibility, were not included, Robins being unavailable and Peebles having lost his leg-break almost completely. That left Brown, who had had a brilliant all-round season with Surrey, and Mitchell, who had been taking a lot of wickets for Derbyshire over the last few seasons. Neither was to form a part of the English attack, although Mitchell did play in one Test. English leg-spinners did not do well in Australia as a rule, and the fact that two were in the party illustrates the prominent place that Bradman occupied in the minds of Jardine and his fellow-selectors.

All the interest centred on the fast bowlers, but there was also in the side one of the greatest of all slow bowlers, Hedley Verity. He had a shrewd cricket brain – Jardine said he was the best professional thinker he had come across – and was an effective batsman whose style Robertson-Glasgow once described as 'Sutcliffe gone stale'.

The real greatness of the side lay in its all-round strength. Of the 17, 14 made Test fifties at some point, and 11 took Test wickets. The fielding, too, was of high ability and with the possible exception of the two over-35s, nobody would have to be 'hidden'. Jardine believed that all-rounders were essential in timeless Tests. A side might find itself in the field for two days or more, and four bowlers would be struggling to keep control under those conditions, whereas in each of the five Tests Jardine had at his disposal five proper Test bowlers and two more who took plenty of wickets in county cricket. In the first and third

Tests the team contained ten batsmen and seven bowlers.

To one living in an age when a player's personality is hidden behind a visor and the spectator struggles to discern individual characteristics, sometimes having to invent them, the 1932–33 English tourists appear to have been a wonderfully mixed bunch. They represented not only a wide range of cricketing styles but a cross-section of British Imperial society. There were three miners: Mitchell and the two northern expresses, Larwood and Voce. The Nawab of Pataudi ('Pat' to his team-mates), who ruled a small province south of Delhi, was a keen shot as well as being a billiards and hockey Blue. Leyland was a carpenter and Allen was a member of the Stock Exchange and an Old Etonian. Bowes (described by one writer as the 'platinum blond' of the side) was a member of the Magic Circle and was as popular with his 'illusions' as George Geary had been with his ukelele on the previous tour. Hammond, the Gloucestershire crack, was a keen aviator, and then there was Paynter, the perky Oswaldtwistle bricklayer, and thoughtful Bob Wyatt, who was an expert figure-skater. And who could resist the boyish charm of Freddie Brown, recently down from the 'Varsity.

The 20,000-ton Royal Mail steamer *Orontes* pulled out of Tilbury on 17 September. The crowds waved, the newsreel cameras turned and our boys stood shyly at the rails wearing their double-breasted suits, trilby hats and polished shoes, chatting to each other and watching their loved ones receding into the distance. Seven months away from home, no wives with young children, no girl-friends allowed – a man's only comfort was his golf clubs.

7
Bodyline: The Tour

After a hard season's county cricket the players used the first few weeks of the voyage to relax. There was no vigorous programme of physical training beyond a little light work with the medicine ball for form's sake and dancing in the evenings (at which Freddie Brown excelled).

Many accounts claim that there were numerous planning meetings on board the *Orontes* when the evil plot for biffing Johnnie Convict was finalised, but this is not so. Any planning that was done, was done by Jardine alone in his cabin. He did not discuss detailed tactics with the players beyond saying, ominously, that the only way to beat the Australians was to 'hate them', an expression common in more recent times but one which raised a few eyebrows in 1932. There has surely always been an element of hatred in cricket as in any other hard physical sport. The feelings of the fast bowler towards the batsman at the moment of delivery should hardly be cordial but only recently has he owned up to possessing such aggressive intentions. Had Jardine said to his bowlers, 'Look here, you fellows, I want you to test the Cornstalks' pluck,' they would have understood what he wanted; the phrase would no doubt have been more acceptable, but it would not have expressed the degree of dedication that Jardine required. And it was dedication that distinguished this party from all previous ones.

Jardine's own planning seems to have been comprehensive and to have reached a point where bodyline was only a very short step away. Before leaving England he had discussed field-placings with Frank Foster, the left-arm leg theorist who had taken no less than

32 wickets in the 1911–12 series. Foster's and Larwood's lines of attack were similar (Foster left-arm round, Larwood right-arm over, but wide of, the wicket), and Larwood's eventual bodyline field owed much to Foster. The leg trap, fine leg and square leg positions were sometimes identical, but other parts of the field were differently guarded and Foster usually had one more man on the off-side. Jardine developed his field-placings once bodyline had become a reality. He made continual alterations right through the series; as I write, I have in front of me Larwood's field as mapped out by six different authors, no two of whom agree. This is not to say that they are inaccurate, merely that there were a great many variations on the theme.

Foster was later to express regret in print that his advice had been used for what he regarded as evil purposes. He had been accused himself of bowling at the man and was very touchy about it. The merest suggestion that Jardine's men were attacking the batsmen and not the wicket was enough to make Foster dissociate himself from their methods. (He was a highly eccentric individual. In 1934, 20 years after his retirement, he kept pestering Bob Wyatt to give him a place in the England side since he was convinced he could get Bradman out.)

Jardine had also examined Bradman's record, scrutinising scoring diagrams of some of his major innings. He watched a film showing play in the final Test at the Oval in 1930 when Bradman was seen to flinch from some of Larwood's deliveries. 'I've got it,' he is said to have declared, 'he's yellow.' This conviction, although incorrect as we shall see, gave Jardine and his men a confidence that had been lacking since the terrible summer of 1930.

On board the *Orontes*, some of the professionals formed a male voice choir and performed on certain nights in the smoking room under the conductorship of Bill Voce. Jardine would occasionally look in to see how they were getting on but on the whole he kept himself apart from his men during the trip. It was quite deliberate, since he felt that a leader should be remote and even unpredictable; it kept people on their toes.

The whole campaign, whatever one might say about it, was conducted with a fine sense of theatre. From start to finish he kept everyone guessing and no journalist, official or player approached him without a certain amount of trepidation. He was like one of those great Victorian men of action, possessed of a deeply sensitive and reflective nature but hiding it behind his more obvious qualities of courage and imperturbability. He loved to create an effect, to surprise his opponents and even his subordinates. He went about this in a number of ways. One was to issue improbable instructions, as when he told Voce and Bowes to bowl one full toss an over in a Test (the reason being that the lack of a sight-screen made it difficult to judge the flight of a full toss), or when he told Bowes that he could not have one extra man on the leg-side as requested but that he could have five (Jardine's unexplained thinking was that Bowes should attack one side of the wicket or the other but not both). He expected these instructions to be obeyed unquestioningly, which they some-times were not, the men being international cricketers and not troopers in an Afghan campaign. Nevertheless he possessed a nobility and natural authority which men will follow anywhere, however grumpily and unwillingly. And they followed him into the midst of tens of thousands of howling, violent-looking Australians. There were several independent spirits in that party of 17, men who could have made his life considerably harder had they chosen to, but they didn't; they were united in respect for and loyalty to their leader, and of course in their will to win.

A fortnight before the end of the voyage, training began in earnest. Four hours of deck games in the morning, two more hours in the afternoon and then a run round the deck before dinner. Net practice was started but it did not last long; Jardine stopped it after an unexpected lurch of the ship caused Voce to injure his ankle while bowling. But by the time they reached Fremantle on 18 October they were a very fit side, well prepared to go the distance – 25 matches, five of which promised to last a week or more each. Fitness had been high on Jardine's list of priorities from the start and it became noticeable as the series progressed that the all-rounders were worked hard and not 'saved' for their batting or their bowling.

Jardine and Australia wasted no time in re-establishing the old feelings of mutual dislike. One of Jardine's first actions on arriving in Perth was to deliver a withering snub to a journalist, Claude Corbett of the Sydney *Sun*, who had asked him if he could release the team selections in time to meet the paper's deadlines. Jardine said that he had come to play cricket, not to provide newspaper scoops. By contrast, the first thing Chapman had done four years earlier, even as he was coming down the ship's gangplank, was to make a bet with a docker on the outcome of the series. That was not Jardine's way unfortunately.

Relations with the press deteriorated rapidly and anti-British feeling began to spread. When the team was 20 minutes late taking the field for the first match of the tour, the story was put about that the delay was due to Jardine's decision to go shopping instead. Needless to say, the barracking also began before long and so within a week it was clear that in ambassadorial terms the tour was going to be a disaster. Poor old Warner wrung his hands and tried to smoothe things over but Jardine was not interested in making placatory gestures as long as his team was being subjected to barracking. The press, being denied what they considered their rightful access to the captain's opinions, were obliged to use their own imaginations. Consequently more 'scoops' appeared than would ever have been possible under more friendly circumstances.

Several of the likely Australian Test players travelled all the way across the continent (four days in a train) to play in the second match of the tour for a Combined Australian XI, Bradman, Richardson, Fingleton and McCabe were all anxious to test the strength of the English bowling while Jardine, not surprisingly, was equally anxious to disappoint them. Voce, Bowes and Larwood were left out and Allen, who at that stage seemed destined to sit out the Tests on the subs' bench, was the only fast bowler picked. However, he decided to make the most of his opportunity and applied himself fiercely and with impressive results; he sent Richardson's middle stump spinning and worried Bradman with several short ones before having him caught for 10. The Combined XI managed to save the game but Jardine was left with the comforting thought that if Allen could cause trouble, what might not Larwood and Voce do?

The full-blown English pace attack was not revealed until the fifth match, in Melbourne against an Australian XI. Leg-theory was used successfully; Larwood (who got Bradman twice), Voce and Bowes all took wickets and caused a fair amount of ducking and swaying. Allen hardly bowled at all but looked dangerous enough with his few overs of off-theory. Captaining the side was Wyatt, not Jardine as might have been expected at such a crucial stage in England's build-up to the first Test. But it is only in retrospect that it seems such an important match. Up until then the only firm policy that had been decided upon was that

Bradman should be attacked with at least one fast bowler for as long as he was in, a plan which Wyatt was perfectly capable of supervising, and so Jardine took the opportunity to go off with his fishing rod and relax before the first Test. It was because of the Australian XI's failure to handle fast, rising balls that this match became a turning-point.

Bob Wyatt has told me that although leg-theory was bowled in this match with great speed and hostility, he is certain that none of the English bowlers bowled short *outside* the leg stump as they were later to do. It was effective enough, if not quite bodyline. Jardine listened with interest to Wyatt's report. Bradman and Woodfull, England's two main worries, had been found out, it seemed, by the concerted pace attack. At that point the leg-spinner, Freddie Brown, and the medium-pacer, Maurice Tate, might as well have gone home.

Larwood was rested for the match against New South Wales which immediately preceded the first Test. Voce played, however, and took six wickets bowling *apparently* at the man. It was bodyline and, as was to happen on subsequent occasions, the batsmen showed that it was possible to fight through the barrage for one innings but not for two. For instance, Bradman's second innings ended when, anticipating a bouncer from Voce, he leapt in the general direction of point only to see his middle stump knocked back. 'Apparently' because, although the New South Wales batsmen were certainly hit a good many times, it is important to remember that they were following the new fashion of moving across their stumps to play the ball. Had they stood clear of the leg stump, as was the orthodox manner in those days, they would have been in far less danger of being hit. An orthodox player himself, Jardine was genuinely amazed at the Australians' efforts to play everything into the on-side. At about this time he wrote to Fender in England saying that his (Fender's) information about the Australians' new technique had proved correct. Fender no longer has the letter (one of several) but he remembers this sentence: 'I find I now have to have four or five men on the leg-side and if this goes on I shall have to move the whole bloody lot over.' In fact, at one stage in the New South Wales match Voce was bowling to a seven-two leg-side field.

Bradman, the superstar, had failed in six consecutive innings against the English tourists. It would be no exaggeration to say that it shocked the country. When he was out for 10 at Perth the crowd looked on in stunned silence as he bustled back to the pavilion, head down, like an actress leaving a divorce court. His failure was due only in small part to the high quality of the English bowling. He was suffering from the effects of four years of non-stop cricket, his health was not good and he was also in the middle of a row with the Australian Board of Control. He had been contracted by the Sydney *Sun* to write (unghosted) reports on the forthcoming series, but the Board had a ruling which forbade this and they enforced it in Bradman's case while allowing another Test player (Fingleton) to write on the grounds that he was a full-time professional journalist. There was no love lost between Bradman and the Board of Control, and he had been in conflict with them before over a trifling technicality. The roots of the trouble were, in reality, his phenomenal success and the fact that he gave every appearance of enjoying it. The Board, an unwieldy and autocratic body, resented such individualism and possibly felt threatened by it. If Bradman was to play in the Tests, it seemed that either he or the Board would have to give way, and neither party showed the slightest intention of doing so. Fortunately, part of the problem was solved by the *Sun* newspaper releasing Bradman from his contract. However, he was still unwell and was ordered by his doctor to take a month's rest. He withdrew from the first Test and went off with his wife to the seaside, there to work out some sort of answer to the new form of bowling.

Informed Australian opinion was by no means unanimously opposed to the English tactics at this point. Many of the old brigade found themselves with a dilemma: wishing on the one hand to condemn the tactics as new-fangled and unfair and, on the other hand, wanting to make it quite clear that Trumper or Macartney would have been able to play bodyline one-handed with a walking stick, and still have made a hundred before lunch. Attitudes changed as the series progressed, but even during the 'Battle of Adelaide' there were those who thought that the Australian batsmen were simply not up to it. The general cricket-watching public, heavily influenced by the popular press and the sight of their heroes falling, were firmly opposed to the English tactics even before the full horror of bodyline had been seen.

On the morning of the first Test, in his second over, Larwood made the ball fly off a length in a way which silenced the crowd. It seemed inconceivable that he could have increased his pace since the last tour but he had and, what was more, he was getting the ball up off a length. Hobbs said it quite frightened him sitting in the press box. Larwood's regular practice during the series was to bowl ordinary off-theory for two or three overs while the shine was still on the ball. This was when he was at his fastest. During one of these spells, in a match at Adelaide, Bob Wyatt remembers standing within 30 yards of the boundary – a position approximate to fine third man on a moderate-sized ground – but he was standing *in the slips*. He still thought he was unlikely to catch anything but Jardine refused his request to go further back, saying that he was just being silly.

There were a number of reasons for Larwood's increased pace in Australia: the pitches were on the whole faster; his boots had the long studs necessary for English conditions, and on the dryer Australian turf he got a much firmer grip and thus more leverage; he put on nearly a stone and a half during the tour and felt much stronger for it; the atmosphere of the Tests lifted him and the barracking geed him up nicely; dental treatment he had undergone in England left him less tense than before; and also, a little-known fact this, he used to take a snort of snuff sometimes to give himself a bit of a buzz before gliding in on that deadly run of his.

As for the extra lift he achieved off the pitch, this was something that surprised everyone. The Englishmen had expected to find the same deadened wickets they had encountered in 1928–29, and in fact, the practice of over-preparation had actually increased over the four years, with special top-dressings being added in greedy expectation of record-breaking scores and attendances. In theory the wickets should have been slower and more benign of bounce, but it did not quite work out like that in practice. The new surface gave a slightly uneven bounce and, perhaps more importantly, the ball tended to bite more than usual on pitching. This helped some bowlers more than others. Bowes, for instance, delivered the ball from a great height and although he was able to get plenty of lift, it was slowish lift. Pace off the pitch decreases in proportion to the angle of flight and so the slowness of the pitch negatived Bowes' effectiveness.

With Larwood it was different. As he was only 5 feet 9 inches, his flight was much flatter so he lost far less pace off the pitch. The 'bite' was less pronounced but enough to make the ball lift appreciably. In principle it was not unlike skimming flat stones across water, or perhaps it would be more apt to compare it to Barnes Wallis' bouncing bomb. In their respective attempts to give the Aussie and the Hun a dose of the short stuff, Larwood and Wallis were faced with the necessity for pin-point accuracy, but Larwood had an advantage in that his extreme pace meant that it was almost impossible for him to bowl a bad-length ball. He was also extremely accurate for a fast bowler, and so with the assistance of an occasionally inconsistent bounce, just about every ball he bowled posed a serious threat to the batsman. Some deliveries might rear up off a length and some might not, so it was not uncommon to see batsmen guessing wrong and ducking into balls that rose barely to stump height. The danger to which the batsmen were exposed came from the wicket as well as from Larwood.

Of course there has always been uneven bounce, and until simulated grass pitches are universally adopted there will continue to be uneven bounce, but on this tour it was particularly pronounced. It wasn't only Larwood who took advantage of it, the bowlers generally had a better series than they or anyone else could have expected. 322 fewer runs per Test were scored than in 1928–29, with roughly the same number of wickets falling.

The word 'bodyline' was coined on the first day of the first Test at Sydney. It was a piece of journalist's telegraphese which appealed to a *Melbourne Herald* sub-editor, Ray Robinson, whose job it was to write up the cabled report for the evening edition. He used the word and it caught on immediately.

Ironically, that day was one of the least successful in bodyline's brief history. Stan McCabe, whose batting was usually better if Bradman either wasn't there or failed, was 127 not out at the close and was 187 not out when the Australian innings finished on the second day. It was, by general agreement, the best innings of the series. It was also the luckiest, and this by McCabe's own admission: he thought it could not be done again and he was proved correct (Larwood was not fully fit when Bradman scored his 103 not out in the second Test). The Australian batting folded in the second innings and they lost by 10 wickets.

Larwood's match figures were 10 for 124 in 49 overs. Most of his wickets came as a result of sheer pace at the start of a spell and not from bodyline. Voce, whose bowling was more blatantly intimidating throughout the series, took six wickets using the full bodyline field. According to Kevin Perkins in *The Larwood*

Story, Cyril Ritchard, who was appearing at Her Majesty's Theatre, Sydney, in *Our Miss Gibbs*, slotted this topical verse into one of his numbers while the first Test was on (Cyril Ritchard was an accomplished 'light comedian' possessed of one of those marvellous vibrato voices and also a rather large head):

> Now this new kind of cricket takes courage to stick it,
> There's bruises and fractures galore;
> After kissing their wives and insuring their lives,
> Batsmen fearfully walk out to score.
> With a prayer and a curse they prepare for the hearse,
> Undertakers look on with broad grins;
> Oh! They'd look a lot calmer in Ned Kelly's armour,
> When Larwood the wrecker begins.

Jardine was shrewd enough to see that McCabe's innings, brilliant as it was, was something of a flash in the pan. Without having been tried in a Test against Bradman, bodyline was not yet a completely proven success, but there was clearly every reason to persevere with it. Jardine was unmoved by the angry reactions of the crowds and sections of the press, and his own men were left in no doubt that they were expected to lay aside all else in order to achieve their purpose. In one sense the Australians' antipathy helped Jardine since it had a unifying effect on the team. Discipline was strict and inevitably there were occasional rows, but on the whole the players saw that Jardine's style of leadership was the most likely to bring success and when the going became rough in the middle of the tour, to a man they remained loyal.

The campaign was conducted almost along military lines. Fraternisation with the enemy was not encouraged, and those players who took full advantage of the prodigious hospitality extended to all touring cricketers were reprimanded. (This applied particularly to Brown and Pataudi, who liked to keep things jolly. It is significant that as the tour progressed, these two played less and less part in the campaign.) In Perth, a whisky firm wanted to present each of the team with a sample of their product, but Jardine would not allow it, sensibly perhaps, since an image of sobriety might well have unsettled the Australians. It was all very different from the previous tour. Chapman's side had been pictured in advertisements for mustard baths ('A. P. F. Chapman – Absolutely Prefers Famous Condiment') and had also received talent money from Wolfe's Schnapps (Jardine had picked up £7 4s, incidentally).

Discipline was evident, too, on the field. Jardine insisted that the ball was always returned to the wicket-keeper unless a run-out was being attempted at the bowler's end. Australian observers found this practice over-fussy, but England's alertness in the field brought them five run-outs compared to Australia's two.

Another practice that Jardine sometimes adopted, and which brought criticism even from his own players, was assembling all 17 of the touring party changed into whites before the start of a match and then only pinning up the team shortly before he went out to toss. His object was obviously to foster a feeling of team spirit and to involve those who had little chance of playing in any of the Tests. But it just made everyone very nervous and so Jardine abandoned the idea.

When Jardine's captaincy had first been announced Rockley Wilson, his old cricket master at Winchester, remarked that Jardine would probably win us back the Ashes but that he would also lose us a Dominion. Wilson knew only too well what was required of a touring captain in Australia. He had been there himself in 1920–21 under Douglas, when the barracking had been particularly noisy. The Englishmen took it in good part to begin with, but when the crowd jeered Hobbs for being slow in the field (he was injured and in pain, as was obvious) Wilson and Fender took action and cabled reports of the incident back to London. This enraged the crowds and things got very nasty. Douglas asked for police to be stationed around the boundary but the request was turned down. As it happened, no pitch invasions took place. Australia won that series 5–0 and it is interesting in view of the result that the barracking was so bad. It seems that on every English tour of Australia there have been complaints, formal or otherwise, about the barracking.

Wilson's joke shows that anyone who knew Jardine and knew Australians could have predicted trouble. With this in mind, perhaps, the selectors had decided on sending two managers; Warner, one of the most respected figures in the game, particularly in Australia, and R. C. N. Palairet, a no-nonsense sort of chap who knew Jardine well, having recently retired as Surrey secretary. Neither of these men was able to influence Jardine either in his attitude or in his tactics, but it is open to doubt whether they really tried to. The bad feeling that resulted from bodyline made their job harder, but Warner for one was desperately keen to win. (When Paynter made the Ashes-winning hit at Brisbane, Warner burst forth with 'Now thank we all our God'.) There is no doubt that Warner disapproved of bodyline, but officially, tactics were entirely Jardine's province and it is unlikely that even the great C. B. Fry himself, had he been there, could have deterred Jardine from following his own plan.

Warner was not alone among Englishmen in his distaste for bodyline. Allen, Wyatt and Hammond also disliked it but made no public denouncement at the time. Some think that it would have been better if they had, and it has been said that Warner should have stopped dithering, resigned and taken the next ship home. But before passing moral judgements upon these men, accusing them of conniving at the use of bodyline as long as it suited them, it should be remembered that they were only human. As Gubby Allen has said, 'What could I do? I could have gone home, I suppose, but I wanted to play for England.'

After the first Test the team went to Tasmania, and there Jardine made his only public comment on his tactics of the tour: 'These so-called new tactics are nothing new at all. They have been used for a very long time. At all events they have been very successful and I hope they go on being successful.'

He ran into trouble with the press again in Tasmania. It was during the Christmas match against the island at Hobart. The weather was bad and there had even been a light fall of snow. The local authorities were anxious to get started what was, for them, the biggest match for four years, but Jardine maintained that the ground was too muddy. However, he had to accede to the umpires' insistence and, after losing the toss, he squelched out onto the field at the head of his side. As he soon realised, the ground was too slippery to risk his front-line bowlers, so he bowled himself (10–2–21–0), Paynter and Ames. Duckworth behind the stumps had his face splattered with mud, and Paynter bowled with his trousers rolled up. All this was taken as an insult to the people of Tasmania and an affront to the traditions of the game.

The atmosphere was therefore well and truly hotted up for the second Test at Melbourne. Bradman returned to the side after his convalescence and the public were confidently awaiting his humiliation of Larwood. It was to be the fastest in the world against the record-breaker. Such a contest greatly appealed to people in those days. It was the age of speed and of broken records. Scarcely a month seemed to pass without some land, sea or air conveyance travelling faster than ever before, and the amount of attention these speed trials received greatly exceeded anything one might expect nowadays. People flocked to see fearless young men and women jumping in countless novel ways from high buildings, diving boards and bridges. Danger as always was a vital element in the appeal of these activities, and therefore bodyline easily qualified as a crowd-pulling spectacle. Arthur Mailey thought that it satisfied the blood-lust of the masses in peacetime. One only has to look at the behaviour of crowds today for proof of this theory.

Despite Jardine's confident announcement from Tasmania, he was not entirely convinced that 'fast leg-theory' was going to win the Ashes. He had appeared rather jittery during McCabe's great innings, moving fielders to where the last ball had been hit. However, he decided to gamble on an all-out pace attack in the second Test. Bowes was brought in to replace Verity, which meant that England took the field with four fast bowlers, a thing they had never done before.

Shortly before the start of play there was a row which nearly resulted in one of those bowlers pulling out. The trouble was between Jardine and Gubby Allen, good pals off the field but holding different views on bodyline. During the first Test Jardine had suggested that Allen bowl more bouncers, but Allen had resisted, saying that he did not think that was how cricket should be played. Jardine pressed him again before the second Test and again Allen refused. A row developed. Allen said that he was quite prepared to take the next ship home (a much used threat, this), and that once he was back in England he would make public everything that Jardine had said. Since a captain's encouragement to his fast bowlers is seldom couched in the sort of terms one would normally associate with the Noble Game, this might have been very embarrassing for Jardine. Allen stumped off to sit on the pavilion balcony, where he said he would await notification of whether he was required to play or not. He played.

Bodyline or no bodyline, Allen was one of the most hostile bowlers around at the time. He did not spare the batsman's ribs, and he had the temperament to go with it. Bob Wyatt remembers being hit over the heart by him in a county match. 'So you're yellow are you?' growled Allen as Wyatt staggered back in pain.

Newsreel footage of the 1932–33 series shows an Australian playing and missing and the unlucky bowler, Allen, having a mini-tantrum – not, I hasten to add, anything like as demonstrative as one sees now but more of a period tantrum, dashing the air with his fist, stamping and saying, one imagines, 'Oh, hang it!' or something of the kind.

One has to admire the stand Allen took. How was he to know that the Australians would not find a means of combating bodyline? It might even have become respectable in the way that other new methods have done. If Allen had walked out and these things had happened, he would have looked a bit foolish.

A question that arises here is, would Jardine have dealt differently with conscientious objection from a professional bowler? Would Larwood, for example, have been sent back steerage on that 'next ship home'? The most likely answer is that it would simply have depended on how valuable the bowler in question was. Jardine was concerned less with asserting his authority than with winning. It was not necessary that his will was seen to triumph always. Possessed of a natural authority, he found no need for shows of strength. He admired anyone who stuck to his principles, professional or amateur, and if Larwood or Bowes or Voce had refused to bowl bodyline then, provided they were prepared to withstand Jardine's initial fury, their conviction would have been respected. Whether they would have been sent home or not would have depended on their worth as orthodox bowlers. Larwood naturally would have been retained and for that reason he can be said to have had a choice in the matter. As the fastest and best fast bowler in the world he had a certain freedom of choice, and to depict him as a forelock-tugging pro. carrying out his master's orders is to lay too much of the responsibility for bodyline on Jardine's shoulders.

More people than had ever watched a cricket match before cheered Bradman to the wicket on the first day of the second Test. So much was expected of him and the English bowlers were most definitely 'after him'. But one thing he did not lack was confidence – in fact the English players, the Australian Board of Control and some of his own side thought he had a deal too much of it. Confidently, he faced his first ball. It was a long hop from Bowes, the kind of ball that Bradman put away through mid-wicket without thinking about. This one, however, he dragged into his stumps. There were cries of anguish around the ground and then silence. It was one of the happiest moments of Jardine's life. Bowes remembers him doing a most uncharacteristic little jig as the wicket was broken.

The pressure on Bradman when he went out to bat in the second innings must have been tremendous; seven consecutive failures against the tourists and another record-breaking crowd expecting nothing less than a hundred. It is doubtful, though, whether Bradman felt the kind of pressures that ordinary people feel. Discussing his first-ball dismissal only recently in the Melbourne *Age*, he said that the trouble with the shot he played was that it was *too good*. Whatever his feelings, he scored 103 not out out of a total of 191, easily his best innings of the series and one of the best of his career. It ought to be said, however, that Larwood was not at his best (he was suffering agonies from a new pair of boots).

The wicket had begun to crack up by then and England badly needed the spinner they had left out. The Australians had made the same mistake on the same ground four years earlier but this time they included Ironmonger and O'Reilly. These two made short work of England in the fourth innings and bowled their team to victory by 111 runs.

The affair of Larwood's boots was the cause of much ill-feeling between captain and main bowler. What happened was that Larwood split his left boot bowling on the first day. He went off and changed into another pair belonging to Duckworth, who took the same size, but again the left one split under the strain of his explosive delivery stride, and he was obliged to leave the field a second time. The crowd thought he must be going off for a drink or a shower and started to have a go at him. Some minutes later he walked back onto the field, to a furious reception, wearing a brand new pair of boots. These tore the skin off his toes as soon as he started bowling. He consulted his captain, who was now pretty well fed up and testily told him to go off and change. But Larwood was reluctant to do so, fearing a lynching from the crowd. After a brief but heated exchange it was decided that if he was going to stay on, then he would have to bowl. In considerable pain, he carried on, but his match return of 4 for 100 was his worst of the series.

The rift that had opened between the two men widened when, four days after the Test, Jardine selected Larwood to play in a country game. It was not a particularly important match as far as

England was concerned and Larwood felt, with some justification, that he should be allowed to rest his toes. The two wouldn't speak to each other for days.

The annoying thing for Jardine was that Bradman had been able to build up his confidence without having to face the full fury of bodyline. And with the series now standing at one-all, there was less room for experiment.

Another more personal worry was that he was having a bad run with the bat. After a start almost as good as the one he had made four years earlier, his form had fallen away. 98 against the Combined XI was followed by a cautious 108 not out against South Australia, but his next seven innings brought only 75 runs, and in the Tests he made 27, 1, 0. He felt that he ought to stand down for the third Test, not just because of his lack of form but also because of the barracking he seemed to attract. He thought the side might have an easier time of it if he withdrew. However the selection committee (Warner, Sutcliffe, Wyatt and Hammond) would not hear of it.

The reason for his failure seems to have been a not uncommon one – the burden of captaincy. In the dressing room he was like a cat on hot bricks before he went in, pacing to and fro, muttering nervously about the state of the game. 'You're bloody mad,' Wyatt had told him. In an attempt to calm him down it was decided that for the third Test he should open the innings with Sutcliffe. He did not like opening and, since his Oxford days, he had only done so in emergencies, but he agreed to give it a try. And so in the Adelaide Test he became the only man to have opened an England innings with both Hobbs and Sutcliffe. The experiment was half successful. He made 3 in the first innings and 56 (lbw to Ironmonger) in $4\frac{1}{4}$ hours in the second. However, it is not for Jardine's batting that the Battle of Adelaide is remembered.

England made a terrible start and were 30 for 4 at one point. But then Wyatt joined Leyland in a do-or-die stand. The way they carried the attack was not only thrilling but quite against the captain's orders; Jardine had told them to take things steady. They added 156 and put England right back in the game. Wyatt remembers that when he hit his first six, Jardine disappeared from the balcony.

As soon as Australia began their reply it was evident that there was life in the wicket; perhaps there always is when two really fast bowlers are inspired, as Allen and Larwood were that afternoon. Jardine's reason for opening with Allen instead of Voce was that Fingleton seemed to have a weakness against him on the off stump. The plan worked perfectly and Fingleton was caught Ames, bowled Allen for 0. Larwood opened with the wind behind him, operating, as was his custom at the start of an innings, to an off-side field. With the last ball of his second over he hit Woodfull a fearful thump over the heart. The batsman staggered back and the crowd, who were spoiling for a fight, howled with rage. Not just the ordinary punters but grey-haired members were up on their feet, shouting imprecations. Jardine walked across to sympathise with Woodfull and then made his way to Larwood at the other end. Hammond was already there, telling Larwood not to be put off by the crowd's behaviour. 'Well bowled, Harold,' said Jardine loud and clear, as much for the non-striker's ears as for Larwood's (Bradman had come in on Fingleton's dismissal and was not looking at all comfortable).

During the previous over to Woodfull, Larwood had found that he was making the ball swing in to the batsman. This surprised him, as throughout his career he had only ever been able to make the ball swing away. Woodfull, too, had been taken by surprise but at that moment was more concerned about whether or not his heart would continue to function than he was about the mysteries of swing. Needless to say, Jardine had spotted it and discussed it with Larwood while Woodfull was rubbing his bruise. A logical course of action under the circumstances would have been to switch to a leg-side field. There is no evidence that Larwood and Jardine agreed to change the field at the start of his next over, but it seems likely.

Bradman scored two boundaries off Allen in the next over, but it was clear by now that Australia were on the run. As Larwood was about to bowl the first ball of his third over to Woodfull, play was held up (by Larwood according to Jardine, and by Jardine according to Larwood) and the leg-side field was set. This provoked further storms of protest from the crowd, to whom it seemed as if the English were kicking a man when he was down. It looked and sounded as if a riot was about to take place, and some of the English players have said that they were ready to grab a stump to defend themselves. It is a reflection on the conditioning of the times that no invasion did take place. In his book on the tour, Jardine wrote, 'Had he [Larwood] or I realised the misrepresentation to which we were to be subjected, neither of us would have set that particular field for that particular over.' Diplomatically it was a disastrous move but tactically it was correct and Jardine's conviction, remember, was that cricket was a game for 22 players, and the crowd had no business to interfere with the play.

Woodfull somehow managed to hang on against Larwood, despite having his bat torn from his grasp by one delivery. Bradman went quickly, though, jabbing a good length-ball to Allen in the leg trap. McCabe left in similar fashion. Woodfull was eventually bowled by Allen for 22, but that was the extent of the English success that afternoon. The two bowlers had shot their bolts and Richardson and Ponsford were able to play out time.

Woodfull meanwhile was nursing his bruises in the Australian dressing room. Having allowed a decent period of time to elapse after his dismissal, the English managers, Warner and Palairet, presented themselves to offer their sympathy. They hoped that he was not too badly hurt and that he would make a swift recovery – one imagines them standing there like Basil Radford and Naunton Wayne, Warner doing the talking and Palairet murmuring agreement, with the Australians watching silent and stony-faced. Woodfull uttered the famous remark that there were two sides out there but only one was playing cricket. Warner and Palariet made a dignified exit – well, there wasn't much a chap could say if the fellow was going to take that sort of tone.

The incident was leaked to the press by someone. It was just the sort of story that was needed to revive the interest in bodyline, an interest that had flagged rather since Australia's win in the second Test. It will probably never be known who leaked the story. Bradman says it was Fingleton, Fingleton said it was Bradman and Leo O'Brien (the twelfth man) further confused the issue by revealing in a recent interview with *Wisden Cricket Monthly* that neither Bradman nor Fingleton was in the room at the time of the exchange, but Ryder and Kippax, who were both reporting the matches in one way or another, were. Fingleton was for many years believed to have been the culprit, but of the four he was the least likely 'mole' since, as the only player allowed to report on the series, any 'shock horrors' would immediately be attributed to him, and he had to keep his nose clean if he wished his priviliged status to continue. Whatever the source, the story was all over the newspapers and when the match resumed after the week-end, anti-British feeling, which already existed to a greater or lesser extent in the hearts of most Australians in those days, was well and truly roused.

Policemen were stationed around the boundary and a substantial force of mounted police was also on hand, ready to intervene. Indeed, it seemed inevitable that they would have to do so if another Australian was hit. But the first session of play passed without accident.

The wicket had lost its life over the week-end and, with the ball now over 100 runs old, none of the English bowlers was able to achieve any lift. After lunch Larwood took the new ball. Oldfield, who had played extremely well for 41, got a short one, tried to hook and played the ball onto his head. Pandemonium broke out as he hit the ground, but amazingly there was no invasion. The England fielders gathered round him and, to their relief, found that he was alive. It was perhaps the apparent seriousness of the injury that kept the crowd from swarming over the fence. The horror of the spectacle may have shocked them, if not into silence, at least into immobility.

Oldfield had sustained a small fracture which was to put him out of action until the final Test. He was able to walk, assisted, from the field and even managed a smile. His own fault, he said, for hooking. The crowd was less ready to absolve Larwood and, during the short time it took him to polish off the Australian tail, they hooted and yelled and counted him out.

The English began their reply with a lead of over 100, and were clearly intent on wearing down the bowling and building up an unassailable lead. Jardine, wearing his Harlequin cap, took 4¼ hours to score 56 and one can't help feeling that it was the crowd that he wanted to wear down as well as the bowling. England took two days to score 412 runs.

The crowd resigned themselves to the fact that Australia could not possibly score the necessary 532 to win, and there seemed to be far less antagonism towards the Englishmen in the fourth innings.

Fingleton went for 0 again, this time bowled by Larwood. The Englishmen were especially pleased with this since they rated Fingleton, along with Richardson, as just about the best player of bodyline in the Australian side. Warner, too, was pleased since he blamed Fingleton for the press leak and had offered Larwood a

quid if he could get him out quickly. Larwood scattered his
stumps, bowling, one imagines, not so much for the money but to
show that he could, when he put his mind to it, knock anyone's
stumps over. Fingleton was dropped for the rest of the series and
did not make the 1934 tour of England, a fact which illustrates the
kind of confusion induced by bodyline.

Fingleton gave an indication of the lasting impression with
which one was left after facing Larwood with the new ball. In a
letter to me dated 16 March 1981 he wrote,

> Funny thing. Only this morning I had a dream about re-playing the
> Test again and I was going in to bat determined to resist [protect] the
> off stump, hold my bat handle higher and go for strokes from the
> start. The dream was too short to know how I went, but it was good
> while it lasted.

– 48 years on and still dreaming about it.

Woodfull again played Larwood bravely, the pitch making his
job a little easier than in the first innings. Ponsford went quickly
to Larwood and then Bradman came in. It was clear from the start
that he was going for runs and, what was more, doing so in an
unorthodox way. He had shown glimpses of this method while
scoring his hundred in the Melbourne Test. Some thought it
reckless and irresponsible, others thought it plain cowardly. But,
whether it was mistaken or not, Bradman's answer to bodyline
was the result of level-headed and careful planning.

As the ball rocketed towards his throat, he would step outside
the line and try to swat it into the vacant off-side area. He scored
runs very quickly like this although the method was not entirely
successful, firstly because of the risk involved in leaving his wicket
unguarded and secondly because, if Larwood saw Bradman
starting to edge away to leg just before he delivered the ball, he
would 'follow him'. The acrobatics Bradman performed in
pursuit of his method smacked of weediness to many of those
playing with and against him. One may easily understand the
feelings of his fellow-Australian batsmen sitting black and blue
in the dressing room watching his antics. The feeling was that it
was all very well to swan around scoring quadruple-hundreds on
featherbed pitches against ordinary bowlers, but where was the
Boy Wonder when the heat was really on? Dancing about outside
the leg stump, that was where he was. Bradman was so quick on his

feet that he could have remained at the crease all day simply dodging the bouncers and not making any attempt to score, but as he has made clear with some feeling, this would have pleased people even less. He also made the point that any fool could stand there, brave and upright, and allow himself to be beaten into a pulp. As he saw it, his job was to score runs *and* avoid serious injury. He managed to score more runs and at a higher average than any other Australian, but even so his scores fell a long way short of the expectations of his adoring fans (0, 103 not out, 8, 66, 76, 24, 48, 71). Before the tour Jardine would probably have 'settled out of court' for 150 per match from him.

Both Jardine and Larwood thought Bradman was wrong to adopt the measures he did. The existence of the leg trap had persuaded him, and several other Australians, that the hook was not on. By opting not to play the stroke they denied themselves the opporunity not only of scoring, but also of scattering the close field and thereby giving themselves a bit of breathing space. It has to be said, though, that hooking Larwood was something that one might attempt but not necessarily survive.

Jardine's conviction that Bradman was frightened of Larwood, a serious charge in the days when 'pluck' was king, was born more out of wishful thinking than factual evidence. Bradman denies that he flinched from Larwood at the Oval in 1930 and on subsequent occasions in 1932–33, but there is some evidence to suggest that he did. Arguing this point might seem rather silly in view of the fact that facing Larwood at all must be counted an act of lunatic bravery – it was not unknown for tail-end batsmen simply to lift their bats up to the first ball they received – but Bradman's apparent discomfort was widely discussed at the time. He claimed that his method of darting to leg, or sometimes right across in the other direction, exposed him to greater danger than if he had stood his ground. It is easy to see that his wicket was at greater risk but not so easy to see how the physical danger was increased. He also argued the other way, saying he would not have been much use to Australia with a broken head, but that did not quite carry the weight then that it would now. In any case, flinching, being a reflex action, can hardly be considered an expression of poltroonery. Ponsford flinched at Larwood but overcame the impulse to jab at the ball by turning his back and allowing it to hit him. Proof of pluck, surely. Not for Jardine: he believed in standing up to short-pitched bowling and using his bat to defend himself. It is impossible to say whether or not he would have survived a whole series of bodyline by using this method, but certainly he and Sutcliffe, out of all the 33 men who played in the series, were the most likely to succeed against it.

After the early dismissals of Fingleton and Ponsford, the Australian cause was lost. Woodfull, and later on Richardson, played stubbornly, their pluck being duly recorded. But Bradman used his 'cut and run' method to score 66 in even time. It was an innings of sheer genuis, but to some, it looked suspiciously as if he wasn't trying, and Woodfull is said to have wanted to drop him from the side. The crowd loved it, though, and their excitement was further heightened by the extravagant ducking and weaving that the Australians had taken to – this practice was adopted in varying degrees throughout the rest of the series, much to the annoyance of the English bowlers.

This was the day on which the Australian Board of Control fired the first shot in the cable war that was to occupy so many minds over the next 11 months. This is the text:

> Body-line bowling has assumed such proportions as to menace the best interests of the game, making protection of the body by the batsmen the main consideration. This is causing intensely bitter feelings between the players as well as injury. In our opinion it is unsportsmanlike. Unless stopped at once, it is likely to upset the friendly relations existing between Australia and England.

No 'respectfully submits', no 'hereuntofors', just a straightforward expression of opinion.

As a response to the English tactics it was the diplomatic equivalent of Bradman's batting – unorthodox, spectacular, but ultimately doomed to failure. Just as it was not done to cross-bat straight balls into the off-side, it was not done to use such emotional language to an Imperial governing body. MCC declined to accept the implied urgency of the situation and took its time to think things over. The reply which whizzed down the wire five days later was unplayable:

> We, Marylebone Cricket Club, deplore your cable. We deprecate your opinion that there has been unsportsmanlike play. We have fullest confidence in captain, team and managers and are convinced

that they would do nothing to infringe either the laws of Cricket or the spirit of the game. We have no evidence that our confidence has been misplaced. Much as we regret accidents to Woodfull and Oldfield, we understand that in neither case was the bowler to blame. If the Australian Board of Control wish to propose a new Law or Rule, it shall receive our careful consideration in due course.

We hope the situation is not now as serious as your cable would seem to indicate, but if it is such as to jeopardise the good relations between English and Australian cricketers and you consider it desirable to cancel the remainder of the programme we would consent, but with great reluctance.

From the lofty ignoring of the word 'bodyline' to the threat to cancel the rest of the tour, the cable was a tribute to the legal expertise of those who drafted it. Cancellation of the remaining Tests would have deprived the Board of Control of about £20,000 and also any remaining shred of credibility they commanded. They were in no position to demand anything. It was like arguing with the headmaster.

There was no independent body to whom the Board could appeal for a judgement on bodyline. The people who decided whether it was fair or not were the people whose representative XI was now using it, and for the moment they were saying it was fair.

The English team took exception to the word 'unsportsman-like' just as their superiors at Lord's had done. In addition to this, other slurs began to appear in the Australian press about dissension within the team. One story alleged that Maurice Tate had thrown a glass of beer at Jardine. As a result of the general hostility being shown towards the team, Jardine decided to call a meeting to discuss what action, if any, should be taken. He had, as he said in his book, made no secret of the fact that he would not take the field against Australia until the 'unsportsmanlike' stigma had been removed. He also believed, and this is not normally acknowledged since it confuses an image of unwavering ruthlessness, that Australian hostility had now reached such a level as to make it impossible for the team to give of their best. For this reason alone, he was prepared to consider abandoning 'leg-theory'.

The English team decided amongst themselves to issue a statement to the press to the effect that there was no dissension and that they were all entirely loyal to their captain under whom they hoped to achieve 'an honourable victory'. They all signed it, even Gubby Allen (the statement made no mention of bodyline), and it was grudgingly published, though not necessarily believed. Enough of the players, it seems, were unwilling to go into the fourth Test with the 'unsportsmanlike' charge hanging over them to make cancellation of the rest of the programme likely. This display of solidarity was remarkable, even in an age when team spirit was practically a way of life. Support for Jardine was all the more remarkable since there were not a few grumbles going around: Allen, as we have seen, was unhappy, as was Tate, who was wondering why he had been brought over in the first place. The touring party was too big and, with a specific plan of attack, it meant that too many had too few opportunities. Certain of the younger element were not responding too well to the strict discipline imposed, either. But it was clear to all of them that, in spite of the fact that Jardine's poor batting form made him something of a passenger, he had the strength of character to lead them through the remaining six weeks, and to do so competitively without cracking under the strain. He was not only moved but surprised by their demonstration of support.

Gubby Allen has said that Jardine did not expect to continue as captain after the first Australian cable had been sent. He doubted that Lord's would back him. But when Allen pointed out to him that the Board of Control could not possibly expect to get away with using the word 'unsportsmanlike', Jardine cheered up a bit.

Many Australians were embarrassed by the Board's precipitate cable, and even members of the Board themselves privately expressed regret. Publicly, however, they took a little longer to do so, and then only after a ticking off from their own government. The Board's climb-down began at the end of January and continued for the best part of a year. Shortly before the fourth Test they cabled Lord's thus: 'We do not regard the sportsmanship of your team as being in question ... It is the particular class of bowling referred to therein which we consider is not in the best interest of cricket.'

The fourth Test went ahead after all. It was played at Brisbane in temperatures of over 100° for most of the time. The match will always be remembered for Paynter's heroic innings of 83. He had gone into the match not feeling at his best but had kept quiet about it. By the end of the second day he was in hospital with tonsilitis. Jardine visited him on the rest day and suggested that if necessary he should bat for England whatever his condition and regardless of the consequences. Paynter of course agreed. He remained in bed for the rest of Sunday and most of Monday. Meanwhile, at the 'Gabba things were proceeding at a funereal pace. Partly through boredom and partly through the debilitating humidity, the barrackers were almost polite. England were batting extraordinarily slowly and, crucially in view of their depleted resources, they were also losing wickets – half the side was out for under 200. Jardine decided to send for Paynter. Warner expressed concern about the risk to Paynter's health, but Jardine swept this aside, saying, 'What about those fellows who marched on Kandahar with the fever on them?' Warner, who liked to think of cricket in terms of nineteenth-century military history, was instantly won over by this allusion and the message was sent. Paynter said that he left the hospital as soon as he heard that England were in trouble, so it seems that Jardine's summons arrived afterwards.

At any rate, when the sixth wicket fell Paynter tottered out to the middle. He was plainly far from well but he kept his end going until the close, by which time he had made 24. He spent the night in hospital and then went on the next day to make 83. It gave England a small first-innings lead. There was only one word for it – pluck.

Larwood sent down nearly 50 overs in that Turkish-bath atmosphere, taking seven wickets in all for 150 runs. His stamina was incredible for someone of such a small, wiry build. Jardine believed that the sips of champagne with which he fed him had something to do with it. Barnes and Foster had bowled on champagne on the 1911–12 tour, and in fact most English touring teams seem to have got through a fair bit of the stuff. (The tradition dated back to when the old amateur captains were given an unlimited champagne allowance – chamateurism?).

Jardine had found that his fast bowlers worked best if they had a drink after the first over of a new spell. Whether the advantage was physical or psychological he was not sure, but as with any other minutely favourable condition, he exploited it meticulously. This meant that the drinks waiter had to keep his eyes peeled for bowling changes. The job was usually assigned to Pataudi in the latter half of the tour, and one can't help feeling that Jardine thought a spot of fetching and carrying would do him no harm at all. Once, during the fourth Test, he came off the field carrying a tray of empty glasses and tripped up the pavilion steps. The whole lot went flying and there was a good deal of cheering and applause. Pataudi raised himself and said, with a crack in his voice, 'At least I still have my public.' Like Jardine, many of his jokes were either misunderstood or not understood at all. He undoubtedly had the common touch, though, and while Jardine was having insults, obscenities and orange peel hurled at him from over the boundary, Pataudi was telling the barrackers to call him 'Pat' and taking all the Gandhi jokes in a most cheerful spirit. He liked neither Jardine nor his approach to the game, and the feeling was entirely mutual. He once teased Jardine after seeing him flinch when in a close fielding position. Later (taking his lead from Ranji, perhaps who had publicly denounced bodyline), he declined to field in the leg trap, and from then on he had no place in Jardine's plans.

England cut things pretty fine in the final innings of the fourth Test. They took 80 overs to make the necessary 160 runs, and this with rain imminent for most of the time. When Paynter made the winning hit an electric storm was just beginning. Nobody could understand England's caution, since O'Reilly and Ironmonger could have gone through them in a session on a drying wicket. Jardine at one stage played 82 balls without scoring off one of them. He was openly shamefaced about this innings, saying he had batted like an old maid defending her virginity, but in explanation of his side's performance he merely said that the bowling was good and that they could not afford to take any risks. Still, the Ashes were won and that was that.

Larwood and Allen asked Jardine if they could miss the fifth Test, Allen because of a back injury that was troubling him and Larwood because he had never sat and watched a Test match before. Jardine tersely turned down their requests and made it clear that he wanted a 4–1 result to the series.

The match was played at a rather more sedate pace, although it was not without incident. There was further friction between Larwood and Jardine when, after being in the field for nearly two days and having bowled 32 overs, Larwood was sent in as night-watchman. Jardine did not explain that he merely wanted him to get his innings over with so that he could have a good long rest before bowling again. Larwood thought he was being victimised and began batting as if he meant to get out as soon as possible. This affair is often quoted as an example of Jardine's bad management, but the fact is that Larwood was so cross with his captain that he scored 98 runs. He was given a thunderous ovation, incidentally, as he returned to the pavilion. Larwood was a man who, while possessed of a gentle nature, kind to his mother and no doubt to dumb animals too, also had a streak of ferociousness which, when roused, could produce startling results. Jardine knew all about this, having had ample time to observe his behaviour on the previous tour, and he made every effort to exploit it. He had seen what happened in 1928 when Ponsford let it be known that he didn't think Larwood was all that fast. Larwood had ripped out his leg stump a few times and then, the point having been made, had put him out of action completely by breaking his hand. And so at Sydney a high-handed 'Larwood, you will bat at no. 4' produced similarly gratifying results.

A high proportion of Larwood's runs were made off the fast, short-pitched bowling of H. H. 'Bull' Alexander, the same man who had bowled bodyline unsuccessfully at Jardine at Melbourne on the previous tour. He was fast and aggressive and the crowd urged him to 'knock the bastard's head off' as he charged in to bowl to Larwood. It is hard to see for what purpose Alexander had been brought into the side if not for retaliation. He was not really a Test bowler, as his match figures of 1 for 154 would suggest, but, to use an expression of Warner's, he knew how to 'bump her', and therein lay his appeal to the selectors. He did not bowl proper bodyline – his field was different from Larwood's – but his deliveries were undoubtedly designed to intimidate.

The Englishmen made no murmur of official complaint, as was only proper in view of what had gone before. What they did object to, however, was the fact that Alexander followed through on the wicket. This had been noticed and objected to on the previous tour; it was not quite as bad now as it had been then and he had made efforts to eradicate the problem, but it was still unfair. For much of the time in this match the Australian attack was carried by Alexander and, at the other end, Ironmonger, the left-armer, who was able to pitch his deliveries on a spot which Alexander was roughing up directly on a line with the right-hander's leg stump. The Englishmen felt especially bitter about this since Ironmonger's action was considered by them to be highly suspect – he was never picked for a Test outside Australia. Sutcliffe complained about Alexander's follow-through in the first innings to no effect, but in the second Jardine was more persistent. A short altercation took place amid much hooting from the crowd. Jardine suggested that if Alexander could not run off the wicket, then he should not wear studs. Woodfull intervened, saying that Alexander had always bowled in studs. Alexander then said that he would bowl round the wicket and, just as he had done to Jardine four years ago almost to the day, he proceeded to bowl a succession of bouncers aimed quite obviously at the batsman. The crowd understandably loved it. Bob Wyatt, who was Jardine's partner at the time, remembers it well since he actually had to suffer the major part of Alexander's resentment (36 deliveries to Jardine's 24).

There were exultant cheers when Alexander eventually scored a resounding hit on Jardine. Typically, there was no doubling up with pain, no rubbing of the afflicted area, only the merest delay while Jardine waved away the sympathetic fielders. 'Let's get on with the game' he said. He was dismissed shortly afterwards having a hit at Ironmonger, but Hammond and Wyatt knocked off the necessary runs to give England an eight-wicket victory.

If the match made less than gripping watching from a purely cricketing point of view, it contained moments of high drama. The most tragic of these was Larwood's breakdown. It happened when he was bowling in the second innings and the cause indirectly was Bradman. By that time Larwood had dismissed him four times out of seven and he was keen to get him once more. For the only time in the series, Larwood landed a blow on Bradman, but it was only a glancing one on the arm. Bradman at the time was trying to square-cut a ball wide of the leg stump – he had edged away and Larwood had followed him.

Larwood continued to tear in, hammering the ball into the pitch, his knuckles scraping the grass on his follow-through, and Bradman was dashing at the ball in what was now the accustomed manner. But their final duel was to be undecided, for Larwood broke down in his eleventh over. After $4\frac{1}{2}$ months of crashing his left leg down in the delivery stride a bone finally snapped, and at that moment his Test career ended.

Ironically, the injury was caused by one of the very factors that enabled him to achieve such unprecedented speed, namely his studs. In England the turf normally allowed his feet some 'give' in the delivery stride, but the rock-hard Australian pitches offered no such cushioning effect. Larwood's English studs were longer than the ones normally worn in Australia and they gripped the ground more firmly, giving him added leverage but also putting more strain on his left foot as it slammed down in the act of delivery.

Jardine would not let him go off, thinking that the affair of the Melbourne boots was about to be revived, and he made Larwood bowl the remaining balls of his over. These were lobbed to Woodfull who blocked each one, making no attempt to score. Not until Bradman was out was Larwood allowed to leave the field. Jardine felt that his very presence, lame or not, was enough to intimidate the pride of Australia. He was right, too. Bradman immediately tried to take advantage of the respite and before very long he was bowled when trying to hit Verity.

The greatest fast bowler and the greatest batsman in the history of the game left the field together in silence.

8
Bodyline:
The Aftermath

Bodyline tamed Bradman but it destroyed Larwood and Jardine. It might not have destroyed two lesser men, but then lesser men would probably not have had the resolve to pursue their policy in the face of such passionate opposition.

No-one knew at the time the extent to which the affair had wounded Jardine. He remained outwardly impervious to the waves of hate that came rolling over the boundary fences in his direction. His desire to maintain an appearance of invulnerability was obsessive. When the aboriginal fast bowler, Eddie Gilbert, hit him on the hip, he showed no sign of being in pain until some time later when he was out. Once inside the England dressing room he asked for the door to be closed, then collapsed onto the massage table, saying through clenched teeth, 'This hip, it's giving me hell.' Just as he concealed his physical pain, he nursed in secret the wounds to his pride and his honour. When those he liked and respected spoke out against bodyline, he said nothing.

It was the Winchester way; monumental toughness and unfailing confidence in one's convictions makyth man. However severe the punishment, justified or otherwise, one did not show that it hurt. Jardine was more than just a product of the system, however, all the nineteenth-century fantasies about chivalry and purity seem to have been embraced by him at an earlier age and, what is more, he hung on to them into adulthood. One could say that he was an instinctive Victorian, and he followed the code to extremes that even the hardiest of his Winchester contemporaries would have been stretched to match.

In this respect he was out of step with his generation. Even cricketers – a most conservative lot in the main – were rebelling against the old order, while Jardine's philosophy was firmly nineteenth-century romantic. He was clearly proud of being anachronistic, as much of his writing reveals, and inevitably his friendships tended to be with people older than himself. Photographs taken of him as a young man show him dressed expensively and immaculately but not particularly fashionably. Other photographs and snatches of newsreel of official occasions record his scrupulous politeness: listening avidly to the speeches of mayors and association presidents, even bowing from the waist as he shakes hands with the armies of local worthies. All very formal, an ideal defence against attempts at mateyness of any kind. His values were not those 'Victorian values' of which we hear so much these days, and there was no middle-class industriousness in his make-up; earning a living was always a chore. In thought and deed he was an aristocrat, standing above the common herd, to whom it was unthinkable that he should reveal his innermost feelings.

It seems that secretly, he liked to cast himself in the role of a classical hero. He called his book *In Quest of the Ashes* and in many ways the tour was for him a knightly quest. 'One crowded hour of glorious life is worth an age without a name' he used to quote to his men as they sat in the dressing room having one last fag or applying a dab of Brylcreem before taking the field.

He carried his singular brand of honour onto the field. He had a rigid and to most people, contradictory set of standards which admitted merciless adherence to the letter of the law and at the same time gestures of magnanimity well beyond the wider limits of the spirit of the law. (In an important match against New South Wales he allowed the opposition to replace their injured wicket-keeper with one who was not even in the original twelve.) If such a combination of attitudes was puzzling in 1933, it would have been less so 50 years earlier, when a more brutal form of chivalry prevailed on the cricket field. Again the anachronistic streak.

To one who had the morality and chivalry of the game so much at heart, the charge of bad sportsmanship was especially wounding. Hurt and, at the same time, contemptuous of those who had in his view broken the code by making such a charge, he reacted with haughty silence. There was little to be gained, he felt, by descending to the Australians' level to defend himself. He was aware, too, that to have done so would have been difficult without implying that the Australian batsmen were cowards. Even if he thought privately that they were, to have said so publicly would have brought the argument to an even more undignified level. All he would say was that he would not play until the charge was withdrawn. Unfortunately his silence was taken in some quarters as an admission of guilt, and it caused some uncertainty at home as well. English cricket followers were certain that he had done nothing to contravene the spirit of the game but they could have done with some form of denial as reassurance. He said later that he thought the policy of silence had been overdone and that he should have offered some words in explanation of his tactics for the benefit of those who could not see for themselves. Perhaps it was as well that he did not, or the row might have developed still further.

He was not without favourable representation, however. Bruce Harris of the *Evening Standard*, in return for being the only journalist favoured with Jardine's co-operation, wrote approvingly of the English tactics. But Harris was inexperienced (he was really a lawn tennis correspondent) and his accounts were not very authoritative. Later he became a well-respected cricket writer and the book he wrote after the tour (*Jardine Justified*) shows how quickly he acquired the skills; it is an interesting read and not the whitewash job one might expect. Then there was Jack Hobbs who, with the 'assistance' of Jack Ingham, dispatched reports of a similarly uncritical nature to the *Star*. Hobbs did not like bodyline but was reluctant to criticise his county captain and so the account was rather colourless, despite the efforts of Ingham, the zip and pep specialist. The pair of them fell foul of Jardine early on in the tour for criticising Sutcliffe's slow batting and their job must have been a little harder for that. (Ingham, incidentally, was once heard to say, when Cardus' name came up in conversation, 'Oh yes, he's the bugger who pinches all my epigrams.') The only other English writer out there was Maj. the Hon. E. G. French, who strongly disapproved of bodyline on aesthetic grounds, but his voice was not heard since no-one would publish him (his mammoth manuscript account is astonishingly uninteresting). The Reuters correspondent, Gerald Mant, whose reports appeared in *The Times*, was Australian and therefore suspect in Jardine's eyes. His reports were comprehensive but strictly factual and impersonal, as was Reuters policy. So the British public knew virtually nothing of the atmosphere in which the Tests were played.

Even when all the books of the tour came out in the summer of 1933, the English public was none the wiser. It was difficult to explain the sheer menace of a huge Australian crowd to a race of cricket watchers accustomed to a suspension of play if an aircraft passed overhead. The actual level of noise was to increase over the years, but on very few occasions can there have been such a dangerous atmosphere at a Test match.

Before sailing for home, the Englishmen made a short tour of New Zealand. The visit was highly successful, with both hosts and guests anxious to demonstrate, for different reasons, how much they preferred each other's company to the Australians'. Australia had tried to stop England making the tour, feeling that it would diminish the importance of the main series of matches in Australia. New Zealand was offended by this and was subsequently delighted when the Englishmen so obviously enjoyed their visit. 'If only,' said the Englishmen as they travelled about the islands, 'if only Australians were as civilised as New Zealanders, there would not have been all the trouble.' The display of mutual affection reached its peak at the City Hall, Wellington, where the English team solemnly processed down the central aisle with the organ playing 'See the conquering hero comes'. They played two drawn Test matches, remarkable for Hammond's successive scores of 227 and 336. Then they sailed for home via Fiji, Hawaii, Vancouver and across Canada by train then a boat home across the Atlantic.

As soon as the Australian series finished, work began on nearly a dozen books of the tour. Written from different points of view and some in the heat of indignation, they tell very different stories although the Australian authors made more of an effort to understand the English position than the other way round. For instance, *Anti-Bodyline* by Alan Kippax and E. P. Barbour is a more balanced book than the outraged *Bodyline?* By Larwood and his ghost.

Jardine's book, the least easy read of the lot, is in the form of a legal defence. Each anti-bodyline argument is clearly set out and compliments paid to the ability and reputations of the opposition, but the case for the prosecution is then destroyed with a mixture of sarcasm and logic, and pity is even expressed for those unfortunate enough to hold such misguided views. The defence is overstated and therefore ultimately unconvincing. The narrative frequently boils over with rage. Had he waited a little longer before committing himself to paper, a more balanced account might have emerged but, as it was, six months of bottled-up resentment flowed across the pages of *In Quest of the Ashes*.

It has been suggested that the book was ghosted but the style is unmistakably that of Jardine's other published works – slightly pedantic and self-effacing, with a reluctance to refer to himself in the first person. The *Times* reviewer was obviously disappointed, saying that it was 'hardly a helpful book' and of Jardine's tactics he wrote somewhat cautiously, 'his position seems sound enough'. The reviewer also suggested in answer to Jardine's frequent complaints about the barracking that crowds might conceivably behave better if they were not provoked in the first place. This was an unusual approach to the problem from the English point of view. Hitherto the Australian ground authorities had been blamed for not keeping the customers under control, Jardine going so far as to say that it might be better to suspend the fixture until the responsible bodies had managed to improve the situation. Quite how 80,000 people were to be kept quiet was rather harder to say, but Jardine suggested notices posted in easily visible places saying that any misbehaviour would result in the automatic suspension of half an hour's play. *The Times* clearly thought that this was not the answer to the difficulty, and one suspects that Jardine only suggested it to illustrate his point that, if the crowds would not behave, it was better not to play at all.

All this is not to say that public opinion was turning against Jardine. Far from it. He was a national hero, cheered wherever he took the field and sympathised with for the ordeal he had been through. To the public it was simply a case of the Australians not being able to take a beating and, not having seen bodyline in action, the concept of unfair bowling was almost as incomprehensible to them as unfair batting.

At the end of April the Board of Control sent MCC a proposal for an amendment to the Laws which would put a stop to direct-attack bowling. MCC rejected the proposal and at the same time asked the Board of Control if they would please do something about the barracking problem. Their high-handed reply belied the fact that the whole affair was now causing a good deal of anxiety not only in inner cricket circles but also in diplomatic ones.

Correspondence published in E. W. Swanton's *Follow On* reveals how the British government were made aware of the strength of feeling in Australia. Sir Alexander Hore-Ruthven (the then Governor of South Australia) wrote to J. H. Thomas, (the Secretary for the Dominions) in June, presenting the Australian side of the argument and explaining that Australians felt they had been unfairly treated by both the English press and MCC. Thomas, who was regarded by his Labour party colleagues as an imperialist, was particularly keen to maintain cordial relations and intervened. The disagreement was a source of irritation to both governments, whose time was more than occupied by trying to deal with the Depression, and they were both annoyed with their respective cricketing bodies for having allowed the argument to get out of hand. I can find no record of Thomas' discussions with the MCC although, as Laurence Le Quesne states in *The Bodyline Controversy*, they undoubtedly took place. In fact hardly any records of discussions have survived, which is a shame, although they may not have held any astonishing secrets since it was one of those disagreements solved by informal chats rather than formal negotiations. Lord Hailsham, for instance, as both Secretary of State for War and President of MCC, was in an ideal position to have quiet words in a number of influential ears. This high-level connection between MCC and the Cabinet may explain why there was no formal discussion of bodyline at Cabinet meetings.

MCC's position was complicated; as the neutral figurehead of international cricket, sponsors of the English team and as a private club, any action they took was bound to be considered partial in one way or another. They held a rather half-hearted inquiry into the events of the winter. The testimonies of Jardine, the managers and several other players (though, significantly, not those of either Wyatt or Allen) were heard. The exact findings of the inquiry are not known but in their June cable to the Board of Control, MCC promised to keep an eye open for any unfair tactics during the 1933 season. Of course this was very far from an acknowledgement that the Australians had a point, but it does seem to suggest that Warner's report on the series was critical of Jardine and his tactics.

The potentially far-reaching consequences of Anglo-Australian disharmony became clear to the British Government shortly after the end of the tour. A representative of the Australian Government (Stanley Bruce) arrived in England to negotiate a loan conversion. Australia already owed Great Britain £500m but their economy was in a very bad way and they needed more. At a meeting with Bruce, Neville Chamberlain offered a further loan of £84m to be spread over a two-year period. Bruce demanded a much more rapid scheme of conversion and, what was more, at a lower rate of interest than they were paying on the existing loan. He pointed out that feeling in Australia was 'very strongly moved' and even 'explosive'.

Bodyline was by no means solely responsible for the anti-British feeling in Australia, as there had been a succession of wrangles over duties which Australia had unilaterally imposed on imported British goods – farm machinery mainly, but also such items as sheet glass, socks, egg-pulp and felt hats! These were emergency measures which the Australians felt justified in taking in view of their desperate economic situation and they had also devalued, thus making British goods even less competitive. The British Government, not unnaturally, found this unreasonable, and the Australians felt they were being unsympathetically treated. The marked fall in the sale of British goods at the time of the bodyline row may have been due as much to anti-British feeling as to the fact that the Australian consumer had to pay through the nose for his British egg-pulp and felt hats.

Bruce's request was challenging to say the least and, if Chamberlain had it in mind to tell the fellow to take his hands out of his pockets and accept his more than generous offer, Bruce took his breath away by saying that if he didn't get his money pretty quick, Australia might be forced to default in repayments on the existing loan.

The Cabinet seemed a bit shaken when Chamberlain reported Bruce's threat to them. For Australia to have defaulted would have been an act of economic suicide, but more importantly it would have set a dangerous precedent which might have had an unsettling effect on the whole of international trade. It was a very serious situation and President Roosevelt, no less, was said to be 'terrified of a default'. Chamberlain told his Cabinet colleagues that with a bit of a juggling it would be possible to accommodate the Australians without the legislation that would normally be necessary. It was essential that the proposal was not put before the House of Commons since anything that looked like submission to colonial threats would certainly have been thrown out. The cabinet decided that the loan should go through in secret. A month later, however, the Australian Government cancelled plans for any loan conversion and there the matter rested. It therefore seems that Stanley Bruce was over-dramatising the situation and there must be some doubt as to whether he had authority to make the threats that he did (Chamberlain suspected that he was trying to pull off a coup to further his career).

Bodyline thus added popular fuel to the political fire of disagreement that existed between the two countries. The argument over the import duties was far more significant politically and indeed, many people were directly affected by it, far more than could be said to have been affected by bodyline. The press, though, saw better copy in bodyline, which provided an opportunity for Australians to give vent to their resentment both in the press and in the cricket grounds themselves. Jardine noted in his book that he felt the barracking was not always directed solely at the players.

It has been suggested from time to time that bodyline very nearly caused a break-off of diplomatic relations, but such a move would have been in neither government's interests. Britain was having quite enough trouble with the nationalist movement in India, and to have fallen out with Australia at the highest level would have been poor Imperial policy. And Australia, being dependent on Britain for financial aid, would also have had nothing to gain from severing relations.

The idea that Australia tried to secede from the Empire seems to have emanated from reports of another argument going on at the time. There was a strong independence movement in the state of Western Australia which made frequent representations to the British Government. It was no more anti-British than it was anti-Australian; they simply thought that they would be better off on their own, and their campaign had nothing to do with cricket. A delegation was in London at around the time of the bodyline row.

Clearly, then, there were other threats to Imperial unity at the time and bodyline, in itself, was not the political menace that has been suggested. Nevertheless, J. H. Thomas said that it caused him more anxiety than anything else during his ministry.

As to the question of whether it was all worth it, the answer must be a resounding 'no', particularly in Jardine's case, although he never admitted as much, perhaps not even to himself. The hurt he suffered was deeper and more lasting than any knocks sustained by Woodfull and his men. In spite of the withdrawal of the 'unsportsmanlike' charge, the stigma was never completely removed, and once the law had been amended to prevent bodyline being used, the English victory of 1932–33 acquired a dubious value. This is a shame because England's was an excellent team performance. Jardines's captaincy was almost faultless and he inspired the team in a way that was remarkable given the cumbersome size of the party. Bob Wyatt remembers the united resolve to return to England unbeaten, and they very nearly did it. The English players's accounts of the tour all refer to the excellent team spirit and to the renowned Australian hospitality which, amazingly, was undiminished by the events on the field. But on whether the means justified the end, there is less agreement.

On the other question of whether England could have won without bodyline, opinions of those who were there are evenly divided. The form, for what it is worth, was as follows; Australia held the advantage in the first six batting places because of Bradman, and England had a slight advantage in the bowling department owing to Larwood's presence. The balance, however, was tilted slightly England's way by the fact that they batted right down to no. 9 or 10 whereas Australia only batted down to no. 7 or 8. As to the possible effectiveness of Larwood without bodyline, three factors need to be taken into account: his extraordinary pace throughout that particular series, his ability to get the ball up off a length and the Australian practice of walking across the stumps to play the ball. The first two qualities would have certainly brought him wickets, though how many is of course impossible to say. The injuries to Woodfall and Oldfield were caused by balls pitching on off and middle stumps, so we may assume that if Larwood had not used bodyline the Australians would have suffered plenty of bruises by 'walking into' him – more, perhaps, since the intimidatory bouncer would have come unexpected. The main effect of bodyline was to tame Bradman, but if it had not been used and he had averaged, say, 100 as opposed to 56, the extra runs coming from his bat would still not have been enough to affect the outcome of the series. Indeed, the almost incredible fact is that the English winning margins were so large that all the Australian players could have scored at a higher rate than their overall Test averages (Bradman 99.94, Woodfull 45.82, McCabe 48.36 etc) and on paper the result of the matches should have been the same.

9
The Other Abdication

Jardine was surprised and touched by the warmth with which he was greeted on his return. MCC gave him a five-star welcome when he arrived at Euston station. Several committee members were there to meet him, including Lord Hawke, Lord Lewisham and Sir Kynaston Studd, with Findlay, the secretary.

All along, he had expected MCC to place Imperial harmony before national loyalty, but in due course he was invited to captain England in the forthcoming Test series against the West Indies. His appetite for international cricket had abated considerably by then, but a refusal might well have been misinterpreted and under the circumstances he felt obliged to accept the job.

The first part of the 1933 season was a honeymoon period. He was a celebrity and much in demand. He was the principal guest at a Foyle's Literary Lunch where he was introduced ironically as 'The monster from the Antipodes ... Douglas The Killer' and the speech he made was typically Jardinian in its references to ancient Greece and the romance of cricket. He was cheered by a capacity Lord's crowd when he walked out to bat for MCC against the tourists and he was similarly received wherever he led Surrey onto the field. Happily, too, he regained his batting form and made hundreds against Sussex and Yorkshire.

His business commitments allowed him to make only a few Championship appearances and the Surrey side, as a result of being captained alternately by Fender, Jardine and Allom, suffered from acute cricketing schizophrenia and had an unsuccessful season. Jardine, however, proved to be one of the side's main run-getters, averaging 55 in his nine innings.

To the British public, bodyline was a figment of the spoilsport Australian imagination and, despite Warner's efforts to explain to his fellow committee members what he saw as the evils of the method, MCC stood firmly behind Jardine – for the time being.

It was not until the University match in July that officialdom was provided with a practical demonstration of bodyline. Farnes, the Cambridge fast bowler, took seven wickets in the match, bowling one batsman off his neck and causing another one to break his own wicket after being hit in the same place. From that point, opinion began slowly to change. There was a lot of mumbling about it being dull to watch – not dangerous, but dull. It was the same criticism that had been applied to leg-theory for years and, by making it, the critics avoided making a distinction between what they now saw to be Jardine's tactics in Australia and old-fashioned leg-theory. It ought to be said, too, that any bodyline that was bowled in England was, of necessity, more blatantly intimidating. Farnes and his fellow-practitioners could not rely on lightning-quick pitches and unpredictable bounce for results, they really had to bang the ball in short on the line of the batsman's body.

The depths of 'dullness' were reached in the second Test at Old Trafford, when Hammond had his chin cut open by Martindale. The West Indies had decided to give the new method a try in this match, it being the only one in the series of three in which they were able to play both their fast bowlers, Constantine and Martindale. They felt that bodyline would have to come from both ends if it was to have any chance of success. They were by no means confident that it would succeed, but they had been badly beaten in the first Test and the risk seemed justifiable. The Old Trafford wicket was one of the slowest the tourists had come across but they still managed to give the English batsmen a hairy time, particularly Hammond who, as well as having his chin cut, was hit on the back when he ducked into a ball from Constantine. 'If this is what the game has come to,' he is supposed to have said as he left the crease, 'it's time I bloody well got out.'

There was an element of 'feeling' in the West Indians' decision to use bodyline. Constantine and Martindale were fast, not as fast as Larwood and Voce but quick enough to hurry the best, and it seemed to them that some of the English pitches had been doped to take the edge off their attack. Of course they had, but with the object of frustating all bowlers, not just Constantine and Martindale. But the West Indies felt they had been unfairly treated and took action accordingly.

Learie Constantine's book, *Cricket and I* (1933), contains a frank chapter on how, when and why he used bodyline (he was quite happy to use the word). He explains, better perhaps than anyone before or since, the fast bowler's ambivalent attitude towards the batsman – the desire to frighten and to hurt but not to injure. It is probably difficult for those who only watch the game to detect any logic in that idea and Constantine's book is strongly recommended to them. Perhaps it is enough to say that there was as much bluster in MCC's assertion that it was inconceivable that an Englishman would bowl at the man as there was in Jeff Thomson's claim 40 years later that he liked to see blood dripping from the batsman's head. The truth has always lain somewhere between the two.

Constantine also said that both Jardine and Hammond had shown no great liking for the short stuff during the previous series in 1928. Jardine had demonstrated his feelings in the usual way, walking into the bowler's half of the wicket and patting the pitch. Relations between Jardine and the West Indians had been further soured by an incident in the second Test of that year. Jardine was on his way to his 83 when he played a ball from O. C. Scott to square leg and, as he started on his run, he slipped and broke his wicket. According to Constantine, umpire Morton's finger was on its way up when Jardine said firmly, 'I had completed my shot.' Quite correctly, though much to the West Indians' annoyance, the umpire ruled not out. (Many years later, the law was altered and a batsman would now be out in such a case.)

And so five years later, almost to the day, and while the Australian series was still under discussion, a full-scale bodyline attack was launched at the Englishmen. Jardine was the main target, of course, and even he must have known that he was due for it. In Jardine, Sutcliffe and Wyatt, though, England had three of the best players of fast, short-pitched bowling in the world. But Sutcliffe ran himself out when he was on 20, and Wyatt fell to a freak catch when he had made 18. The score was 134 for 4 when Ames came out to join Jardine. Ames was a fine player of fast bowling himself (he once hooked Larwood for six) and hung on bravely with his captain. He was clearly finding it tough going, though, and at one point Jardine called to him for all to hear, 'You get yourself down this end, Les. I'll take care of this bloody nonsense.'

Jardine played it superbly. He got right up on his toes, using his full height, and managed to play the ball with a dead bat straight down in front of him. Sometimes the point of contact was close to his face, but the bat would be there, perpendicular to the ground and controlled almost entirely by the left hand, the right hand being pulled away at the moment of impact.

After tea the pair had a respite from bodyline while the West Indians were waiting for the new ball, and in this period they were able to push the score along in comparative comfort. But once the 200 was up and the new ball taken, Constantine and Martindale resumed and Ames was soon caught fending a ball off his hip.

With the arrival of the next man, James Langridge, the attack was intensified by a fifth fielder being brought up into the leg trap. Jardine contrived to take most of the strike and looked as steady as ever, even if he was obliged to duck a couple of deliveries from Martindale. He appeared not to mind when another ball whizzed through an inch or so outside his chin. After 2 hours 50 minutes of Spartan batting he hit Martindale for 10 runs in one over and brought up his 50 in the process. Langridge was out at 234 but Robins managed to stay with his captain until the close.

The next morning Robins and Jardine continued their partnership and when Robins was out they had put on 140 in two hours. Jardine went in the next over (reluctantly, to a low catch at point) and the innings folded. England were left one short of the West Indies first innings total of 375.

Jardine's 127 took a little under five hours. He hit five fours and does not appear to have offered a chance. The pressures on him were such that it must be counted as one of his greatest innings. He had to score runs both for himself (he had only managed to pass 50 once in his last 11 Test innings) and for his side, who were definitely in trouble when he went out to bat. Above all though, he had to demonstrate that runs could be made against bodyline. It was just the sort of situation to bring out the best in him.

Historians have rightly pointed out that conditions at Old Trafford were vastly different from those experienced by the Australian batsmen six months previously. The pitch and the bowling were slower. Constantine wrote that if he and Martindale had bowled bodyline on the faster pitches of Lord's or the Oval, Jardine 'might have made his hundred but he would have had to adopt different tactics. He would have had to move to the off-stump or turn and hook. But to stand up and play defensive strokes as he did at Old Trafford would have been quite impossible.' By 'impossible' Constantine meant that Jardine would have been hit repeatedly and that, with the ball coming on more quickly, it would have been harder to control and a catch to the leg trap would have been offered sooner or later. He possessed the hook but had long since excluded it from his repertoire at the highest level, and it is unlikely that he would have used it against Constantine and Martindale under any circumstances.

Constantine suggested that moving across the stumps might have been another answer and, since Jardine's first movement against fast bowling was to bring his back foot across, it must be assumed that Constantine was advocating the more exaggerated Australian method which involved a proper 'walk' across. Not having seen the Australian series, Constantine was probably unaware that this method was doomed to failure, against the very fastest bowling anyway.

The fact that Jardine was one of the best leg-side players in the world made it unlikely that bodyline would be very effective in containing him. Added to this was an amazing *sang froid* which had enabled him to develop an excellent technique for controlling the fast, rising ball. Being tall, using a lightish bat and having a strong left wrist, he was able to alter his shot late and play the short ball down directly in front of him with a certainty unequalled at the time.

Having thwarted the West Indian bodyline attack, Jardine then used Clark to bowl it at them. The West Indians managed to play out time and the match was drawn.

Rather than being seen as a vindication of Jardine's argument, and indeed MCC's stated position, the demonstration served to add momentum to the sway of opinion against bodyline. *The Times*' correspondent, in his description of Jardine's innings, used for the first time the word 'bodyline' without either inverted commas or the prefix 'so-called', which was in itself a small acknowledgement that the Australians might have a point. *Wisden*'s report of the match contained the following sentence:

The fact that Jardine showed that it was possible to meet it without suffering physical injury or losing his wicket through any impatient or wild stroke, did not, however, make the sight of it any more welcome, and most of those watching it for the first time must have come to the conclusion that, while strictly within the law, it was not nice.

A week after the Old Trafford Test, Jardine was injured playing against Kent at The Oval. In the first over of the third day he took a brilliant catch to dismiss Woolley off Gover and almost immediately afterwards Ashdown cut a ball from the same bowler straight at Jardine in the gully. The ball hit him just below the right knee and he had to be helped from the field. The right knee was the one that had given him so much trouble in his Oxford days and, not wishing to take any chances with it, he played no more cricket that season.

The third Test against the West Indies saw Wyatt's return to the captaincy and significantly, there was no more bodyline. But MCC's position regarding the Australian Board of Control remained unchanged and, as a further demonstration of support for Jardine, they appointed him captain of the England side to tour India that winter. It was a brave move on MCC's part for, whatever the rights and wrongs of bodyline, the fact was that Jardine's presence in Australia had caused trouble, and there was a risk that the same thing might happen again in India. And if there was one place where the British government could do without an upsurge of anti-British feeling it was India. MCC would have been 'for it' if their loyalty to Jardine had turned out to be misplaced and it is interesting that they were not prevailed upon to choose another captain.

Laurence Le Quesne, in *The Bodyline Controversy*, quotes the MCC Main Committee minutes for 10 July, 1933: 'After a prolonged discussion it was decided to invite Mr D. R. Jardine [to captain the team in India] and to ask the President and Treasurer [Lords Hailsham and Hawke] of the MCC to have a talk with Mr D. R. Jardine when the official invitation is extended to him.' It seems more than likely that the purpose of the 'talk' was to advise Jardine of the possibly disastrous consequences of antagonising Indian crowds and Indian cricket officialdom.

In view of his declared dislike of political intervention in addition to his two previous experiences of touring, it is surprising that Jardine accepted the job. Two factors influenced his decision: the first was the prospect of seeing again the land of his birth; the second was the necessity, pointed out to him by friends, to show that he was not going to admit defeat over bodyline. To have rejected MCC's gesture of support might have looked like surrender.

Apart from Jardine, only Verity remained from the victorious 1932–33 side. The party was strong enough though, the other players were Walters, Valentine, Barnett, Townsend, James Langridge, Bakewell, Arthur Mitchell, Gregory, Harry Elliott, Nichols, J. H. Human, Levett, Clark and Marriott. 'Selection of such a team a disgusting insult to India. Will recommend tour be cancelled unless more stars added. Indian Cricket Board of Control.' was the message which fluttered through the MCC letter-box after the team was announced. But before another international storm could break, it was discovered that the cable had been sent by a clerk at the Indian Telegraph Office, who clearly did not want to miss out on all the cablegram fun that was going on at the time.

There had been two previous attempts to stage an Anglo-Indian Test series in India. The first in 1930–31 was cancelled because of the civil disobedience campaign, and the second in 1931–32 was called off because of threats of boycotts to all matches played in Bombay. However, the political situation was now thought to be stable enough to allow a tour to proceed.

The structure of Indian cricket was unwieldy, part Indian and part European controlled, and with the selectorial processes made difficult by the sheer size of the country. The most important influence was the participation and patronage of the wealthy native aristocracy. Relations between them and the governing bodies were not always smooth but had to be maintained in the mutual interest. The game needed the money and by providing it the Indians were able to gain a certain amount of political influence. But the great patrons, such as the Maharaja of Vizianagram or the Maharaja of Patiala, were no mere cynical exploiters of the game, they were passionate devotees. Patiala, for instance, ran his own private side at considerable expense. Top English professionals would be brought over to play for him, Sutcliffe, Hobbs and Larwood among others were on his payroll at various times, although Larwood claims he returned to England empty-handed after sitting in scented ante-rooms for three weeks and Hobbs, or more importantly his wife, Ada, did not care for the place at all.

The ordinary Indian cricketer did not have much chance of advancing himself unless he belonged to one of the big princely circuses, or unless he could force his way into one of the clubs in the major cities. To do the latter he would have to be either phenomenally talented or, harder still, socially acceptable. The system was the cause of much bitterness and resentment, particularly when it came to the selection of representative sides. The selection process is still fraught with jealousies and accusations of favouritism, but 50 years ago the situation was even worse. Decisions were taken by a committee of whom the majority of members were British, so you had Englishmen saying which Indians should play against England.

It was all part of the old idea that India was too large and its people too disparate to manage on its own. It could be argued that the selectors were impartial and that there was no State favouritism. Whether or not this was true in practice, even in theory the advantages of the system were lost on the majority of Indian cricket followers. It was precisely that kind of paternalism which was being so strongly called into question at the time.

The most sensitive issue that the selectors had to face was the captaincy. They had to decide whether to give the job to an Indian or a white man and in either case whether he should be the highest-ranking or the richest or simply the best cricketer. In the event they made a wise choice and as popular a one as was possible – C. K. Nayudu, an aggressive all-rounder who had performed well as India's captain in their only previous Test. He held the rank of major and was socially well-connected.

Oddly enough, Jardine had himself been a candidate for the job at one time. It was thought in 1930, when the first Test tour was being planned, that Jardine might be going to settle in India, in which case he would have been a good man to lead the first All-India side. Much as he would have liked to live there, an old tradition of the Raj prevented him from doing so. Every third generation of an English 'Indian' family had to follow a career at home in England. The fear was that the family might lose its Englishness and become totally naturalised or, even worse, might start to turn brown. Jardine's father and grandfather had spent their working lives in India and so, whether or not he believed the superstition, he obeyed it at the expense of his personal happiness, for he loved India.

There was no question of his approaching the tour as any sort of a holiday. He intended, as always, to win, and he impressed on his relatively inexperienced team that nothing but total commitment would do. The Indians were stronger than they had been 18 months earlier, and this time they would also have the home advantage. The itinerary was to be extremely tough – 50 matches in 5½ months. And with only 14 men in the party, the team would occasionally be comprised of those men still standing.

Jardine's attitude was made clear to the opposition even before the team arrived. He cabled from the ss *Mooltan* to Karachi where the first matches were to be played and asked for details of the ground conditions – length of matting wicket, height of sight-screens, state of outfield etc. The Indians were taking things just as seriously, it seemed. A message was radioed to Jardine from Nayudu, its tone jovially menacing: 'Wait until you meet me.'

The team arrived at Bombay amid great excitement. They received, among many others, a telegram of welcome from the Viceroy, Lord Willingdon, himself an ex-first-class cricketer. Jardine threw himself into the diplomatic side of his job with a relish that had been notably absent in Australia. He responded to the extravagant welcome accorded the MCC party by making a broadcast speech. That he managed to do this with the crowd jostling him and often drowning out his words was a source of amazement to many, but then he had nothing but the warmest of feelings towards Indian crowds. This is an extract from the speech which may or may not have been heard over the air waves:

> We are delighted that we have landed at Bombay first. Kipling called Bombay the Queen of cities and I have a great love for the place.... We bring to you old friends of cricket in India a message of welcome from the premier cricket club of England. I understand that there has been some disappointment at the absence of some cricketers with great names who are not with us, but I assure you that the team is the best that the Marylebone Club could send. It is not for me to extol the virtues of my team but you will have the pleasure of seeing men whose names will be household names in the cricket world in the future.... Finally, may I express the hope and belief that both on and off the field this team, which the Marylebone Cricket Club has sent to India, will be deservedly popular, for we represent the goodwill which

the Premier Club bears to all lovers of cricket throughout this great Indian Empire. No one could be more jealous of their good name than myself or more sensible of the honour done to me by the Marylebone Cricket Club when they asked me to lead their team in the land of my birth.

Even in 1933 such sentiments had to be passionately believed if the speaker wanted a sympathetic hearing. There is no doubt that Jardine did believe them and that he saw his role on this tour as a political one as well as a cricketing one.

He said on a number of occasions that too much was expected of cricket tours in the way of forging links between different peoples, but in the case of India he seemed to make an exception. As the team travelled about the sub-continent, he gave full vent to his slightly anachronistic (but unquestionably well-meaning) feelings about the Empire and the brotherhood of Anglo-Indian cricketers. At countless civic receptions, banquets and 'at homes' he spoke lucidly and entertainingly about the far-reaching benefits of the tour. He paid many tributes to the charm and the ability of Indian cricketers and the sportsmanship of the crowds. He predicted that India would one day be pre-eminent in international cricket (a prophesy which in terms of one-day cricket, came true exactly 50 years later) and he hoped that when that happened, her cricketers would not forget about the club who started it all.

It seemed incredible that in Australia he had been thought a poor speaker, but then everyone performs better if they feel the audience is with them. He felt at home in India where the late Victorian/Edwardian way of life survived, unlike Australia where, as Bruce Harris wrote, 'free and easiness runs riot'. The frequent use of Kipling in his speeches characterised his old-fashioned values (Kipling was thought of as a bit of a joke by Jardine's contemporaries, or those of similarly discerning tastes, anyway). Photographs taken on the tour show a relaxed and happy man, an image which contrasted with the one projected in the Australian photographs of a rather hunted individual who seemed to be thinking as he faced the press, 'They'll get me if I don't get them first.'

His batting form was as good as it always was at the start of a tour, and he made a hundred in the first first-class match, against the relatively minor province of Sind.

Nayudu carried out his threat when he made 116 against the tourists in his first encounter with them. The merit of the achievement was rather doubtful, however, since it was Jardine's policy at the start of the tour to allow himself a thorough examination of the likely Test candidates. Consequently, when Marriott had Nayudu dropped twice in his first two overs, he was quickly taken off and replaced by a less dangerous bowler. The Indians played into Jardine's hands in this respect, the best players following the MCC team about the country and strengthening the sides of this or that province so that local sides were seldom more than 50 per cent local. They came to be known as 'Nayudu's Roving Circus'. It defeated the object of the exercise from the Indian point of view, which was to give local players the opportunity of learning by playing against the best. A number of people, including Jardine, pointed this out, but the fear was that the MCC side would be far too strong for most provincial sides.

It could not have been easy for the MCC players to concentrate their minds on winning when some of the distractions offered them were irresistible. Maharajas, Nawabs and European dignitaries vied with each other in providing hospitality for the team, and a certain amount of 'tactical' entertaining took place. According to E. W. Docker's *The History of Indian Cricket*, when the MCC were playing against Patiala there was a banquet at the Maharaja's palace which lasted until three or four in the morning, then at seven the players were woken up and taken on a deer hunt, and after that there was a full day's cricket. Another writer, Jarmani Das, stated confidently that 'members of the British team indulged in merry-making with the dancing girls and drank Scotch whisky and the choicest wines.' It may not have been quite as orgiastic as that, but who knows? With 'Bouncer' Human and 'Hopper' Levett in the party things must have been fairly lively. There was a second session of merry-making during the match, followed this time by a panther hunt. The match itself was rather slow and dull and was drawn.

As if to repay the Maharaja for his kindness, Jardine invited him to play for MCC in the next match against Delhi and District C.A. Being an MCC member, the Maharaja was perfectly entitled to do so, and in fact he appears to have been made an honorary member of the party, for there is a photograph of him, tubby and turbaned, wearing the famous blue touring blazer with the St

George and Dragon crest. However (again according to Docker) no less a person than the Viceroy thought that it was a bad idea for him to turn out for MCC and communicated his feelings to Jardine. Jardine thought this meddlesome and, if such a concept had existed then, he might even have thought it racist, so he refused to reconsider his selection. He wasn't going to be mucked about by any Viceroy, least of all a Cantab Viceroy. The Vicereine was also said to have tried to persuade him but was equally unsuccessful. The Maharaja played and made 54. The early history of Indian cricket is peppered with instances of Maharajas making fifties and then being out shortly afterwards, but Patalia was not at all a bad player and his innings was one of genuine merit. He was some way past his best at the age of 42, but with 360 concubines to look after, that is not altogether surprising.

Jardine had another brush with the Viceroy indirectly in the very next match. MCC built up a huge first-innings lead over the Viceroy's XI, and before the home side batted again, the groundsmen rolled the pitch for a good 20 minutes. The MCC ruling allowed for only seven minutes' rolling and so Jardine demanded an apology. Eventually he got one but he would not, he said, have taken the field without it even if the King of England were playing on the other side. The home side made only 63 in their second innings and it could not have been entirely coincidental that Maurice Nichols bowled a particularly fiery spell of 45 balls, 5 wickets for 7 runs. There were plenty of short deliveries but the field-setting, it seems, was orthodox. Nevertheless, there were cries of 'Bodyline' from students in the enclosure.

It was another example of Jardine's strict adherence to the rules, a demonstration not so much of fussiness but of his extraordinary reverence for the Laws as laid down by MCC, and of the Victorian idea of the sanctity and antiquity of the game. It was as if God had framed the laws and presented them on tablets of stone to some ancient prophet in an MCC tie. And, like the Ten Commandments, the Laws could not be 'got round' or bent. 'Thou shalt roll the pitch in between innings for no longer than seven minutes.' No one was above the laws, not the Viceroy, not even the King-Emperor. The fact that MCC eventually beat the Viceroy's XI by an innings and 208 runs was, in Jardine's view, quite beside the point.

Although there were a number of such upsets, the feeling

between the players was invariably friendly and the ultimate success of the tour was due entirely to this. Nevertheless, the matches, particularly the more important ones, were definitely played with the gloves off, and with four such fierce bowlers as Clark, Nichols, Nissar and Amar Singh, there were some nasty moments for batsmen on both sides. There were, in fact, more injuries than on the bodyline tour even though hardly any proper bodyline was actually bowled.

The Indians were not ones to capitulate meekly against fast bowling; they had a go at it. In fact they had a go at most bowling, and that was their main weakness. Their cricket was hot-blooded in every department. Fielders sometimes made no effort to save runs and at other times they threw wayward or unnecessarily hard returns (during the first Test, Amar Singh threw so hard to the bowler, Jamshedji, that he was unable to continue for several minutes). Their strokeplay, when it came off, was exhilarating to watch. Slow bowling was very much in its infancy, and one Indian official, making a speech at a reception, bemoaned the fact that schoolboys who practised slow bowling were considered cissies. By far the greater part of their bowling was fast or medium.

The English batsmen countered the pace attack in their various ways, and Jardine was not slow to spot the protective qualities of the solar topee in this respect. They had all been equipped with these articles at the start of the tour. In one of the early matches, Bakewell was walking out to open the innings in a cap, but when Jardine noticed that he was about to face the bowling of Nissar, he called the batsman back and made him swap the cap for a topee. The sixth ball of Nissar's first over cracked into the brim of Bakewell's topee, leaving the batsman entirely unharmed. Photographs show that thereafter, topees were the standard rig for the English team.

The fact that each side possessed a pair of fast bowlers of approximately equal menace probably served to maintain a balance and prevent any acrimonious feelings. They were able to match each other bouncer for bouncer in a way that had not been possible in Australia the previous year. The sportsmanship of the two sides was of an impressively high standard. Two random examples illustrate this. The first happened in the First Test when Amarnath had just completed his maiden Test hundred. Two spectators ran onto the field to garland the batsman. Nayudu, his partner, who had just completed a run when he saw the invaders, set off down the pitch intending to shoo them away and also to congratulate Amarnath. At the point when he left his ground, the ball was still in play and was being returned to the wicket-keeper, Elliott. Elliott took the ball and, as a compliment to a good piece of fielding, whipped the bails off. He then realised that Nayudu was out of his ground, but Jardine firmly stopped him from appealing and allowed Nayudu to get back to his crease in his own time. It was not done for fear of provoking the crowd – Jardine had taken on tougher crowds than that – but was a purely sporting gesture. Nayudu responded in the next Test when India were struggling to bat out time and avoid an innings defeat. At the fall of each Indian wicket, rather than using up the maximum time allowed, the outgoing batsmen crossed with the incoming batsmen on the field.

The two men had a high regard for one another. Jardine said that he had learnt from Nayudu's captaincy and, as a batsman, compared him to a right-handed Woolley. Nayudu reckoned Jardine to be the best tactician in the game. Nayudu gave long service to cricket in India, and he suffered a number of politically motivated 'hate' campaigns with dignity. He could be awkward, though, as when he refused to play under Wazir Ali's captaincy in 1935. And Bob Wyatt remembers batting against him once when he needed one for his hundred off the last ball of a dead match. Nayudu deliberately bowled wide of the stumps to prevent him scoring. It was odd, because there was no ill feeling between the two off the field. Nayudu was by far the best man to lead India and, under him, it was generally thought that they had the potential to win a Test if not the series.

There was great excitement, therefore, before the first Test in Bombay. Preparations had been going on for weeks on the Esplanade Maidan ground. Special restaurants had been built and also a new, two-tiered stand which held 7,000. It looked rather precarious and, with only three exits for the spectators on top, it seemed a very risky eight rupees' worth for the day. A crowd of Australian proportions packed the ground before the start of play. The band was playing and the flags were fluttering. Let *The Times of India* take up the story: 'The stage was set for the greatest cricket drama in Indian history. Then Jardine, at the head of his men, left the pavilion and a nipple (*sic*) of applause went along the line of tents.'

The Indian batting was disappointing. Eight of the side got into double figures but none got as far as 40. England in their reply made the game safe with a big total (Walters 78, Valentine 136 and Jardine 60). India needed 219 to avoid an innings defeat and started badly, losing two early wickets. But then a thrilling partnership followed between the 22-year-old Lala Amarnath, playing in his first Test, and Nayudu. They added 186 and, as we have seen, Amarnath's century caused wild jubilation (the band even struck up 'God Save The King'). Sadly, it was his only hundred in his long Test career (but 50 years later, his younger son, Mohinder, enjoyed a similar triumph when he won the Man of the Match award in the World Cup Final of 1983). That was the extent of the Indian success, and they went from 207 for 2 to 258 all out. England were left with only 40 to make in the fourth innings. With a storm about to break any second it was not certain that they would have time to do it, but Walters and Barnett slogged out and won the game in seven and a bit overs.

The game was followed with great interest throughout the country. As well as the quarter of a million or so people who were actually present, there were many who listened to the broadcast commentaries and even more who read the extraordinarily lengthy reports of E. H. D. Sewell in *The Times of India*. Never can a sports correspondent have been given as much space as Sewell was over the months of the tour. His reports sometimes ran to over 7,000 words, and in addition to this, he covered the matches for *The Times* in London. It was an output of Victorian proportions. His dispatches read like leaves from the diary of an old Imperial adventurer. He made liberal use of Indian words and expressions, as in the tantalising remark, 'Amar Singh bowled round the wicket and gave the batsmen plenty of dikh' or in the evocative 'A delay after tiffin was caused by a screw coming loose in Barnett's boot.'

His estimation of Jardine as a batsman and as a captain was high and not once did he criticise his tactics. In fact, all along he had nothing but praise for all the English players, while the shortcomings of the local Indian sides irritated him increasingly. The progress of his relationship with Jardine is interesting to follow. Early on, it seems that Jardine could do no wrong. After one aggressive display of cutting, driving and hooking, Sewell wrote that he was 'in danger of becoming known as the Jessop of India'. But in the second half of the tour such compliments became noticeably more scarce, and finally non-existent. There was no actual criticism, merely coolness. The turning point seems to have been a hunting trip they both went on as guests of the Maharaja Scindia of Gwalior. They had to cover a certain amount of rough ground, some of it on their hands and knees, and it may well be that Jardine was not quite as respectful to Sewell as the latter felt his 61 years merited. Anyway, for whatever reason, a strictly factual account of Jardine's doings was related to the readers of *The Times of India* from that point and, by the end of the tour, Sewell was recommending that Percy Chapman be re-instated as captain of England for the coming series against Australia (Chapman had finished one hundred and thirty-seventh in the previous season's batting averages).

The hunting trip referred to was one of nearly a dozen that Jardine undertook. There was no shortage of invitations for so distinguished a guest, and the facilities that the Maharajas offered were, it seems, a big-game hunter's dream. It was a point of honour with them that no guest should leave without having shot something. Jardine was a fairly good shot and so no rigging was necessary in his case. He accounted for a fair number of animals and his bag at the end of the tour included a lion, a tiger, a panther, several stags, a bear and innumerable smaller creatures. The rest of the team managed to reduce the animal population still further though none, with the possible exception of Marriott (a tiger and three crocodiles), was as successful as Jardine. Two hunts in which most of the party were involved resulted in beaters being severely mauled by wounded animals.

There was very little free time and such jaunts were always short. Jardine did manage, when he was in Bombay, to visit his childhood haunts and he even sought out his old servant, Lala Sebastien. He had photographs taken to record their reunion and he also found time to take the old man to the Sewri cemetery so that he could lay a wreath on his wife's grave. After Lala Sebastien had paid his respects, he said he felt unwell and asked Jardine to walk on ahead, saying that he would catch up in a few minutes. Jardine tactfully withdrew, thinking that he wished to be alone with his thoughts for a while. He waited, and then returned to find that the old man had collapsed. Jardine got him to hospital but he died shortly afterwards.

The second Test began under the threat of a boycott. The match was to be played in Calcutta and local cricket followers, annoyed at the lack of Bengali representation in the Indian side, had announced their intention to stay away. Attendances were down on the Bombay match but it could not be said to have been a boycott. The match followed a similar pattern to the previous one – India fighting first to avoid an innings defeat and then having to attempt to occupy the crease for as long as possible. Thanks to exhibitions of maddening patience from the Nayudu brothers (C.K. 38 in $2\frac{1}{2}$ hours and C.S. 15 in $2\frac{1}{4}$ hours), they managed to use up all but the last half-hour of the final day. England needed 82 to win and did not go for them.

Jardine made 61 in his only innings. He had looked set for a hundred when he was out in a curious way. Mushtaq Ali, playing in his first Test, was put on to bowl to him. Ali was so delighted with his new topee which bore the crest of the national team that he was unwilling to remove it, even for bowling. As his arm came over, it knocked against the brim of the new headgear, causing the ball to be slower and shorter. Jardine was effectively beaten in the air, he hit too soon and C. K. Nayudu at cover took the catch.

This match ended what was, for Jardine, a highly uncharacteristic run of dropped catches. Shortly before the first Test he had sprained his left wrist, and no sooner had that recovered than he injured his right hand. As invariably happens in such cases, the ball seemed to follow him around wherever he placed himself. In the Bombay Presidency match, he dropped two catches off successive deliveries. But then in the Calcutta Test he made up for it by taking five good ones. (On the bodyline tour he had taken more test catches than anybody including the wicket-keeper – nine to Ames' eight. And on the Indian tour he took more than either wicket-keeper. His rate of catches per Test is 1.2 as opposed to Cowdrey's 1.1 and Hammond's 1.3.)

After the second Test the circus moved to Benares, where MCC were due to play the Maharaja of Vizianagram's XI. The 'home' side was culled from all over India and included six players from the Calcutta Test. The wicket was a matting one such as the tourists had had to play on from time to time and on which they were none too keen, especially the bowlers, who found their run-ups impeded by having to step from grass onto mat as they approached the stumps. This particular mat was, for some reason, navy blue.

It was a low-scoring game and MCC were left to make the highest score of the match in the fourth innings. They started badly but then Jardine and Townsend shared a useful partnership which brought MCC to within easy reach of victory. But in a dramatic last few overs they collapsed and were beaten by 14 runs. The main reason for this, their only defeat of the tour, was that the captain of India got the wickets of Nichols, Jardine and Verity, all lbw; the decision being made in each case by the same umpire. Jardine was not at all pleased.

The umpire was the veteran all-rounder, Frank Tarrant of Victoria, Middlesex, MCC and Patiala. Like his ancestor, 'Tear 'em' Tarrant, he was one of that much-maligned type, the cricket mercenary. He was employed at the time not, as was uncharitably suggested, by the Maharaja of Vizianagram but by the Maharaja of Patiala. He did have close contacts with many princes on account of his talent for spotting a good yearling, and he later made a great deal of money buying and selling racehorses in India and in Australia. Whether or not his decisions were influenced by factors other than the appeals of C.K. Nayudu is impossible to say, but his Indian connections were well known to the MCC team and so, if he was going to assist the home team, he would surely have found a more subtle means of doing so.

To 'Vizzy', a win over MCC must have been the proudest achievement of his life. He was chaired from the field all the way back to his palace, even though his contribution to the victory had been modest. Such moments cannot be bought, although not everybody would have agreed with that at the time. Jardine seemed to bear him no ill-will since he went off on a shooting trip with him immediately after the match.

Ten days later the English opening batsmen's hearts sank as they walked out to bat at Secunderabad and found that there behind the stumps again was none other than 'the Maharaja's friend', Frank Tarrant. There was very nearly a repeat performance and the home side must have known they were onto a good thing since Sewell counted 12 leg-before appeals in quarter of an hour. In spite of 10 lbw decisions going againt MCC, the match was drawn slightly in their favour. The tally of lbw's in the last two matches in which Tarrant had stood was 14 against the Englishmen and four against the Indians. But Tarrant had also stood in the first two Tests, and there the tally was five against England and six against India.

Jardine felt that some sort of action was called for. It was cable time again. He notified Lord's of the situation and asked for guidance which came a short while later. It is not known what was said in any of the cables as the press were not told, and we only know that they were sent at all because Sir Stanley Jackson let it slip while addressing the annual meeting of the Yorkshire Club.

The upshot was that the Indian Board of Control informed Tarrant that he would not be required to stand in the third Test since his eyesight was defective. Tarrant made furious protestations, of course, and said that Jardine was just making a fuss because he didn't like being given out. Nobody took much notice of him, though, and he was replaced at Madras by J. B. Higgins, the ex-Worcestershire amateur.

The barracking, which hitherto had only been sporadic and on nothing like the scale of Australian barracking, became more voluble in the third Test. The crowd was initially roused when Clark laid out Naoomal Jeoomal. The Indian opener had to be carried from the field and was unable to take any further part in the match. Batsmen on both sides had been hit before without any substantial reaction resulting, but a significant factor in this case was the absence through illness of Mohammed Nissar. This meant that the balance of fast bowling power was tilted in England's favour – India did not have the means to retaliate. At the end of Clark's destructive over, he went to his position on the boundary whereupon someone threw a stone at him. He quietly picked it up and placed it outside the rope, an act certain to enrage an Australian crowd but which silenced this one.

Jeoomal's absence did not greatly alter the result of the match, which England won by 202 runs. They were only once in any trouble, in their first innings when they were 208 for 7, but Jardine, with a three-hour 65, was helped by Verity to repair the damage. The Indian first-innings total was 190 short of England's but Jardine very sensibly did not enforce the follow-on. England batted again and Jardine declared, leaving India 452 to win. They never looked like getting them.

Jardine's scores against India, including the 1932 Test, were 79, 85 not out, 60, 61, 65, 35 not out (average 96.25). India, with all their brilliant potential, had the misfortune to come up against Jardine at his methodical best in all four matches. He had always been one of the more disheartening sights for the bowling side as he approached the wicket, but India seemed to suffer more than other sides. Faced with having to bowl at Jardine in the first Test, Mohammed Nissar was seized by stomach pains at the start of his run and had to be assisted from the field. His captaincy, too, was at its most meticulous on the Indian tour. When choosing ends for his opening bowlers, he even took into consideration the direction in which the grass had been flattened by the roller on its final run.

With the Test series over and won, the last leg of the tour took the MCC team to Ceylon. It was not a happy fortnight. On the second day of the match against All Ceylon there was a fair bit of noise coming from students in the one-rupee enclosure. The remarks were mostly aimed at their own players, but Jardine took exception and held up play. This had the effect of turning the crowd against him and the whistles and catcalls started. At the next interval Jardine insisted that the police remove the main offenders. This was reluctantly agreed to and eight people were ejected (having had their one rupees refunded). Hardly anyone turned up to watch the last day's play.

There was more trouble two days later when half the MCC side failed to arrive in time for the start of a one-day match against Galle. The players were being driven the 75 miles from Colombo in four taxis. Play was due to start at 11 and by 12, only three of the cars had turned up. Jardine's party was stuck about 10 miles from the ground. Not entirely surprising perhaps for, as the *Ceylon Observer* pointed out, 'They are the about the most disgraceful cars that could be found ... The car in which Jardine was travelling, for instance, had several punctures on the way, and carried no spare tyres or tubes. Later, with so many punctures, the tubes, it is said, commenced to rip.' The stranded party was offered lifts by passers-by but, in order to make a point perhaps, Jardine said that he would wait until the repairs were carried out. They turned up two hours late. 'MCC Team Disappoint Galle Crowd' ran the headline in the local paper.

The next day Verity and Barnett, while travelling in another disgraceful car, were involved in a crash and were unable to play in the final match against an India and Ceylon XI. This match saw the ugliest incident of the tour. Towards the end of MCC's second innings, Clark and Marriott, the last pair, were trying to give some respectability to the team's worst batting performance. Since they were two of the worst batsmen in the history of first-class cricket, however, they weren't having much success. Clark decided that there was no point in mucking about any longer and at the end of an over he began to roughen up a spot on a length in line with the leg stump. His action momentarily paralysed the other people on the field, so extraordinary was the sight of this batsman ploughing up the wicket with his studs. One of the umpires was the first to find words and asked him what he thought he was doing. Clark made no reply but prodded the spot with the corner of his bat and returned to his crease. The partnership was broken shortly afterwards and the teams came off.

Valentine, who was captaining the side in Jardine's absence, told Clark to go and apologise to the opposing captain but Clark refused, claiming that he had merely been patting down a spot. Valentine and Marriott then went to the home dressing room and expressed abject apologies. These were accepted and the teams took the field again.

MCC then brought off what had seemed to be an impossible win with (and this must have been especially galling for the losers) Clark taking 4 for 38. Nobby Clark was a highly temperamental character who nevertheless behaved well enough under Jardine. He was notably absent from the side that played the final match of the tour (a specially organised game at Bombay, the proceeds of which were to go to victims of a recent earthquake), but he received no public reprimand and was chosen to play for England in the 1934 series against Australia.

The MCC party left Ceylon with some relief and sailed for Bombay to play the charity match, and then home. There had been speculation in the English press about whether or not Jardine would continue to captain Surrey and England. Arthur Gilligan, writing in the *News Chronicle*, believed that the Surrey Club had sent three telegrams to Jardine in India asking him if he wished to continue but they had received no reply. It was a measure of how highly Surrey valued his services, knowing as they must have done that he would be unlikely to play full-time.

As for the England selectors, they would not have required a definite commitment from Jardine so early in the year, but it seems that they were giving considerable thought to his position. A hard series against Australia lay ahead and there simply was not another candidate in Jardine's class. On this there was general agreement, but Warner fervently believed that Jardine should not be re-appointed and he had managed to gain some support, his point being that the restoration of friendly relations between cricketers of the two countries was more important than the retention of the Ashes. In a letter (published in E. W. Swanton's *Sort of a Cricket Person*) to Sir Alexander Hore-Ruthven, the then Governor of South Australia, Warner wrote:

> The real trouble is Jardine. Is he to be Capt.? At present I say 'No' unless he makes a most generous public gesture of friendliness and then I am not sure I would trust him. He is a queer fellow. When he sees a cricket ground with an Australian on it he goes mad! He rose to his present position on my shoulders, and of his attitude to me I do not care to speak. It is hoped he may retire at the end of the Indian tour, but in many quarters here – where they do not know the truth – he is a bit of a hero. If he is captain in First Test and is not friendly he will not capt. in the 2nd but I would not have him at all.

On 5 March the Surrey Club issued a statement to the effect that Jardine had told them that he was unlikely to be able to play regularly and that he thought it better to appoint a regular player as captain. With great reluctance the club had agreed and E. R. T. Holmes had accepted the captaincy.

On 10 March the majority of the English team sailed for home while Jardine went off for a month's shooting in Mysore with 'Vizzy', and then on to Torai and Nepal. He deserved a holiday after playing cricket almost solidly for two years. And although he hadn't had the barrackers to cope with on the Indian tour, there had been other strains. Shortly after the second Test he was told that his father was seriously ill with influenza. Contrary to expectations, M.R. recovered, but his 90-year-old mother, who lived with him, caught it and died.

On 31 March the *Evening Standard* published an announcement by Jardine: 'I have neither the intention nor the desire to play cricket against Australia this summer.' It was a puzzlingly blunt way to inform MCC that he was not going to be available, for he was and remained a devoted, loyal member of the club. He certainly had no great respect or liking for some of the old buffers in charge at Lord's but he knew well enough that they had supported him when it had not always been easy for them to do so. However, since the very first cable had been dispatched by the Australian Board of Control 14 months earlier, he had had to live with the possibility that MCC might abandon him at any moment. The pressure on him must have increased as time went by and he may have felt that it was better to resign before he was asked to do so. Alternatively, MCC may have contacted him in secret, asking for an assurance that, if selected, he would not use the bodyline tactics. It may even have been that, like Larwood and Voce, he was asked to apologise for using those methods. This would certainly explain the tone of his announcement. It would also explain why, after indicating to Surrey that he might be able to play one or two matches, he decided that he had had enough of first-class cricket altogether.

A third possible reason, and the one which his eldest daughter believes to be the correct one, was that he simply could not afford to spend another summer playing cricket. Before leaving on the Indian tour he had become unofficially engaged to be married. With new responsibilities, the need to earn a living was more pressing than keeping the Australians in their place. His future father-in-law, Sir Harry Peat, was keen for him to apply himself to some sort of career, preferably the law, since that was what he was qualified for. But Jardine preferred to supplement his bank clerk's income by signing up to write reports on the forthcoming Tests against Australia for the *Evening Standard.*

And so, at the age of only 33, he retired from competitive cricket. His record as England's captain was: played 15, won 9, lost 1, drawn 5. He scored 1296 runs in 33 innings at an average of 48. Those figures establish him among the very best in both categories: no-one, with the exceptions of Len Hutton and, possibly, Peter May, has succeeded so consistently both as a captain and as a batsman. But the fact is that he did not play quite enough to be considered among the great. One more series against Australia would have done it. Had he played in 1934 it is extremely unlikely that England would have lost the series and his standing would have remained to this day unchallenged. But it was not to be.

10
The Stigma Borne with Dignity

When the Australians came in 1934, they found Jardine in the press box. This made life easier for them and also for those attempting to heal the wounds of bodyline but the public were not keen on the arrangement. 'We want you out there, Jardine,' called a voice from the crowd as Bradman neared 300.

A feature of his writing from the start of his journalistic career was his generosity towards the players. He felt very strongly that the game was a great deal harder in the middle than in the pavilion, and he invariably excused a rash piece of play as one of those things that happen in the heat of a Test match. On the other hand he was merciless in his treatment of officials, especially selectors. Their mistakes were described in minute detail. The first blunder he discussed was the treatment of Larwood. Having recovered from his foot injury, Larwood had been playing for Notts, but just before the first Test he had declared himself unfit and consequently he was not selected.

Before the side for the second Test was to be picked, Jardine wrote an article for the *Evening Standard* in which he said that if Larwood was to be chosen his selection must be unconditional and there should be no restrictions on his fieldplacing. The chairman of selectors, Sir Stanley Jackson ('Whiskers', as Jardine used to refer to him privately) replied to the article saying that if Larwood was picked, he, like everyone else, would be under instructions from no-one but his captain. The captain, though, was Bob Wyatt, who disliked bodyline and would not have allowed Larwood to bowl it. The fact that Jardine thought it necessary to condemn so vehemently the idea of extracting some kind of promise from Larwood suggests that he suspected that something of the sort was going on.

It was, of course, Sir Julian Cahn, the then president of Notts, approached Larwood confidentially and explained that if he apologised for his Australian tactics, it would considerably increase his chances of playing again for England. Larwood refused, then ruled himself out completely by authorising the publication of an article in his name which appeared in the *Sunday Dispatch* just before the side was picked. 'I have definitely made up my mind not to play against the Australians in this or any of the Tests. I doubt if I shall ever play against them again – at least in big cricket.' The pressure on Larwood had been steadily building and it was with a sense of some relief that he pulled out of the 'decider' between himself and Bradman.

The announcement was not entirely unexpected, since Carr had hinted in an article in the *Evening Standard* that Larwood might not wish to play. In this article, which appeared soon after Jardine's, he re-stated the arguments and added that his own club was attempting to prevent him from using bodyline. This argument over restrictions was purely one of principle, as Larwood had more or less given up bodyline. His reduced pace since his foot operation and the quality of English pitches combined to make it not a worthwhile method of attack. He was also doing very well with ordinary off-theory (6 wickets for one run in a recent spell against Lancashire).

The articles by Carr and Jardine would have reached a large readership and they had a considerable effect on public opinion, which is never particularly well disposed towards selectors. Incidentally, the *Evening Standard's* team of writers consisted of Jardine and Bruce Harris, who favoured the continuance of bodyline, and C. B. Fry and E. W. Swanton who disapproved of it but did not actually say so.

Neither Jardine, Larwood nor Voce played in any of the Tests and the eventual Australian victory was received with only qualified satisfaction in the Australian press. But interest in the series was as intense as ever. Film companies competed for the rights to the matches, and barrage balloons were put up round Trent Bridge to stop pirate film crews filming the play from the air. The company who bought the rights also erected searchlights in order to dazzle out the cameras of rival crews.

The front page of Jardine's paper was devoted to details of play on each Test match day, even when nothing of any great consequence had happened. Jardine's reports were written in the present tense, as seems to have been customary in the popular press then. To begin with his style was suspiciously 'snappy', but as the series progressed he seems to have been left to his own devices and a more lucid and considered prose is allowed to stand.

He also signed up as a commentator with an Australian radio station to do a six-minute live summary of play during the tea interval on each Test match day. Jardine wrote a book on the series, too, *Ashes and Dust* (acknowledgements to Bruce Harris for help with the proofs). In it, he continued his attack on the selectors:

> The blunder of taking the field with only one fast bowler, which was to be repeated in the fourth Test match at Leeds, is easily explained by Sir Stanley Jackson's naive admission after the last Test match that: 'Things have changed tremendously since I played. We never thought of having more than one fast bowler in the side.' For all that, it does not seem much to expect the Chairman of a Selection Committee to know that the last rubber in Australia was won with three fast bowlers.

Warner had removed himself from the selection committee by then, with some sense of relief one imagines, and poor old 'Whiskers' was now under fire. (M. R. Jardine had hammered his bowling in the '92 Varsity match and now D.R.J. was attacking his chairmanship.)

Jardine was absolutely right to criticise the lack of fast bowling, as the Australians really did seem to have a weakness against it at this time. In the 1934 series, fast bowling on average took a wicket every 9.86 overs whereas the spinners only struck once in 16.76 overs. Jardine noticed that some of the Australian batsmen edged away from Clark and Farnes – Woodfull, Bradman and Darling in particular, while Ponsford, as always, turned his back on anything short. Bradman began the tour as though he was still facing Larwood at Adelaide; it was almost as if he was trying to make a point, demonstrating perhaps that he always batted like that, and it was nothing to do with Larwood. His form was predictably erratic, and it was not until he resorted to more othodox methods later on that the big scores came consistently.

At the end of the 1934 season, Jardine was married to Irene

Margaret Peat at St George's, Hanover Square. The merging of the two families appears to have been a fairly important event, no fewer than 24 of the wedding guests being titled. Jardine's best man was Major the Hon. Arthur Child-Villiers, the East End philanthropist. Like many of Jardine's friends, he was quite a bit older than himself. (Over the years he showed great concern for Jardine's financial advancement, frequently encouraging him to put everything he had into cabbages.) After the wedding the couple left for East Africa. The honeymoon was spent big-game hunting, an activity at which the young bride excelled. There were only three cricketing names on the list of wedding guests (Robertson-Glasgow, Palairet and Fender), indicative perhaps of Jardine's growing disenchantment with the top-class game.

In the close season of 1934–35, cricket was undergoing its biggest change for 60 years. Playing for Nottinghamshire, Voce's use of bodyline against Lancashire, the Australians and Middlesex had met with disapproval and formal protests, and had caused a number of injuries. Bodyline was effectively outlawed, or at any rate 'persistent and systematic bowling of fast short-pitched balls at the batsman standing clear of his wicket' was outlawed. And the lbw law was finally changed so that a batsman could now be out to a ball pitching outside the off stump, provided that the point of contact with the pad was on a line between wicket and wicket – victory for R.H. Lyttleton in his eighty-second year.

Jardine opposed both these rule changes. The first he believed to be unfair to counties (such as Notts) who were strong in fast bowling:

> The amount of bowling required of professionals today has reduced the number of counties possessing really fast bowlers to four, where, before the war, every county had one, if not more, such bowler. Rather naturally, those not blessed with a fast bowler had (in 1934) no objection to reducing the efficiency of those that were.

The answer, he felt, was to reduce the amount of cricket played and also to reduce the number of first-class counties. The balance of fast-bowling power would then be restored without recourse to such artificial restrictions as banning fast leg-theory. (It does seem to be that short-pitched bowling only causes trouble when one side has an overwhelming advantage in the pace department: Gregory and McDonald, Larwood and Voce, Lillee and Thomson.)

His opposition to the lbw alteration was just as strong, and he was supported in this by a number of other top players including Sutcliffe, Wyatt and Fender. He even spoke against the proposal to the MCC Committee. There were two main fears: the first – that matches begun on rain-affected wickets would be finished by tea on the first day – proved groundless, as batsmen managed to adapt their techniques and there was no catastrophic drop in gates resulting from shortened games; but the second objection – that the alteration would discourage classical off-side strokeplay – is now believed by many to have been borne out. Jardine believed that the new rule should be given a trial, however, and not 'turned down for financial reasons by representatives of the counties'.

Jardine's distaste for the financial element in first-class cricket further exemplifies his Victorian conception of how the game should be played and organised. It may seem a somewhat naive view given the state of the game in 1934 and the fact that it could not have existed without the big money-spinning Tests and a steady income through the county turnstiles. But the point is that he did not think much of the state of the game in 1934; he deplored the kind of nationalism which Test matches stirred up, he deplored the cult of the individual, particularly the superstar treatment of Bradman, and he deplored the clubs' greedy preparation of batsmen's wickets. It was not the game he had learnt at Winchester, the game of Fry, of Scofield Haigh and of Tom Hayward. He believed that MCC should set its face against commercialism and make its decisions for the good of the game and not for the financial well-being of a few of the less successful county clubs.

In 1934–35, cricketers and their governing bodies badly wanted to put the bodyline row behind them. For a year and a half it had threatened to start again with renewed vigour, and Jardine's continued involvement in top-class cricket had not made the peacemakers' (or appeasers', if you prefer) job any easier. However, legislation had at last been passed. Jardine's departure from competitive cricket was seen as a symbolic end to the affair, a ritual casting out of the great evil. This is not to say that there were attacks on him in the press or public expressions of relief by club officials. His ostracism was of a more subtle kind – he was simply not mentioned.

In *Wisden's* review of the 1934 Surrey season his name does not appear. Much is made of the new captain, Holmes, and his fresh and sporting approach to the job, even though Surrey had their worst season for 30 years, but nothing is said of the early retirement of one of the most successful England captains ever. Compare this to the attention given to Brearley's retirement in the 1983 *Wisden* (a six-page article and a photograph) and one begins to appreciate the conspiracy of silence that existed. Having been the object of such intense public scrutiny for so long, Jardine must have felt rather like a star turn leaving the stage to the sound of his own footsteps.

It is really only within the last couple of years that his standing as a batsman and as a captain is once again being recognised. There is no longer a need to apportion blame for bodyline in the way that there was in the past. For many years, it seems, a scapegoat was necessary, and Jardine fulfilled this role up to and beyond his death in 1958. After 1958 there was more open condemnation of him as a man and a leader. Larwood was portrayed as a forelock-tugging retainer who had no say in what happened to the ball once it was in his hands. It is very noticeable that historians have repeatedly chosen to ignore Larwood's frank admission that bodyline would not have been possible without his own firm commitment to it; the phrase 'bowling under orders' appears in most accounts.

All these years later, those who played with him and knew him retain a strong loyalty to him. It is more than just the loyalty of a dwindling generation for one of its members. There is a certain amount of that but, in hearing and reading the opinions of his contemporaries, I have found, without exception, genuine admiration and respect. Wyatt, Allen, Fender and dozens of others freely admit that he could be pretty severe on those who did not see things quite his way, but he is remembered with great affection nevertheless. The feeling is that his reputation as a batsman has been obscured by the notoriety surrounding his captaincy.

He was in the top flight of English batsmen between the wars, a time when English batting was probably stronger than it has ever been. Even with such people around as Duleepsinhji, Hobbs, Hammond, Woolley, Sutcliffe, Leyland and Hendren, it would have been difficult to leave him out of any England side of the 'thirties, and on the 1928–29 tour he was preferred at various times to Mead, Leyland and Tyldesley. It was his defensive game that served England so well, and he averted disaster on perhaps a dozen occasions coming in at no. 1, 2, 4, 5, or 6. He was only twice on the losing side in 22 Tests, and it is interesting that those two games were his least successful with the bat (0 and 19 in Melbourne in 1928–29, and 1 and 0 in Melbourne in 1932–33.

The acid test of his batsmanship and one which, if passed, would have pushed him up into the category of greatness, would have been to face Grimmett and O'Reilly in England in 1934. He had shown a slight weakness in footwork against the Australian spinners in Australia (10 of his 16 Test innings there were ended by spinners) and the fact that Grimmett and O'Reilly were if anything more effective in England meant that, going on form, Jardine should have struggled against them. He had scored hundreds against them, however, as well as losing his wicket to them. He never experienced undue difficulty against the English spinners, with the possible exception of White, and it seems likely that if his footwork was quick enough for them on English pitches, it would also be quick enough to keep out Grimmett and O'Reilly.

His most attractive innings were not played for England or for Surrey but, appropriately enough, for the Gentlemen. He appeared for them 12 times and captained them four times. He was never able to lead them to a victory, but in fact they won only once during the entire period of his career, and on that occasion he was not playing. It was a fixture which attracted variable interest. Sometimes the sides would be heavily depleted by the Championship matches that were taking place at the same time, but at Lord's each year the strength of professional and amateur cricket was represented and the place was usually packed. Jardine managed to achieve something notable on each of his six appearances at Lord's (his scores were 85 run out, 123, 86, 40 run out, 49, 2, 64, 59, 19). The hundred he made in 1927 was a turning point in his career, the innings which placed him among the top batsmen of the time. *The Times* said he played 'in the manner of a master' and referred to his 'contemptuous ability to score runs on the leg-side'. But more important from Jardine's point of view was the fact that Warner was there to see it. Warner wrote that it was a 'very fine innings indeed', which may not sound much nowadays when such performances are described in more colourful terms, but, romantic as his vision of cricket was, Warner was not given to excess in describing individual performances and his words were the very highest praise. Warner had long been an admirer of Jardine's batting and this innings convinced him that he was an England batsman and possibly captain as well. Warner had considerable influence and, although Jardine would have become an international cricketer anyway, he might not have been given the captaincy as early as 1931 without Warner's assistance. As Warner was to write bitterly in the letter to Hore-Ruthven in 1934, 'He rose to his present position on my shoulders.'

Jardine also made two hundreds in the Oval matches. The first was in his best year, 1928, when he made 193, his highest first-class score in England. The crowd barracked his slowness in reaching three figures and then cheered his strokeplay as he made the next 93 in just over an hour. Overall he had the highest average (64.31) of all batsmen who represented the Gentlemen in the 157-year history of the fixture. Only Grace with 16 and Fry with four scored more centuries for the Gentlemen.

Although his career in competitive cricket ended in 1934, he made several subsequent appearances in first-class cricket between then and 1948. In 1937 he played for Free Foresters against Cambridge. He made 50 and 47, but it seems that the stigma of bodyline still clung to him since those whose job it was to report on the match did not seem at all excited at seeing him since the reports of the match record only the barest details of what was a most successful reappearance after 3½ years.

He played regularly at the more sedate level of sides such as the Butterflies, Free Foresters, Harlequins and I Zingari – the amateur game in which the spectators, if there were any, behaved themselves. It is perhaps necessary to point out again that his preference for the world of the brightly coloured cap was not a snobbish one. It was not that he disliked the company of professionals or the way they played. Far from it: it was the fact that first-class cricket had gradually become more and more of a business. That was what he found distasteful. Necessarily, he found himself playing in a standard of cricket well below his own, but he still managed to find ways of keeping his interest going. R. L. Arrowsmith remembers playing with him for I Zingari against Lord's and Commons at the Oval in 1938:

> Lord Ebbisham was bowling: he was a charming man and bowled very slow with lots of air: he was 70, but still took his 100 wickets a season. However, clearly he was not a bowler to bother Douglas, who could

doubtless have taken 24 off him an over quite safely, despite lots of men on the boundary. But that would not have been the 'correct' way to play him (it was trying to do that lesser players got out), so for half an hour or so Douglas took a single off every ball – and everyone was happy, Douglas because he was giving a good lesson, the old man because he was keeping the great batsman relatively quiet and the rest of us because we thought it mildly comic. I also remember from the same match Douglas saying that he always bought his I.Z. ties in the lavatory at King's Cross – where he doubtless paid 3/6 against 7/6 at Foster's. This was typical of a sardonic sense of humour which endeared him to his friends and is important in any assessment of him. One of his great Wykehamist cricket friends, Gerald Hough, shared this style of humour (one of the reasons why he was not an unqualified success as Secretary of Kent). Gerald told me that he and Douglas, neither of whom took golf very seriously, played together at West Surrey against a fellow Wykehamist who was a class player. They refused any handicap except the right to say 'Woof' three times. Gerald said that Douglas was a great artist at making the most of this handicap. They won without using a single 'Woof' and their opponent was in such a state of nerves that at the 18th he drove three consecutive balls into the woods. Whenever he was going to play a shot, there stood Douglas with his mouth open, apparently on the point of uttering the hateful word.

(Jardine liked a good practical joke – he sent Sutcliffe an umbrella on the first day of his benefit match.)

In 1939 he was back in the press box again, this time as correspondent to the *Daily Telegraph*. He covered nearly a full season of Championship matches and the first two Tests against the West Indies, and in this period he produced far and away his best cricket writing. The slightly long-winded style had tightened up considerably. He was as generous to the players as ever and even found a kind word or two for the selectors. He seemed to have acquired the greatest of all cricket writers' skills: knowing when to write about something else if the cricket is boring. His reports (lengthy by modern standards) often contained leisurely and entertaining musings on players and matches past and present but he was not given to making unfavourable comparisons with the glories of the past, and he was so modest about his own place in the game's history that when he referred to incidents on, say, the 1928–29 or 1932–33 tours he did so as if he hadn't been there at all.

By the beginning of August 1939 the amount of space devoted

to cricket in the *Daily Telegraph* reflected the national preoccupation with the impending hostilities. Jardine ended his description of the Surrey v. Yorkshire match with the words, 'This is the last county match I shall see for some time as I am off to camp with the Territorials.'

Shortly afterwards, he was commissioned into the Royal Berkshire Regiment and went with the British Expeditionary Force to France where he served with distinction. In 1982, this story appeared in *The Observer*: 'He was sent by headquarters in Dunkirk into Belgium to discover why troops there had not made contact. Jardine found them all dead, commandeered a troop carrier and drove himself back through enemy lines.' I have not been able to verify this story but such an act of cold courage would have been quite in keeping with Jardine's character. He was fortunate enough to get back from Dunkirk but, like so many who had been through it, his feet were badly cut about. He volunteered to go back and help to hold Calais but his commanding officer turned him down. They were taking on single men only and not only was Jardine married but his wife had just given birth to their third child.

Over the next few months he was stationed at St Albans as a staff captain and the family rented a house nearby in Harpenden. The British Expeditionary Force was in the process of reorganisation and Jardine's responsibility was arranging transport for troops joining newly formed regiments. Being rather older than his fellow-captains and majors, he made no intimate friendships, but one fellow-officer remembers that he was in no way aloof. In fact, everyone was surprised by his diffidence and shy politeness, which was not at all what they had expected of the terror of Adelaide. He was frequently pressed to discuss the bodyline tour but he refused to be drawn, although he did once remark that, knowing the War Office, his next posting would be as Liaison Officer with the Australian Army.

As it happened, he spent the rest of the war in India – first of all in Quetta and then in Simla, where he was a major in the Central Provisions Directorate. He had a great liking for Simla and its incongruous English architecture, and he loved the historic landscape of the North-West Frontier, which he planned to explore extensively after the war. He became fluent in Hindustani (his daughter remembers that he often used to break into it at home), and he involved himself, albeit rather formally, in the social life of the base. An officer stationed there at the time wrote, 'In the evenings he always wore blue patrols, as ram-rod stiff as a Spy cartoon.' He was perfectly friendly though never intimate. He used to enjoy a game of snooker in the club but would discreetly withdraw when people started to bet on his skill (which was considerable).

He gave a series of lectures to the troops, mainly on cricket and fishing. He even managed to play a few games of cricket, but had little opportunity to show what he could do since the local umpires were as keen to take his wicket as were the bowlers. There was one first-class match however. It was in early 1944 at Bombay and its purpose was to raise money for war charities. Jardine captained a Services XI against an Indian XI led by Mushtaq Ali. Hardstaff and Jardine shared an attractive stand and both players made runs, but the Indian XI won an exciting match with 12 minutes to spare.

It may seem strange that a man with such exceptional gifts of courage and leadership should have been allowed to while away the latter half of the war doling out provisions. It has been stated that he was kept out of things because of bodyline, but this is quite untrue. The explanation, and one is certainly needed, is not so convenient. He had never been a great respecter of authority, or maybe it would be more accurate to say that he was unwilling to submit to the sort of authority for which he had no respect. In the army, his concern for the problems and welfare of those under his command lessened his effectiveness as a leader in the eyes of his superiors. Humanity, the very quality he has been said to have lacked, prevented him from being given more crucial work.

Like many in 1945, he found himself newly demobbed and without prospects. He had hoped to come back to a job in coal mining which had been promised to him, but he found that the job had disappeared and he had to look around for something else. Meanwhile Margaret Jardine had moved the family into an old manor house at Drayton, in Somerset. The move was not altogether successful, Jardine's temperament was not suited to rural tranquility and this, combined with his urgent need to find a job, resulted in another move to Radlett in Hertfordshire. He was then appointed Company Secretary to a firm of paper manufacturers in London, Wiggins Teape.

In 1946 he took part in a perfectly stage-managed centenary match at the Oval. It was not first-class but it was attended with ceremony worthy of a Test match. The sides were Surrey and Old England and the match was played in aid of Surrey's centenary appeal. There was festival atmosphere with a band playing, the King present and the sun shining. 15,000 people saw Percy Fender lead out his Old England side which included Jardine, Sutcliffe, Hendren, Sandham, Woolley, Tate and Freeman. Surrey batted first and made 248 for 6 declared. Old England very nearly got the runs thanks to substantial innings from Woolley, Hendren and Jardine. Jardine and Hendren put on 108 with Jardine's contribution being 54. 'D. R. Jardine,' said *Wisden*, 'wearing his Oxford Harlequin cap, was as polished as ever in academic skill.'

When he was fielding he cut a lonely figure, according to one person who saw the match. He was positioned on the boundary and chased the ball with stiff-kneed studiousness, not joining in the conversations at the fall of each wicket or in between overs. It was his first major appearance since the outlawing of bodyline, and perhaps he was as nervous about talking to his team-mates as he was about the reception the crowd would give him. Both were cordial enough, it seems, without being overwhelming.

By 1948, a slight change of opinion had taken place. He was not exonerated exactly, but the need for a scapegoat was not so pressing as before the war. The new attitude was reflected in *Wisden's* obituary of M. R. Jardine, who died in the early part of 1947:

> His son, D. R. Jardine, captained England during the Australian tour of 1932-33 when the Ashes were recovered in the series of five matches made notable by the 'bodyline' description of specially fast bowling, introduced in a manner since copied by Australian teams without objection by England or adverse criticism.

Lindwall and Miller had humbled the 1946–47 English team with the aid of a liberal sprinkling of short-pitched deliveries. It was not bodyline but, because the bumper had been used so very sparingly since 1935, its sudden re-introduction caused a certain amount of consternation. And when Lindwall and Miller persisted with their methods in the 1948 series, there were those who feared that things might be getting out of hand again. The real cause of the trouble was the usual one: one side had fast bowlers and the other did not. The English feeling was that the score had at last been settled. The crime of bodyline had, to a large extent, been expiated and Jardine was no longer quite the guilty reminder to the nation's cricketing conscience.

At the end of the 1948 season, he was persuaded to captain An England XI against Glamorgan, the Champion County, at Cardiff. His reception from the crowd was warm and enthusiastic. He made no specially notable contribution to the match and even declined to go for a win in the final session when it seemed to be there for the taking. His undeniably slow batting passed almost without a murmur; those present had the defeat of England in the Tests fresh in their minds and Jardine's presence was a reminder that when he was in his prime the Australians were far from invincible.

As had been the case after the first world war, there seemed little hope of winning the Ashes for quite a few years. An excellent publication called *The Daily Worker Cricket Handbook 1949*, which one would have expected to have been the least nationalistically minded, was quite distraught at England's inability to knock the stuffing out of the Aussies, and bemoaned the absence of men such as Jardine who had the mettle to put things right. (Just to please the hard-line readership, though, there was an attack on MCC snobbism.) He was missed a great deal more than was generally admitted. Indeed, this is still the case. While researching this book I received letters and listened to testimonies which, while deprecating the use of bodyline, would frequently finish with the statement, or variations on it: 'But we could do with a few more like Douglas now,' And in September 1980 at Lord's I overheard a senior MCC member saying to his pal, 'Of course, the last *real* captain we had was Jardine!'

In 1953 he was elected to be the first presidentof the Umpires Association. This was a job he thoroughly enjoyed. He had always been especially interested in umpiring and had the highest respect for those who undertook it. From 1955 to 1957 he was president of Oxford University Cricket Club, which might be considered a somewhat belated honour since he was never elected to captain the University; he and Lord Harris are the only two Oxonians to have captained England but not Oxford against Cambridge.

He took up journalism again in 1953 for the *Star* but, whether because of editorial constraints or for other reasons, his writing fell some way short of the standard he had set for himself in 1939 on the *Daily Telegraph*. 1953 was the year in which England won

back the Ashes for the first time since Jardine's side had done it in
1933. Jardine had the highest opinion of Hutton's captaincy and
wrote that it was 'a joy to report' his success in that role. Jardine
held different views from Lord Hawke on the subject of
professional captains. He had always firmly expressed the view
that many more professionals could with advantage be appointed
as captains and elected to serve on selection committees. Verity,
he believed, would have made a particularly good captain, as
would Sutcliffe, who proved his ability when leading the Players on
four occasions. In fact, if Sutcliffe had accepted the Yorkshire
captaincy when it was supposedly offered to him in 1927, he
might well have been given the England captaincy ahead of
Jardine when the time came.

Jardine was moderately successful as a cricket commentator on
the radio. His observations were always perceptive and lucidly
expressed, but his delivery was a little slow for post-war tastes. It
certainly lacked the bite of the modern 'I don't know what's
going on out there' school. He undertook these broadcasting and
journalistic engagements more out of a need to earn a living than
as a means of maintaining contact with the first-class game. By
now he had a wife and four children to support. Things weren't quite
as hard as earlier in their marriage when Margaret Jardine had taken to
smallholding, but the extra income was useful and Jardine himself
contributed short stories to the evening newspapers which
brought in a bit more. He tended to worry a good deal about
money but defied the constraints of austerity to the extent of
running a somewhat decrepit Rolls Royce Phantom II, bought
from a chap in Bognor Regis where the family were holiday-
ing.

The family was a very close one and Jardine involved himself
more in the children's upbringing than most men of his class were
accustomed to do at the time. He read to them, played with them,
took them on outings (the circus being a particular favourite),
and his daughter also remembers the family sitting round listening
to 'The Goon Show', which used to make him cry with laughter.
All the children were sent to boarding schools but during the
holidays there would be large gatherings of Peats and Jardines
either at Hockwold Hall or on the estates that Sir Harry Peat
rented in Perthshire. The Peats were a great sporting family; there
was a substantial amount of shooting attached to Hockwold Hall
and about 25,000 acres went with Crosscraigs House on the south

side of Loch Rannoch. The children were all taught to fish, stalk and walk with guns as a matter of course.

To Jardine's great delight, his two eldest daughters, Fianach and Marion, became fond of playing and watching cricket and often went with him to Lord's for the day. His only son, Euan, though, was unable to continue the distinguished cricketing line. Margaret Jardine had come into contact with German measles while carrying him, he was born with a weak heart and suffered from very bad health throughout his childhood. His father was fully aware of the pressure that resulted from having a famous father and a number of contemporaries remember that he was deeply concerned about it.

Jardine was a devoted family man but he was also fond of socialising. They did not entertain much at Radlett and so he tended to do a fair bit of clubbing, lunching and bridge-playing in London. Ian Peebles recalled in *Spinner's Yarn* that 'D.R.J. came to the City at intervals and we saw quite a lot of him. He was a splendid guest with the agreeable habit of particularly addressing his remarks to anyone who seemed shy or left out of the conversation.'

He was chairman of the New South Wales Land Agency, which was a sheep-farming concern. When the company was taken over by the Scottish Australian Company, he was taken onto the board of directors and in 1953 he was asked to travel to Australia on the company's behalf to assess the development possibilities of the property. He hesitated for obvious reasons before under-taking the mission, and he went to the trouble of consulting Jack Fingleton, by now a friend and press box colleague, on the sort of reception he was likely to get. Fingleton tried to explain that Australians do not as a rule bear grudges and that he would be warmly welcomed. With some trepidation Jardine went ahead with the trip and found that Fingleton had been right. There was no pelting with rotten eggs at the airport and he was jovially received, in his own words, 'as an old so-and-so who got away with it'.

A reunion lunch was arranged with Prime Minister Menzies attending, also Larwood, Mailey, Bardsley and Oldfield. Larwood's autobiography includes an account of the occasion, which seems to have been most convivial, with people making jokes about bodyline without any embarrassment. Fingleton remembered that he also gave a talk in the radio series, 'Guest of

Honour', which was very well received. Jardine was pleased but puzzled – he could not understand these Australians at all.

Larwood himself had been even more warmly welcomed when, three years earlier, he had emigrated to Australia. Again this had been at Fingleton's instigation. The ex-Prime Minister, Ben Chifley, had personally paid half the Larwood family's hotel bill when they first arrived.

In 1957 Jardine was obliged to make a similar trip, this time to inspect land which he owned in Rhodesia. It was a working holiday and he took with him his second eldest daughter, Marion, for whom the trip was a twenty-first birthday present. While he was there he contracted a disease called tick fever. He did not respond to treatment as well as was expected, but the doctors felt there was no cause for great concern and recommended a long sea voyage back to England.

On his return, he was admitted to the Hospital for Tropical Diseases, where his condition showed no improvement. He was moved to University College Hospital and tests revealed an advanced state of cancer. Deep-ray treatment was administered, but without success. His wife was then told by one of the hospital doctors about a clinic in Switzerland which was having a moderate degree of success against cancer. Jardine agreed to go, although neither he nor his children knew what was wrong with him. The deep-ray treatment had caused him great difficulty with his breathing and he thought that the Swiss mountain air would help.

The couple travelled to Switzerland and he was admitted to the clinic. It was found that he not only had lung cancer but that it had got to the stomach and the brain as well. There was nothing they could do for him beyond giving him pain-killing drugs and on 18 June 1958 he died. His body was cremated and flown home and his ashes were scattered over the top of Cross Craigs mountain in Perthshire.

The day after his death, the flags were lowered at Lord's where England were playing New Zealand. A few weeks later there was a minute's silence at the Saffrons ground, Eastbourne, on the first morning of a match that had become a regular fixture over the last three years: D. R. Jardine's XI v Oxford University.

The family was shattered by his death, and even after 25 years it is clear that he was the focal point of their lives. His wife, in a state of abject grief, destroyed all his cricket clothes and equipment.

The house was sold and eventually she went with her youngest daughter, Iona, to live in Malta. Of the other three children, Fianach, the eldest, works as a graphic designer in Scotland. Marion is a social worker in Berkshire, and Euan works as a chef in London.

The memorial service, held on 3 July 1958 at St Michael's, Cornhill, was attended by both English and Australian leading cricket figures. The address was given by Sir Hubert Ashton and in it he said this of Douglas Jardine:

My first recollection of him was when he came to Winchester College in 1914; his reputation as a cricketer had preceded him. But in addition to this he had a somewhat unusual air about him. He was mature, tall and determined; clearly a new man that must be treated with respect...

In retrospect it may seem that his cricket days at Oxford were a relatively quiet period and he did not reach his full maturity until he was picked to go to Australia with Percy Chapman's side in 1928–29. He did well and seemed to prefer to make runs when his side was in a tight corner. His 98 in the deciding Test Match will always be especially remembered. Even then he had become a somewhat provocative figure in his Harlequin cap.

Douglas first captained England against New Zealand in 1931 and in the following year he took the England side to Australia ... That tour of 1932–33 in Australia was the most controversial of any and D.R.J. was the central and commanding figure in it. He has written his own views in his book, *In Quest of the Ashes*, and it would be both out of place and out of time to go into these matters here. However, two things emerge quite clearly – his immense moral and physical courage and the tremendous loyalty that he inspired in his whole team. Here indeed was a man and a leader and surely history confirms that in every sphere of life such people cannot but offend in some quarters...

On first acquaintance it might be thought that he was a trifle austere and brusque; I must confess that on occasions he gave me that impression. However, as is so often the case, I have no doubt that this was due to shyness or a lack of self-confidence; perhaps the better and truer word is humility.

People of his nature may go to remarkable extremes to try and disguise the fact that they are in the process of doing a kindly act. I do not suppose that he and I exchanged more than half a dozen letters in the course of our lives. It is significant that the last of these was written shortly before he went into hospital and was to enquire whether I could help a mutual friend who was experiencing a difficult time. He was indeed ever thoughtful of others and when president of Oxford University Cricket Club he gave unstintingly of his time, his experience and his purse.

We live in a world of so much bitterness, anxiety and perhaps disillusionment. For Douglas our hearts too are sad but he would not wish us to leave this service in that frame of mind. He was a man both proud and sensitive – courageous and with a single-mindedness that must surely be an example to us all. Let us then to our various duties, happy in his memory, encouraged by his courage – determined to play a better innings ourselves, however bad the light and however broken the wicket. In that way and in that way only cometh the true victory.

A Victorian tribute to a man whose rigid adherence to the principles of honour and fair play might have won universal praise had he lived in an earlier age, but the last word belongs to R. C. Robertson-Glasgow, his old Oxford team-mate: 'If he has sometimes been a fierce enemy, he has also been a wonderful friend.'

Statistical Appendix

FIRST CLASS CRICKET

Season	Matches	Inns	N.O.	Runs	H.S.	Ave.	100s	Runs	Wkts	Ave.	5 wkts in inns	Ct
1920	8	14	0	317	70	22.64	0	226	13	17.38	1	4
1921	17	28	2	1015	145	39.03	2	270	11	24.54	0	8
1922	4	5	1	87	30*	21.75	0	56	2	28.00	0	2
1923	18	28	4	916	127	38.16	2	6	0	–	0	10
1924	27	38	7	1249	122	40.29	2	49	0	–	0	21
1925	25	36	3	1020	87	30.90	0	3	0	–	0	21
1926	26	36	4	1473	176	46.03	3	363	10	36.30	0	13
1927	11	14	3	1002	147	91.09	5	108	3	36.00	0	7
1928	14	17	4	1133	193	87.15	3	112	3	37.33	0	17
1928–29	12	19	1	1168	214	64.88	6	67	2	33.50	0	5
1930	9	13	2	402	112	36.54	1	12	0	–	0	4
1931	19	30	13	1104	106*	64.94	2	40	1	40.00	0	12
1932	29	39	11	1464	164	52.28	3	107	2	53.50	0	19
1932–33	15	21	2	698	108*	36.73	1	42	0	–	–	15
1933	11	15	0	779	127	51.93	3	26	1	26.00	0	8
1933–34	14	19	3	835	102	52.18	2	6	0	–	0	20
1937	1	2	0	97	50	48.50	0	–	–	–	–	0
1943–44	1	2	0	56	43	28.00	0	–	–	–	–	1
1948	1	2	1	33	23*	33.00	0	–	–	–	–	1
Total	262	378	61	14,848	214	46.83	35	1493	48	31.10	1	188

Jardine reached 50 on 107 occasions in first-class cricket.

His best bowling return was 6 for 28 for Oxford University v. Essex at The Parks in 1920.

The grounds on which he was most successful were:

The Oval	4424 runs	10 100s	ave. 50.27
Adelaide	501 runs	2 100s	ave. 62.63
Sheffield	376 runs	1 100s	ave. 62.67

He played against Yorkshire 14 times, scoring 992 runs at 47.24, including 3 hundreds.

He scored 6249 Championship runs for Surrey at 43.40, including 11 hundreds.

He played for the Gentlemen 12 times, scoring 1029 runs at 64.31, including 3 hundreds.

Dismissals:	
caught	144
c. and b.	11
bowled	93
lbw.	46
run out	15
stumped	8
	317

TEST CRICKET

Season	Opponents	Matches	Inns	N.O.	Runs	H.S.	Ave.	100s
1928	West Indies	2	2	0	105	83	52.50	0
1928–29	Australia	5	9	1	341	98	42.62	0
1931	New Zealand	3	4	3	73	38	73.00	0
1932	India	1	2	1	164	85*	164.00	0
1932–33	Australia	5	9	0	199	56	22.11	0
1932–33	New Zealand	1	1	0	45	45	45.00	0
1933	West Indies	2	2	1	148	127	74.00	1
1933–34	India	3	4	1	221	65	73.66	0
Total		22	33	6	1296	127	48.00	1

Jardine captained England in 15 Tests; 9 of these were won, 1 lost and 5 drawn. He took 26 catches in Tests including 5 in the second Test against India in 1933–34. Bowling in Tests: 1–0–10–0 (v Australia, 3rd Test 1928–29).

Bibliography

The books consulted in the researching of this biography are too numerous to list in full here. The majority were used as a means of building up a historical context in which to set the story of Jardine's career. Those works from which I have quoted or from which facts have been taken are listed below.

John Arlott, *Jack Hobbs. Profile of 'The Master'*, John Murray & Davis-Poynter, 1981.
Neville Cardus, *Days in the Sun*, Grant Richards, 1924.
A. W. Carr, *Cricket with the Lid Off*, Hutchinson, 1935.
A. J. H. Cochrane, *Records of the Harlequin Cricket Club*, Eyre and Spottiswoode. 1930.
L. Constantine, *Cricket and I*, Philip Allan, 1933.
H. de Selincourt, *Moreover*, Gerald Howe, 1934.
E. W. Docker, *A History of Indian Cricket*, MacMillan, 1976.
E. W. Docker, *Bradman and the Bodyline Series*, Angus and Robertson, 1978.
'Eskari', *C. K. Nayudu: A Cricketer of Charm*, Illustrated News: Calcutta, 1945.
P. G. H. Fender, *The Turn of the Wheel*, Faber and Faber, 1929.
W. H. Ferguson, *Mr. Cricket*, Nicholas Kaye, 1957.
J. H. Fingleton, *Cricket Crisis*, Cassell, 1947.
Maj. the Hon. E. G. French, *An account of the MCC tour of 1932–33* (unpublished MS).
W. Frindall, *The Wisden Book of Cricket Records*, Queen Anne Press, 1980.
C. B. Fry, *Batsmanship*, Eveleigh Nash, 1912.
C. B. Fry, *Life Worth Living*, Eyre and Spottiswoode, 1939.
W. R. Hammond, *Cricket My Destiny*, Stanley Paul, 1946.
B. Harris, *Jardine Justified*, Chapman and Hall, 1933.
E. T. R. Herdman, *Winchester 1916–1921*.
J. B. Hobbs, *Fight for the Ashes 1932–3*, Harrap, 1933.
Christopher Hollis, *Oxford in the Twenties*, Heinemann, 1976.
Two chapters by D. R. Jardine, *The Game of Cricket* (Lonsdale Library) Seeley, Service & Co. 1930.
D. R. Jardine, *In Quest of the Ashes*, Hutchinson, 1933.
D. R. Jardine, *Ashes and Dust*, Hutchinson, 1934.
D. R. Jardine, *Cricket*, J. M. Dent, 1936.
D. R. Jardine, *Cricket – How to Succeed*, Evans Bros, 1936.
A. Kippax and E. P. Barbour, *Anti-Bodyline*, Hurst and Blackett, 1933.
Harold Larwood, *Bodyline?*, E. Mathews and Marrot, 1933.
Laurence Le Quesne, *The Bodyline Controversy*, Secker and Warburg, 1983.
  (This is the most authoritative of all the accounts and is highly recommended to anyone interested in bodyline.)

R. H. Lyttleton, *The Crisis in Cricket: The lbw Rule,* Longmans, 1928.
Arthur Mailey, *And Then Came Larwood,* John Lane, 1933.
Mushtaq Ali, *Cricket Delightful.* Rupa: Calcutta, 1967.
M. A. Noble, *Fight for the Ashes 1928–29,* Harrap. 1929.
L. Palgrave, *The Story of the Oval,* Cornish Bros. 1949.
Ian Peebles, *Spinner's Yarn,* Collins, 1977.
Kevin Perkins, *The Larwood Story,* W. H. Allen, 1965.
K. S. Ranjitsinhji, *The Jubilee Book of Cricket.* W. Blackwood, 1897.
R. C. Robertson-Glasgow, *Cricket Prints,* T. Werner Laurie, 1943.
R. C. Robertson-Glasgow, *46 Not Out,* Hollis and Carter, 1948.
Ray Robinson, *Between Wickets,* Collins, 1948.
Ray Robinson, *The Wildest Tests,* Pelham, 1972.
W. N. Roe, *Public Schools Cricket 1901–1950,* Max Parrish, 1951.
Gordon Ross, *The Surrey Story,* Stanley Paul, 1957.
Ian Sproat, *The Cricketer's Who's Who,* The Cricketer's Who's Who, 1983.
Richard Streeton, *P. G. H. Fender: A Biography,* Faber and Faber, 1981.
H. Sutcliffe, *For England and Yorkshire,* Arnold, 1935.
E. W. Swanton, *Sort of a Cricket Person,* Collins, 1972.
E. W. Swanton, *Follow On,* Collins, 1977.
Ben Travers, *94 Declared,* Elm Tree Books, 1981.
Sir Pelham Warner, *Cricket Betweeen Two Wars,* Chatto and Windus, 1942.
Sir Pelham Warner, *Lord's 1787–1945,* G. G. Harrap, 1946.
Roy Webber, *The Playfair Book of Test Cricket,* Playfair, 1952.
R. W. E. Wilmot, *Defending the Ashes 1932–33,* Robertson and Mullens, 1933.
Wisden 1889–1983.

Periodicals and newspapers consulted: The Advertiser (Adelaide); Ayre's Public Schools Cricket Companion; The Brisbane Courier; The Ceylon Observer; The Cherwell; The Cricketer; The Daily Worker Cricket Handbook; The Evening Standard; The Illustrated Sporting and Dramatic News; The Isis; The Manchester Guardian; The Age (Melbourne); The Morning Post; The Evening News; The New York Times; The New York Herald; The Sporting Life; The Star; The Sunday Dispatch; The Surrey County Cricket Club Yearbooks; The Sydney Morning Herald; The South Wales Echo; The Illustrated Tasmanian Mail; The Daily Telegraph; The Times; The Times of India; The West Australian; Wisden Cricket Monthly; The Wykehamist; The Winchester College Register.

Index